Electronic banking and treasury security

ACT

THE ASSOCIATION OF CORPORATE TREASURERS

The Association is a professional body, formed to encourage and promote the study and practice of finance and treasury management, and to educate those involved in this field. It is the only UK professional body which concentrates and sets professional examinations exclusively on this subject. It is an independent body, governed by a Council of Members whose work is supported by a number of active voluntary committees.

The Association has approximately 450 Fellows, 1400 Members, 850 Associate Members and more than 1300 professionals enrolled on examination courses.

Since its formation in 1979, the influence of and contribution made by the Association have grown steadily. High educational standards have fed through into high technical standards. This has meant that, as an organization, the Association focuses not only on serving its members directly, but also representing them on relevant issues in the public domain. It has influenced proposals for regulatory change and promoted voluntary codes for wholesale market participants. It has also influenced changes in accounting and tax legislation. The Association has contributed to the corporate governance debate and aspects of competition policy, and has been consulted on and successfully contributed to many practical aspects of European Monetary Union. These messages are reinforced at conferences and in the publications it produces.

Electronic banking and treasury security

Second edition
Edited by Brian Welch

NatWest

CRC Press
Boca Raton Boston New York Washington, DC

WOODHEAD PUBLISHING LIMITED

and

THE ASSOCIATION OF CORPORATE TREASURERS

Published by Woodhead Publishing Limited and The Association of Corporate Treasurers

Woodhead Publishing Limited, Abington Hall, Abington
Cambridge CB1 6AH, England

Published in North and South America by CRC Press LLC, 2000 Corporate Blvd, NW
Boca Raton FL 33431, USA

This book was previously published as *Electronic Banking & Security* by
Blackwell Publishers, 1994

This edition published 1999, Woodhead Publishing Ltd, The Association of
Corporate Treasurers and CRC Press LLC

British Library Cataloguing in Publication Data
A catalogue record for this book is available from the British Library.

Library of Congress Cataloging in Publication Data
A catalog record for this book is available from the Library of Congress.

Woodhead Publishing ISBN 1 85573 336 6
CRC Press ISBN 0-8493-0529-2
CRC Press order number: WP0529

Cover design by The ColourStudio
Typeset by BookEns Ltd, Royston, Herts, England
Printed by St Edmundsbury Press, Suffolk, England

Contents

Foreword

Electronic banking is now commonplace, with varying degrees of sophistication, in businesses around the world. Usage is no longer restricted exclusively to the multi-national groups with extensive cross-border requirements: many smaller businesses now also enjoy the considerable advantages to be achieved through using electronic banking services.

Electronic banking service providers have responded by extending the range of products available through electronic access. This has been further fuelled through the effective use of emerging technologies to deliver services, including the Internet. All of these developments, together with the imminent arrival of the European Single Currency, have brought about new challenges and opportunities for electronic banking service providers. Many of these are highlighted in this book.

The first chapter provides a useful insight into the origins of electronic banking. Payments are core to business activity and the chapters which focus on the role of APACS and the issues around BACS highlight some key considerations for businesses.

As technology develops, the global marketplace becomes a reality with many corporates now dealing in such an environment. The chapter on Global Cash Management captures the critical components and analyses the issues involved for businesses when establishing structures to control cashflows on a world-wide scale.

As numbers of electronic banking users have increased, so has the importance of documentation and legal issues, especially in connection with the movement of funds. The book contains two chapters which cover these particular areas in detail.

All sections of the book have a security theme, although Part 2 focuses on this issue specifically. The chapter Managing Treasury Security provides an informative outline of administrative security procedures and protocols: a useful framework for anyone involved in managing a treasury function. There is also a chapter which provides detail about security for the treasury system itself, incorporating key elements such as audit trail, back-up and a useful audit checklist.

A highly topical issue today is that of security on the Internet which is justifiably covered in a chapter in its own right. As Internet usage increases with more businesses becoming aware of the benefits, greater emphasis is being placed on making this particular environment secure. This chapter will put the cynics' minds at rest showing that this is a powerful tool to deliver information in a highly effective and secure manner. Similarly, the chapter on EDI security provides a good insight into the topic, covering the standards now available and the security features involved. The book concludes with a chapter which looks at future developments. In a world so rapidly changing, this is always an exciting area and some interesting issues are raised by the contributors.

NatWest has established itself as an innovative provider of electronic banking services and as an organisation that is committed to extending the range of services available to customers through electronic access. Electronic banking and security are very much linked and for this reason NatWest is pleased to have the opportunity to sponsor this book on the subject.

H A Shaw
Managing Director
NatWest Corporate Banking Services

NatWest Electronic Services

NatWest Corporate Banking Services is the corporate banking arm of NatWest, providing flexible financial solutions to nearly 37,000 Medium and Large Enterprises (MLEs) – companies with annual turnovers in excess of £1 million.

NatWest BankLine

As the UK's leading supplier of Electronic Banking Services and Cash Management solutions we recognize that effective cash management is an important and valuable tool for corporate treasurers of all businesses in building and sustaining competitive advantage in today's ever-changing markets.

Through our electronic banking product, NatWest BankLine, we offer a single electronic access point to our wide range of cash management products and services including:

- Balance and Transaction Information on accounts with NatWest and other banks (including overseas).
- Payment initiation including CHAPS, BACS and International Payments.
- Account reconciliation.
- International trade services.
- Treasury and market rate reporting.

NatWest BankLine has been at the forefront of UK electronic banking since its introduction in 1987. The Windows™ version was launched in 1995 making NatWest the first UK bank to use Microsoft Windows® technology for its electronic banking services.

As you would expect we have been extremely cautious in the way our systems have been developed to ensure information remains confidential and to provide users with the necessary tools to prevent unauthorised access.

NatWest BankLine incorporates some of the most advanced security features available in electronic banking systems to give you peace of mind in conducting your electronic banking transactions including encryption, password protection and Smart Card authentication.

For further information on ***BankLine*** please contact Victor Robinson, National Westminster Bank Plc, Level 2, Drapers Gardens, 12 Throgmorton Avenue, London EC2N 2DL Telephone 0171 454 6641 between 9 am and 5 pm.

NatWest Business On-line

We are committed to the continuing development of innovative electronic solutions. NatWest Business On-line offers a comprehensive suite of on-line information services to help increase business efficiency, improve competitive edge and minimize financial risk through one easy-to-use, quick and secure solution.

Using the latest Internet technology, NatWest Business On-line enables users to:

- Run credit checks on commercial customers and suppliers to reduce business risk.
- Identify sales opportunities and expand commercial base.
- Communicate with customers and business partners via secure electronic mail.
- Access world-wide news from over 700 business sources including major newspapers, trade journals and magazines, and obtain key articles about a specific industry, competitors and market developments.
- Access essential information reports on more than 30 UK industry sectors and 100 countries to help business planning.

- Explore the wealth of information available on the Internet.
- Obtain useful financial and economic information to help management stay briefed.

For further information on NatWest Business On-line please contact Helen Lockstone, National Westminster Bank Plc, Level 2, Drapers Gardens, 12 Throgmorton Avenue, London EC2N 2DL Telephone 0171 454 6719 between 9 am and 5 pm.

Contributors

Brian Welch FCMA FCT FCIS ACIB

Brian Welch is Treasury Consultant with UserCare Limited, with wide experience as a corporate treasurer and with treasury systems. He was Treasurer of Gulf Oil Company – Eastern Hemisphere, Willis Faber, the insurance brokers, and the department store group, House of Fraser. He has also been a consultant with The Bank Relationship Consultancy, concentrating on systems, controls and security, and a Program Manager for Unisys, the international systems provider. He is an active member of The Association of Corporate Treasurers, having served as a Member of the Council, Chairman of the Publications Committee, and currently as Member of the Programme Committee and the Working Party on the introduction of the Euro. He is Chairman of the Board of Peter Symonds' College, Winchester, which is recognised as one of the leading Sixth Form Colleges in the country.

Michael Deakin BA (Com) FCA MCT MIMC

Michael Deakin is an Executive Consultant with Ernst & Young Management Consultants, advising corporate clients, financial institutions and central and local government bodies on efficient and effective treasury management. He is co-author of the keystone study *A strategy for the ECU* and is closely involved in matters relating to the development of European Monetary Union. Before joining Ernst & Young, Michael spent nine years in industry, holding financial and line management responsibilities.

Tony De Caux BA FCIB MIMgt MCT

Tony de Caux is the Chief Executive of The Bank Relationship Consultancy, specializing in international banking, cash management, electronic banking and treasury technology. He was previously with the Bank of America where he was Head of their Cash Management Division in Europe. He held a similar position with the Hongkong Bank. Tony is a well known writer and lecturer. He is co-author of *A Buyer's Guide to Treasury Systems*, and produced a section of the *ACT Manual of Corporate Finance and Treasury Management*.

Tom Fallon BSc AFIMA MCT

Tom Fallon has been the Treasurer of United Utilities Plc since November 1991. He has a degree in mathematics from the University of Aberdeen and spent eight years with Ford Motor Company before becoming Treasurer of Octopus Publishing Plc in 1985, after which he spent four years with Reed International Plc.

Roger Gate CertCM

Roger Gate is Senior Manager, Electronic Commerce and On-line Services, NatWest Group. Roger led the development of, and sits on the examination board for, the ACT Cash Management Certificate. His varied career in NatWest has included positions in large city branches and regional offices. Before taking up his current role developing business to business electronic commerce services, he headed the UK Electronic Cash Management Sales Unit and assisted in the development of the NatWest BankLine range of services.

Claire Goddard BSc FIMC MCT

Claire Goddard is an Executive Consultant in Ernst & Young's Global Investment Banking Consulting Group. She is responsible for advising bank treasuries, global custodians, investment managers and large multi-national corporate clients on commercially effective operational and risk related processes and systems needed for front and back offices, using on and off balance sheet instruments, and for payment links. She is a frequent conference speaker on treasury system and electronic banking issues, and is a regular host presenter at the Association's six monthly Treasury Security and Controls Workshop supported by Ernst & Young. Before joining Ernst & Young, she spent several years with a subsidiary of BET, managing a finance function and implementing computer systems for accounting and order processing.

Tony Palmer MSc MBSC

Tony Palmer is Security Consultant, Group Security Services, NatWest Group, focusing on cryptography and trust infrastructures. Tony has an international banking background and has a wealth of experience in trade finance, money market and international cash management disciplines.

John Sherwood BSc MSc CEng FBCS

John Sherwood is Director of Sherwood Associates Limited, Management Consultants, which offers consultancy on IT Security and Operational Risk Management. He manages a team of highly respected consultants and handles business with a number of financial institutions and other multi-national corporate clients in the UK and the rest of Europe, Scandinavia, the Middle East and the Far East. He is also a member of the UK EDI Security Advisory Group. His previous appointments include Managing Consultant with Computer Security Consultants Limited, Systems Support Manager with Computer Security Limited, Principal Lecturer in Digital Communications Systems at Leicester Polytechnic and Director of the Inner London Educational Computing Centre.

Charles Storer FCIB

Charles Storer is a senior manager in the NatWest Group with a wealth of technical and business experience, and a background in electronic commerce and international cash management. Currently he manages business development of electronic commerce opportunities where smart card technology is a feature. He represents NatWest's interests to government officials in various forums to achieve the Prime Minister's stated objective of Better Government.

His banking career has spanned City of London branches, network strategy, payments consultancy and development and implementation of global cash management solutions. He has often represented NatWest as chairman or speaker at US and European conferences on mobile commerce, global cash management, electronic banking and related legal issues, and the introduction of the euro. He was awarded fellowship of the Chartered Institute of Bankers in recognition of training provided overseas to senior Middle Eastern bankers.

Richard Tyson-Davies

Richard Tyson-Davies is Head of Public Affairs at the Association for Payment Clearing Services (APACS). He joined APACS in 1989 to head a new division to deal with the press, public relations and legal affairs. He acts as spokesman for the payments industry on matters relating to cooperation in the provision of money transmission services. He also represents APACS's interests to government officials and others involved in the formulation of policies and opinions on payment matters. Richard was previously employed at the Bank of England for 28 years, ending up as the Assistant to the Chief of Banking Departments, dealing with national and international payment system matters. Earlier responsibilities in the Bank of England included heading the European Community desk, and close involvement in establishing a division to carry out the prudential supervision of the UK banking sector.

Acknowledgements

My thanks to all of the contributors who have updated their original chapters, and have updated their updates to ensure that this book reflects the up-to-date position in electronic banking and treasury security.

I should also like to thank Lorna Smith and Karen Bond for their advice on updating the BACS practical control issues chapter, and Philip Wood of Allen & Overy for his comments on the electronic banking documentation chapter.

Special thanks are due to the NatWest Bank who have sponsored this edition, and have provided the authors for two very useful chapters. The Bank has shown great patience whilst the various contributors have produced their chapters, in addition to their normal working activities. It is, however, the latest experience of those practitioners which makes this book so useful.

No ACT book is possible without the support of the ACT Publications Department, and in particular Claire Gwinnett to whom I offer my personal appreciation, and my own family who have tolerated my late nights to meet the publication deadlines.

Brian Welch

Part 1

Electronic banking

1

Electronic banking: background and history

Michael Deakin and Claire Goddard

The range of bank services which can be delivered to a customer's office or home by electronic technology has expanded extensively since the first tentative steps were taken some 25 years ago. Banks now use technology to transmit information, receive instructions and to transact and settle business. The quality, range and price of electronic services are an important part of a bank's competitive positioning in its approach to the corporate customer.

The reason behind the spread of electronic services becomes clearer if we consider the following basic banking transactions and the parties they involve:

1 A customer deposits funds in a bank account. Two parties are involved, the customer and the bank.

2 A customer withdraws cash from a bank account. Again, two parties are involved.

3 A customer pays a third party. Within national borders there

will be at least four parties involved – the paying customer, the paying bank, a receiving (payee) bank and the recipient, who is a customer of the payee bank. A fifth party may be a clearing house which is co-ordinating the movement of funds between the two banks.

4 A customer pays a third party overseas. At least one further party may be involved, the paying bank's correspondent bank overseas.

Although it can be longer, the transactional chain may be summed up simply as in Fig. 1.1.

Electronic technology has been applied to each link between the parties involved as follows:

1 Automated teller machines (ATMs) use electronic technology to permit customers to withdraw funds and to make deposits.

2 Electronic funds transfer at point of sale (EFTPOS) permits customers to initiate immediate payments to a third party.

3 Credit cards use electronic technology to set up an accumulating debt for later payment and debit cards, for example SWITCH, to initiate payment at once.

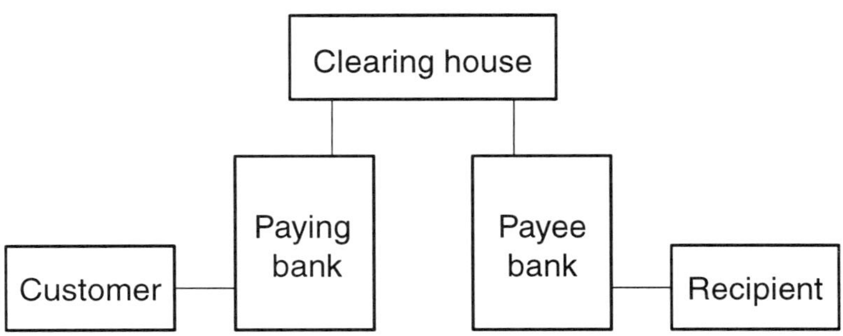

1.1 The transaction chain

4 Treasury work stations permit corporates to initiate payments, to inquire on balances and, in some countries, to access other services, such as making transactions between accounts.

5 Funds transfer systems (or payment systems) pass transactions between banks to complete the payment cycle, whether initiated by paper cheque or by electronic instruction.

The first steps

Technology appears to have been applied first at the centre of the United States banking system. One of the earliest uses of electronic technology was the Federal Reserve Communication System (Fed Wire) which recorded over 700 000 transfers in 1920. Fed Wire is used to transfer reserve account balances from one institution to another which makes it a very specialist electronic banking service. However, it sits at the centre of US bank clearing systems. Electronic technology spreads from this central point through the whole process of bank funds transmissions, finally reaching outside the banks direct to retail customers and corporate treasuries.

At first, the rate of increase in the use of technology appears to have been quite slow. Although Fed Wire was active in 1920, most information flowing between corporate treasuries and banks was still provided by movement of paper in the early 1960s. For example, paper was used to confirm arrangements initiated by telephone and paper provided the legal completion of tentative oral agreements. Where electronic systems were in place at all, mainframe computers provided basic data recording services, fed by data prepared from written documents.

The effectiveness of electronic banking systems was inhibited by the following four main factors:

1 Communication technology was in its infancy and inadequate for local or global coverage – banks and customers could not communicate internationally within their own organizations or with each other.

2 Most companies and banks had incompatible systems – sometimes, even different branches of the same bank had different systems.

3 Computer manufacturers had not yet developed technology standards which would permit data exchange directly between different computer systems.

4 Computer hardware and software were expensive in comparison to the efficiency savings available through automation within an organization, so the latter became the first focus of attention.

The search for efficiency

Electronic banking started in the United States because the clearing arrangements between the large numbers of geographically dispersed US banks were extremely inefficient. Corporate customer pressure for improvements was becoming irresistible. In addition, the early availability of cheap computing power encouraged pioneering work in the United States to achieve savings from more efficient use of the banking system. The creative use of the emerging technology which had been developed for other purposes, and paid for by other industries' research budgets, was fundamental to the progress of electronic banking and the significant savings achieved thereby.

The imaginative use of available computer power was slower to develop within the financial industries in Europe, even though some European countries had banking systems which were as inefficient as the US. The US 'global' banks recognized this difference in the European pace of development and, in the early 1970s, began to use their technology lead to attack the European banks' exclusive hold over European corporate customers.

Of course, the American banks did not have it all their own way. The first ATMs in the world were introduced to the public in the United Kingdom by Barclays Bank in 1969. Once customers became familiar with them, they spread rapidly. By 1985, 160 000 units were run by banks world-wide, with about 9000 in the United Kingdom. By pioneering ATMs, Barclays showed that the United Kingdom was taking the lead in electronic personal banking, although the American banks were still ahead in providing electronic services to corporate customers.

Improving clearing systems

The United Kingdom's paper-based clearing systems were relatively efficient, which meant that pressure for change from corporate customers was much lower than in the United States. In consequence, the UK banks' attention was directed first towards improving services within the banking system, rather than towards developing links with corporate customers which was the greater concern of US banks.

For example, centralized paper clearing of credit transfers was initiated in the United Kingdom in 1960. Increased volumes and the escalating cost of clearing led to the formation of National Giro in October 1968. Although it was initially paper based, National Giro led to an important step for electronic banking, the development of the Bankers' Automated Clearing System (BACS) which opened for business in December 1971. BACS used electronic data processing to offer two-day clearance to participating banks and their customers. Nevertheless, the transfer of data from customer to bank was largely achieved by manual transfer of the output from electronic media in the early days. Even today, electronic data transfer with manual intervention is common.

While BACS offered improved cash movement for domestic clearances, cross-border movements were not included. Corporate customers had to wait for the development of the international payments system co-ordinated by the Society for Worldwide Interbank Funds Transfer (SWIFT) and set up in 1973. SWIFT began operations for international payments in 1977 when it had 239 participating banks in 15 countries.

Thus, although many of the essential elements of full corporate electronic banking were theoretically in place by 1980, the use of electronic banking in UK corporate treasury was still surprisingly primitive:

1 Statements were printed on paper and delivered by mail.

2 Companies obtained balances from branches by telephone. The exceptions were some major corporate clients of US banks who had dumb terminals which were connected directly or through acoustic couplers to off-line computer files of overnight balances. Some of these systems were also able to initiate simple payments.

3 Ninety-five per cent of world payments required at least one or two manual interventions in the bank-to-bank transmission process.

On the other hand, retail services had continued to advance with the introduction of EFTPOS. Barclays combined with four oil companies to run a pilot scheme in 1980 and a French bank, Crédit Agricole, had introduced the first EFTPOS service in Limoges and Clermont Ferrand in 1979 using an off-line system. In 1982, Clydesdale Bank offered an on-line pilot scheme for EFTPOS in the UK but the first on-line commercial EFTPOS system again fell to the French, in St Etienne in 1983.

Progress from technical developments

Further advances in electronic banking for UK corporate treasury use were spurred by the following two technical developments:

1 The introduction of cheap personal computers (it is surprising to recall that PCs and spreadsheets, now ubiquitous treasury tools, were virtually unknown in the UK before 1984).

2 New packet switching techniques which made improved communications available and provided the mechanism for national and international dataflows.

These developments made it possible to link intelligent terminals to bank computer systems for the first time. However, for a few more years, the majority of electronic banking activity continued to be limited to electronic exchange of payments between banks – regulated by membership of BACS and SWIFT – and the UK clearing houses.

Midland Bank became the first UK clearing bank to offer electronic banking to corporate customers in 1982. Immediately, security became a major issue. As customers were unfamiliar with the technology involved they were predictably nervous about possible loss of funds or sensitive information. In consequence, the take up of the new services was halted at first.

Nevertheless banks continued to develop electronic funds transfer systems for their own use and the Clearing House Automated Payments System (CHAPS) opened in February 1984, offering participating banks same-day sterling settlement.

By 1985, electronic banking had progressed considerably:

1 Basic services were well established in the United States.

2 UK banks were responding to the challenge from electronic services offered by Citibank and other US banks.

3 Services in the Middle East and Far East were developing rapidly, using the new communications technology.

4 Growth in the use of personal computers was starting to encourage microcomputer and communication standardization, although mainframes continued to dominate the market.

5 The majority of electronic payments were still between banks but corporate customers were participating more and more in electronic banking transactions.

Personal computer power, usually in the form of a bank work station, gave corporate treasurers the ability to receive and use data directly from banks. A company's daily bank account details and balances could be collected into proprietary spreadsheet packages and used in financial analyses, for managing cash flow forecasts and for carrying out 'what if . . .?' modelling.

Balance reporting systems, designed to deliver the detail needed for uplift to spreadsheets, had started to become popular. Although costs were high, the immediate cash management savings available tended to be high and security risks were considered to be low. Even so, banks using in-house networks and systems to collect information on balances held by other banks were regarded more warily than banks which used commercial networks to collect information.

Weaknesses are uncovered

The usefulness of balance reporting systems was reduced by inadequate and unreliable data, and by interbank tensions. The main weaknesses as in the systems were:

1 *Inadequate and unreliable information* – Bank back office systems, which had been suitable for manual processing, gave reliability problems when they were required to provide rapid direct input to customers' computer systems.

2 *Poor inter-computer communication standards* – Standards were in their infancy. It was not until internationally recognized communication message protocols were developed that global electronic communication links could be established, cutting out reliance on telex and disk transmission.

3 *Interbank tensions* – Some banks refused to supply information through other banks' systems, thus forcing customers using several banks to buy several systems.

Attempts by banks to use electronic banking to tie companies to a single banking relationship often irritated customers and increased the attractiveness of the (largely US) global information providers. On the other hand, the cost of associated banking services and perceived technical complexity made some corporate customers unwilling to disturb existing relationships for 'systems reasons'.

Bank workstations could also provide electronic funds transfer (EFT) but this service was treated by corporate customers with much more caution. The available savings were lower, and the risks were perceived to be much higher. Companies were sceptical about the security arrangements and what was seen as the banks' attempts to reduce their liability.

The banks' concern about the security of payments systems caused the ten bank members of the Clearing House to take action in the UK in 1984. They appointed the Child Committee to examine the issues and to make recommendations for:

1 A new structure for payment systems.

2 New rules of membership.

The Child Report's recommendations were accepted in December 1984, for implementation in 1985, and were effective from 1 December 1985. The report made the Association for Payment Clearing Services (APACS) responsible for the UK payments industry and began a new chapter in the progress of British electronic payments.

Recent times

By 1990, the pace of change had started to accelerate – electronic banking had become the norm in corporate treasuries with electronic links between balance reporting systems and second generation treasury management systems or spreadsheets and from treasury systems to payment systems. The banks had invested in improved security and extended services to corporates, at the same time as presenting a rapidly changing electronic face to retail customers. The move to telephone-based everyday retail services, such as First Direct (from Midland) and NatWest's telephone payment system ActionLine in the UK meant that the use of technology in banking was now an accepted part of many people's experience.

In consequence, corporate treasuries' confidence in electronic systems increased rapidly. At the same time their requirements were becoming more sophisticated in line with the increasingly international nature of business. The 1990s' generation of electronic banking systems delivers an array of automated services including:

1 Cross border and cross currency bank accounts reporting and cash management.
2 On-line access to many banking services including payments, currency dealing, trade finance and account reconciliation.

The range and sophistication of the services delivered, and the technology used, grew in parallel with the development of more advanced security options and devices for protecting the banks and their customers against loss. However, the ingenuity of potential thieves and the opportunities for irreversible errors has also grown. The story is not ended and the stable door has not been shut – vigilance and an understanding of possible weak links in the electronic processes are more necessary than ever in the battle for security.

2

The function of APACS

Richard Tyson-Davies

History and background

The origins of the Association for Payment Clearing Services (APACS) in the UK go back to the Committee of London Clearing Bankers (CLCB) which was formed in the 1830s as a trade association within the London clearing banks. More than 100 years later, during the 1950s and 1960s, the framework of the banking industry experienced a period of major change precipitated by the advent of electronic data processing, a growing requirement for clearing facilities and the concentration of the industry into a small number of major players. With this growing market for payment services, technological change and the emergence of new financial institutions, interest in participation in the payment clearings led to requests for full settlement membership. Although three new participants joined the Clearing House during the 1970s and early 1980s, pressure continued to bear on the industry to allow more open competition and more open membership of the clearings.

In 1984, as a result of increasing public interest in payment systems, the ten banks participating in the Clearing House established the Child Committee to review the membership, ownership and control of the clearings. Extensive research and consultation, including studies of the position in other countries, led the committee to conclude that UK payment systems were among the best in the world but that a series of changes would be required to meet the developing needs of the market-place.

The committee's proposals for more open membership of the clearings – which were compatible with maintaining their integrity and efficiency – were accepted by the banks and by the authorities. The proposals provided for direct and indirect participation in membership of the payment systems. APACS was subsequently set up in December 1985 as an unincorporated association of payment service providers.

Its principal task is to oversee the management, orderly development and operation of the national payment, clearing and settlement systems. This oversight role also extends into money transmission more generally in the UK. It is the voice of the payment industry in dealing with the authorities in the UK and in the European Union, and has established sound liaison with those authorities.

APACS does not itself provide a commercial service. The payment services which customers use are provided by the members of APACS and by other financial institutions which use APACS members as their agents. However, those services often depend on infrastructures which APACS has helped to establish and for which APACS has some responsibility.

The fundamental role of APACS

The essence of APACS' job is to safeguard the financial and operational integrity of payment systems and promote their efficiency while, at the same time, providing for wider participation on a 'level playing field' basis. This aspect, in particular, is relevant to the interests of corporate treasurers in ensuring the soundness and security of payment systems.

APACS structure

The outline structure of APACS is shown in Fig. 2.1. APACS currently has 23 members, who are members of either at least one operational clearing company or the Card Payments Group (see Table 2.1). All members are represented at senior level on the APACS Council, the decision-making body at the top of the 'umbrella'. Membership of the three operational clearing companies (Cheque and Credit, CHAPS and BACS) is open to any appropriately regulated financial institution that can demonstrate its ability to meet fair, explicit, objective published criteria. These basic requirements are an essential safeguard for ensuring the continuing integrity of the payment systems. All APACS clearings settle obligations over members' settlement accounts at the Bank of England. The ability to obtain settlement facilities at the Bank of England for the purposes of settling the particular clearings concerned is an important criterion of membership.

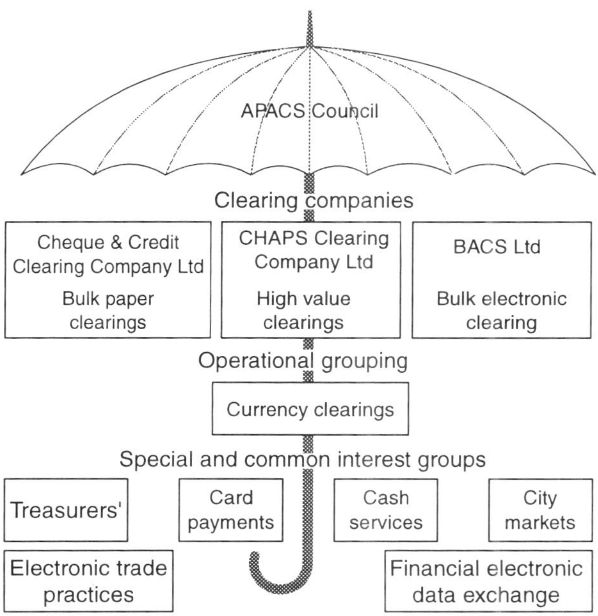

2.1 The structure of APACS in the UK

Table 2.1 Membership of APACS, the clearing companies and Card Payments Group

Members	APACS	BACS	Cheque and Credit	CHAPS	Card Payments Group
Abbey National	x	x	x	-	x
ABN AMRO Bank	x	-	-	x	-
Bank of England	x	x	x	x	-
Bank of Scotland	x	x	x	x	x
Barclays Bank	x	x	x	x	x
Citibank	x	-	-	x	-
Clydesdale Bank	x	x	x	x	x
Co-operative Bank	x	x	x	x	x
Coutts & Co	x	x	-	x	-
Crédit Lyonnais	x	-	-	x	-
Deutsche Bank	x	-	-	x	-
Girobank	x	x	x	x	x
Halifax	x	x	-	-	x
HFC Bank	x	-	-	-	x
Lloyds Bank	x	x	x	x	x
MBNA International Bank	x	-	-	-	x
Midland Bank	x	x	x	x	x
National Westminster Bank	x	x	x	x	x
Nationwide Building Society	x	x	x	-	x
Northern Rock	x	x	-	-	-
Royal Bank of Scotland	x	x	x	x	x
Standard Chartered Bank	x	-	-	x	-
TSB Bank	x	x	x	x	x

Since early 1998 full membership of APACS has also been open to card issuers with more than 1 million cards in issue in the UK, but who are not members of one of the clearing companies.

Within the APACS structure there is a 'currency clearing' which clears a range of paper debit instruments drawn on, or payable at, UK branches of members and participants. Of the ten currencies handled, the US dollar accounts for about half of the number of transactions. Bank-to-bank wholesale payments are excluded from this clearing.

Another important feature of the APACS structure are the Special Common Interest Groups for the member institutions. Currently there are six of these:

1 *The Card Payments Group* which is the forum for high-level discussion of plastic payment card matters, including fraud prevention and the introduction of new technology.

2 *The Cash Services Group* which is responsible for non-competitive industry matters relating to notes and coins.

3 *The City Markets Group* which provides a co-ordinated voice for the payments industry on payment clearing and settlement aspects of all City of London exchange of value markets.

4 *The Financial EDI Group* which provides policy and direction on the developing market for FEDI.

5 *The Electronic Trade Practices Group* focuses on the need to re-engineer existing paper based trading practices and establish best practice for global electronic trade.

6 *The Treasurers' Group* handles issues offering settlement risk and liquidity, including end-of-day transfer arrangements.

A range of other committees and working groups are also serviced by APACS. The central staff of APACS, under its chief executive, numbers around 100 people.

Clearing companies

Cheque and Credit Clearing Company Limited handles bulk cheques and credits in Great Britain. Cheques remain the principal medium for non-cash payments in the UK. Volumes of cheques written have been declining since 1990 and, although they still number around eight million per day across the UK, a further reduction of over 30% is likely by the year 2006 as personal customers turn increasingly to plastic cards for everyday payments. Corporate usage is not expected to shrink as rapidly as personal usage. The extent of decline in this area will depend on the uptake of electronic trade payments and developments such as the purchasing card.

CHAPS Clearing Company Limited handles high-value payments. Clearing House Automated Payment System (CHAPS) provides a same-day guaranteed sterling electronic credit transfer service within the UK. From 1 January 1999 CHAPS has provided a similar service in euro. It is described in more detail later in this chapter.

The Town Clearing, which was a low volume same-day value paper clearing operating within a limited area in the City of London, ceased operation in February 1995.

BACS Limited provides the bulk electronic clearing. It is the oldest and largest automated clearing house in the world, with its roots going back to the Inter-Bank Computer Bureau of 1968. Average daily volumes of around eleven million transactions (direct debits, direct credits and standing orders) can quadruple on a peak day.

In 1997, 99.7% of the total volume (4940 million) of interbank payments were cheques, paper credits and BACS transfers, and only 0.3% (16 million) were high-value transfers. By contrast, those high-value transfers accounted for 92.7% of the value moved (£36032 billion out of £38879 billion).

Card payments

While settlement arrangements for issuers in the various card schemes are not handled through an APACS clearing, APACS does, nevertheless, provide a number of services in the plastic card arena.

Since its inception APACS has been responsible for the management of the Cheque Card Scheme which is responsible for guarantee cards in the UK. Over 60 banks and building societies issue a total of some 52 million guarantee cards for £50, £100, and £250 limits. The majority of these cards now perform other functions, like cash withdrawal and other services from automated teller machines or a debit function (Visa, Delta and Switch).

Future developments in APACS

The payments industry has never faced such a range of complex challenges as it does today, and the next decade will be a challenging one for the industry both in the UK and around the world. There have already been significant changes in terms of the increased automation of the cheque clearing, the introduction of Real Time Gross Settlement (RTGS) in CHAPS and the imminent introduction of CHAPS euro clearing. However there remain very important challenges in areas such as plastic card fraud prevention, introduction of new payment instruments and electronic delivery channels and the implications of the introduction of a single currency.

The European Commission, recognizing the critical role played by payment systems in developed and healthy economies, is becoming increasingly involved in payment matters particularly and, appropriately, is acting as a catalyst in the development of more efficient cross-border payment mechanisms in the single European market. Beyond that, the EU is endeavouring to ensure that payments are handled efficiently as it moves to a single currency.

In all these significant matters, APACS is playing a major role as a co-ordinator of the views of its members and as the voice of the UK payments industry.

Future developments in payment systems and information systems

The 1960s saw the start of a pronounced shift in personal payments from cash to cheques. During the 1980s and 1990s there has been a further shift to automated electronic transfers. This will gather pace during the remainder of the decade, with debit cards (currently Visa Delta and Switch) and on-line products Visa Electron and Switch Solo recording substantial growth in transaction volumes. Figure 2.2 shows the APACS breakdown and forecast of volumes of non-cash transactions.

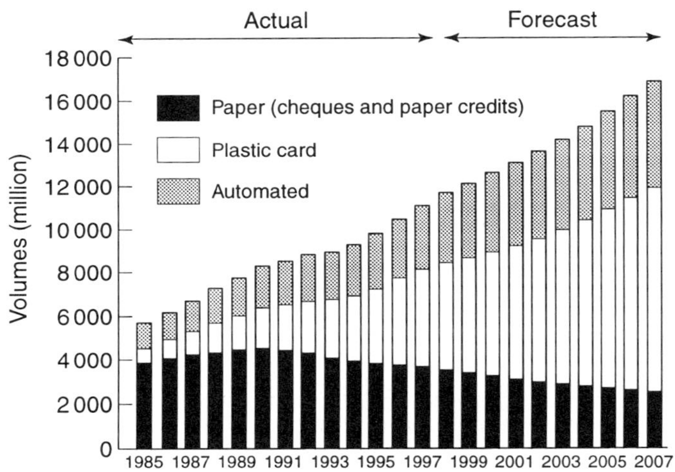

2.2 APACS breakdown and forecast of total non-cash money transmission volumes

CHAPS

Since its introduction in February 1984, CHAPS payment volumes has increased at a rapid rate eclipsing the now defunct Town Clearing (see Fig. 2.3). The fast transfer of huge sums of money has raised a number of issues. Firstly, the importance of maintaining security, and

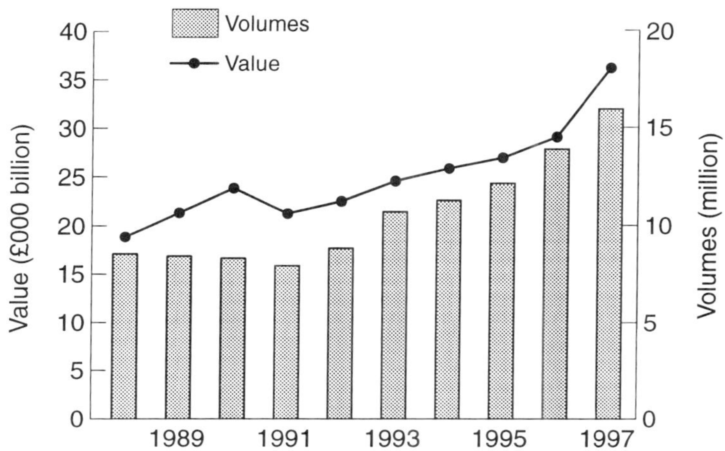

2.3 CHAPS clearing volumes and values (annual number of items)

secondly, the existence of and the means of controlling large 'daylight risk' exposures.

In the business market, automation of information handling is a growth area. Banks now offer ranges of cash management products to suit all levels of corporate user. Indeed, more changes will emerge as we move further towards being an information society and an information economy. In this context, reliable payment structures with high integrity are vital. Moreover, as noted later in this chapter, these arrangements need robust operational standards and security procedures in order to be able to operate in an international environment.

The following sections give more detail about the electronic clearings operated under APACS, CHAPS and BACS, focusing on the security measures they employ.

While the shift from paper-based to electronic payment has enabled greater control to be exercised, not only by the banker but also by the corporate customer, the scope for fraud has to some extent increased. Some major frauds have been attempted in the last few years, and these were only made possible by the availability and use of electronic systems, such as a CHAPS instruction to a UK bank to remit funds by SWIFT to a foreign location. Once there, the perpetrator could withdraw the money and disappear. In the past, in some cases, only luck foiled the successful execution of the crime. Security is therefore vital at all stages, not only in CHAPS which moves the money but also in SWIFT and other systems which handle overseas payment messages.

The amounts handled by CHAPS are immense, with a daily average turnover of £140 billion and peaks of over £230 billion. With sums on this scale, CHAPS' turnover approaches the UK annual GDP figure almost every week.

Security

In a paper-based system, because items are handled physically and the pace of activity is much slower, there is a possibility that incorrect or doubtful instructions will be identified and corrected or stopped before it is too late. Authentication in other systems – such as BACS and electronic data interchange (EDI) – are described in the following chapters.

There is another important factor inherent in electronic systems, namely the greater velocity of the circulation of money. This is clearly demonstrated in the growth seen in high value payment over recent years which is far beyond the growth of the UK economy.

A further consideration is the speed of communication and the interlinking of systems in the major trading centres of the world. This means that an end-of-day problem in Tokyo can be reflected in London and, in turn, in New York, bringing the danger of systemic failure. Therefore, there is a pressing need for effective risk reduction measures.

Although systemic failure was not a potential problem in the BCCI closure, the fact that BCCI was closed in London at 1.00 pm resulted in the completion of the Japanese yen side of a foreign exchange deal but no settlement of the US dollar side in New York.

The proposed establishment of a global arrangement for the continuous linkage of settlement of fax transactions (CLS Bank) will provide a solution.

The banker/customer relationship in the provision of high-value sterling payment services, is a very competitive area. All of the 17 settlement banks in CHAPS offer such services but their precise nature and the terms under which they are offered, differ between them all. In fact, some banks do not mention CHAPS in the services they market but have a proprietary product name which relies on the CHAPS clearing and settlement service along with other services. In broad terms, however, these services fall into two classes:

1 On-line connections between customer and bank.

2 The use of the local branch.

As far as the corporate user is concerned, it is the on-line connections which are of prime concern. Such services may include:

1 Connections via SWIFT (typically, for non-settlement banks – there are over 400 in CHAPS).

2 Mainframe connections.

3 Dedicated terminals.

4 Corporate cash management services.

5 Treasury workstations.

Within the last two in particular, the ability to initiate the same-day value payments is just one of the services which are offered.

Having an on-line connection to your bank provides a number of benefits as follows:

1 Speedy advice of payments received (and many firms consider this to be the major benefit).

2 Control of the content and timing of payments.

3 Improved overall timing by cutting out the time wasted by calling at the bank branch.

4 Linking with own systems.

Whether it is appropriate to have such a link obviously depends on the nature of the business of the company and the costs involved. For the considerations noted above, however, it is necessary to review the security aspects of having an on-line link. This includes the responsibility of the settlement bank to provide security procedures and, most importantly, the responsibility of the corporate customer to use the facilities provided in a well managed and secure manner.

In CHAPS, the settlement bank guarantees each payment it makes on behalf of its customer, so it needs to be absolutely certain that the instruction it receives is genuine. For example, if a customer uses the facilities of a bank branch, that customer will be asked to give a signature whereas, in the case of a direct on-line link, the bank will provide encryption and/or authentication to safeguard its own interests as well as those of its corporate customer.

The bank package will also include a capability for secure input, around which the customer must implement his own procedures. Typically, this will be a two or three stage process – input, authorisation and release – with the appropriate staff signing on with passwords or perhaps even more complex recognition and identification techniques.

It may be appropriate here to say a little more about the security procedures employed in CHAPS for they have been incorporated into the system after drawing on the experience of the member banks from the examination of payment systems world-wide. CHAPS security has now been developed to a level which sets the standard for other systems. The message that a corporate customer sends to its bank is received in that bank's in-house payment system but, before it is passed to the recipient bank, it passes through an authentication process and is dispatched between the computer gateways only after additional encryption techniques have been applied.

Security between the member banks is further enhanced with the inclusion of a system of message numbering and 'hand shaking' procedures between the gateways and between each settlement bank's in-house system and its gateway. As a result, security of the CHAPS system has never been compromised and is regularly upgraded.

Whatever levels of security are applied, the system also has to demonstrate reliability, and the reliability of the gateways in CHAPS and BT's X 25 Network Services which link them is at a very high level. All settlement banks have access to a second gateway, and the fault-tolerant computers running those gateways have duplicates of every significant part built into them.

High levels of security and reliability can be of limited practical value unless the end-to-end service, which incorporates each settlement bank's in-house payment system, is robust and reliable. The member banks of CHAPS continue to invest heavily to ensure that the service they deliver to their customers is the best that can be provided.

BACS

Although procedures for using BACS are covered in some detail in a separate chapter (Chapter 4), the comprehensive range of controls on physical access and system integrity that exist in this system is worth mentioning. In 1997, some 2682 million payments were processed on behalf of more than 35 000 sponsored service providers. Of these payments, 59% were direct debits, 33% were customer credits and 8% were standing orders. Originators submit payment instructions directly to BACS via telecommunication links, with the previous method of submission through computer bureaux (magnetic media input) having been phased-out at the end of 1998.

A comprehensive range of controls protects physical access, and on-system integrity exist at all BACS sites. There are also rigorous checks on the authenticity of the payment instructions received in terms of both source and data content.

Each originator is sponsored by one of the 15 banks and one building society which constitute the settlement membership of BACS Limited (see Table 2.1). The sponsors give BACS precise details of what each originator is authorized to present to BACS, including financial controls on the maximum value of payments which may be made in specified periods.

It is the responsibility of the originator not only to impose effective internal controls prior to submission of payment instructions to BACS but also to make full use of the range of checks provided by BACS to act on the feedback. When transmitting payment instructions to BACS, there is a mandatory 'log on' procedure using a hand-held password generation device and an optional encryption facility based on a 'black box'.

It is only with this level of protection that the reliability and integrity of the BACS system can be guaranteed. Finally, there is no loss of float in using BACS as, despite a clearing cycle spread over three working days, funds for direct debits and direct credits move only on the final day of the cycle.

Settlement risk

Settlement risk may be defined as the risk of a bank failing to settle its obligation in a payment clearing, the consequent disruption of that clearing and settlement process, and the risk of loss to the surviving participating banks and other users of the payment system.

Settlement risk has been the subject of increasing attention and action in many countries in recent years. In the UK, APACS, with the support of the Bank of England, agreed to undertake a study of settlement risk and identify how it should be managed and controlled. It was recognised that the greatest risks arose in the high value clearings – CHAPS and the Town Clearing (up until February 1995). The risks arose in CHAPS because it handles the most high value payments, and its members give value to their customers intra-day, but until recently did not get value for those transactions until the end of the day at the Bank of England.

Although the likelihood of any APACS member failing is remote, the consequences could, in the worst case, have been catastrophic. A settlement default could undermine confidence in the payment system and lead to large losses to members, and possibly their customers, with the consequent risk of systemic collapse. The very highest standards of risk management and control were therefore essential to ensure the integrity of the clearings.

A series of short-term risk control measures enabled the banks to restrict the amount of settlement risk. This started with the introduction in 1992 of Net Bilateral Receiver Limits which allowed each CHAPS member to decide the maximum exposure it would have to each other member. These were supplemented by the introduction of Net Sender Caps which limited the exposure of the whole membership to any one of their number. Finally, the paper-based, high value Town Clearing was closed in February 1995.

Since April 1996 all CHAPS payments have been settled as they occur (in 'real time') across Bank of England settlement accounts, rather than at the end of the day thereby eliminating settlement risk.

Although all other European Union nations are establishing real time settlement in their high-value payment systems, the UK is one of the first countries in the world to implement an RTGS for all its same day payments.

With the introduction of RTGS in CHAPS, the focus of the debate in the high value clearings is shifting. The attention of the long-term risk management programme is concentrating on settlement in the securities market, while further value market, such as real time, deliver versus payment. In the Foreign Exchange markets payments versus payment arrangements are under active consideration by both central banking and commercial banks and are likely to be delivered by the establishment of CLS Bank.

CHAPS was developed as a same day sterling payment facility. However, with the onset of European Economic and Monetary Union, it is recognized that customers need to be able to make payments in euros.

With this in mind the CHAPS Company developed a parallel payment system for euros. Using SWIFT as the messaging network, CHAPS euro allows UK banks to provide same day euro payment facilities. In parallel with the current CHAPS sterling facility, CHAPS euro is an RTGS system with settlement across accounts held at the Bank of England. Thus, CHAPS provides the UK's access route to the Trans-European Automated Real Time Gross Settlement Express Transfer System (TARGET).

3

Global cash management and security

Charles Storer

Global cash management and security is about how to keep secure and manage cash and resources globally and how to obtain maximized returns. The purpose of this chapter is to bring electronic banking and its security into context, by reviewing the broader cash management perspective including the following:

1. The definition and evolution of cash management.
2. Principal cash management components.
3. The issues to consider when establishing a global structure.
4. Potential cash management risks, and security principles.
5. Corporate security requirements and measures.
6. Banking security requirements and measures.

Definition and evolution

There is no single accepted definition of cash management. To many people it is nothing more than the provision of information about funds received and available. To some it is the ability to monitor, move and manipulate those funds to best advantage, and to others, it is as far reaching as availability of funding, market and financial information, and dealing facilities.

A common misconception, however, is that cash management is nothing more than electronic banking. It is certainly true to say that the evolution of cash management has been accompanied by the development of electronic banking, and consequently they are often referred to synonymously. Cash management, however, is about the utilisation of resources in the most effective manner, whereas electronic banking is merely one of the delivery mechanisms available, through which a number of services, including cash management, are provided. Cash management involves decisions regarding the utilization of financial resources; electronic banking helps carry them out ...

The objectives of cash management are as follows:

1 To ensure liquidity – the ability to meet financial obligations when they become due.

2 To maximize investments – the effective utilization of all surplus funds to maximize returns.

3 To minimize borrowing – the effective utilization of all available balances, irrespective of location, to reduce, eradicate, or negate any borrowing requirements.

4 To manage risk – the monitoring and control of exposure to risks, e.g. interest rates and foreign exchange rates.

The concept of cash management had its origins in the US in the 1940s. It was a natural extension of the domestic banking structure, consisting as it did (and still does to some extent) of a large number of banks, but without national coverage by any one individually and with a common acceptance of checks ('cheques') requiring extensive use of the postal system for delivery.

Receipt of checks, and their clearance through the banking system, was particularly slow, (relying totally on the postal system) not to mention the inherent security risk and, as a result, the first lockbox system was introduced in 1947; debtors were able to send their check payments to a local address for the funds to be collected and applied speedily to a local bank account. Postal risks were reduced, although not eradicated. At the same time, low interest rates prevailed, giving little incentive for investment, and surplus funds were left on non interest bearing demand deposit accounts (DDAs), i.e. current accounts.

By the 1960s, interest rates were rising and corporate treasurers were starting to manage their resources more effectively, reducing idle bank balances in favour of better returns. Lockboxes became increasingly popular, coupled with a desire for more effective and detailed information about their contents.

During the 1970s, corporates were able to obtain, and then consolidate, printed reports from their banks about their balance and transaction details. It was the introduction of personal computers, however, that provided the catalyst for the banks to respond effectively to corporate customer demands for electronically delivered balance and transaction information. This first step into electronic banking opened the doors for receipt of electronic funds transfer instructions and the migration from manual cash management techniques to electronic delivery of banking services.

Principal cash management components

The implementation of a cash management structure should be preceded by an evaluation of security. The first step is to understand all the components of the structure, then to relate each component to the business needs, analyse the risks, decide what needs to be managed, and how, and then decide on the security measures to be implemented. There would be no point, for example, in deciding that all office PCs must be protected with smartcard security if, in practice, only one or two individuals are to be involved in transactions requiring that level of protection.

Any cash management structure will consist of a number of intrinsically linked elements. The main components are the *account structures, collections, payments, information*, and *liquidity management. Communication* is critical to the effective operation of the entire package and *telephone/electronic banking* are the mechanisms through which everything is delivered.

Account structures

An average private consumer has one or two bank accounts. Before the introduction of 'telephone banking' his or her choice of institution would probably have been influenced mostly by home or work location, ease of access and convenience. The new 'direct' telephone banking services have clearly changed that buying behaviour.

In contrast, the corporate treasurer has historically focused more on financial support, and the types and quality of services available, requiring more bank accounts, often in more than one location. Company acquisitions and restructuring tends to compound the variety of the banks used, as the internal restructure may not in itself be a reason for changing bankers. The result is invariably a widely spread geographical web of banks and accounts held nationally or multi-nationally.

An optimum structure may involve a rationalization of banks and accounts, and the systems already employed. One of the questions for consideration will be where is it best to locate a company's currency accounts? In the country of the currency, or elsewhere? The answer will largely depend on which location will provide the maximum convenience for collections, payments and liquidity management, whilst offering the best rates of interest payable on surplus balances.

The introduction of the euro provided a whole new dimension to this issue, with a single currency being common to the member states participating in Economic and Monetary Union (EMU).

Collections

The important issues for the treasurer with regard to cash management are how to facilitate earliest possible collection of funds from debtors in the most cost effective manner for both parties and how to find out what funds have been received as early as possible. The location of the account will certainly have a significant impact.

A collection, is, of course, also a payment from the opposite perspective. Like a payment, a collection settles a financial obligation, but the settlement may be initiated by the beneficiary as well as by the debtor. On a global basis, the corporate company, needing to collect funds from trading partners/customers abroad, has in the past had to place heavy reliance on the correspondent banking network, either for electronic transfer of funds initiated by the debtor for documentary letters of credit or for processing of cheques back to countries of origin. The collections process can now be facilitated additionally by the use of lockbox addresses, or international direct debiting.

Lockboxes have already been mentioned. They allow debtors to remit funds to a local address, secure in the knowledge that the proceeds will be advised quickly (subject to the customer's requirements) to the creditor, and either held in a local bank account, or remitted as and when required, back to the creditor. Security procedures are needed to ensure receipt of all payment instruments by the nominated recipient, posting of the funds to the correct customer, integrity of data transmitted to the customer and effective query handling.

International direct debiting extends the principle of direct debiting in the UK (in which the beneficiary of a transaction creates the electronic data to debit the debtor's accounts, and submits them direct to BACS). International direct debiting follows the same principle, but the accounts to be debited may be in other countries. The creditor company submits details of accounts to be debited to its bank and, through arrangements established either through the bank's own network, or with its correspondent partners abroad, the data is transferred into the local automated clearing. Security procedures are needed to ensure that data integrity and authenticity are maintained.

Payments

Payments is the most obvious element of any cash management functionality that requires the application of security measures. The ability to move very large sums of money from one party to another has to be checked and controlled. By the use of stringent security measures, the levels of risk can be greatly assuaged.

Early electronic payment systems relied heavily on the use of identification codes and passwords with encryption of payment messages but more commonly now include the additional use of smart cards and digital signatures.

Information

Information is the key to effective cash management. Without accurate and totally reliable details about available funds and imminent payment liabilities, the corporate treasurer will find it is impossible to maximise liquidity management opportunities, or indeed make properly informed investment or funding decisions.

For private individuals, it will usually be sufficient to wait for a bank statement to confirm receipt of funds, but for corporates that have large trading volumes and may need to know for example that funds have been received before they despatch any goods, the timeliness of the information becomes paramount. Electronic delivery of that information is the logical solution.

The rapid and ongoing development of communications and computer technologies only serve to fuel the demand for more comprehensive information on a 'real time' basis.

Liquidity management

Liquidity management is the optimum use of available funds, in whatever location, whilst ensuring the ability to meet financial obligations when they become due. In the context of cash management, the banking processes most commonly used are termed 'notional pooling' and 'sweeping'. The general principle is to create a 'cash pool' or a 'concentration' of funds in one location.

Notional pooling is where corporate groups with fluctuating account balances commonly have credit balances in some accounts, whilst borrowing in others. A typical requirement of the corporate treasurer is for the banks to acknowledge and compensate for the existence of the credit balances, irrespective of location, in calculating any debit interest (known as interest set-off, or notional pooling). The banks ability to offer notional pooling is influenced and may be restricted by 'capital adequacy' requirements.

Sweeping of balances, by physically moving funds from one account to another, is the norm as, in many countries, notional pooling – without physical movement of balances – is not permitted from a regulatory standpoint.

On a global basis, banking systems are not compatible and sweeping, by necessity, has to occur as a manually driven service. The need for secure procedures to ensure that funds reach the correct beneficiary, and are confirmed as having done so, are self evident.

Other services

Companies do have other cash management requirements, with differing levels of sophistication and complexity; for example, the treasurer will usually want to apportion the benefits of 'cash pooling' to participants in the 'cash pool'. The corporate group may also be very large, consisting of a multitude of smaller companies, all of whom are buying and selling to each other, in which case it may be a requirement to reduce costs by 'netting' out the inter-company payments on a regular basis. In one form or another, all cash management services involve the *passing of information* or the *movement of funds*.

Telecommunications

The telephone plays a crucial role, both in the conventional sense and in the use of computers. A normal telephone call to the bank is relatively quick and simple, but security depends largely on correct identification of the caller and can be breached easily by voice impersonation. Furthermore, the phone's usefulness for a busy treasury department is limited; the amount of information that can be conveyed during a short conversation is restricted and accuracy of information given can easily be compromised if details are incorrectly transcribed.

Telephone banking

The term 'telephone banking' is one that is often misquoted and at best confused. Unlike 'electronic banking', it would not traditionally form part of a corporate's cash management solution, but it is mentioned here simply to put it into context. Telephone banking comes in two forms as follows:

1 *Conversational 'voice telephony'.* National 'direct' telephone services provide instant accessibility, often on a 24-hour basis. Security of contact is maintained by using personal data for identification, e.g. mother's maiden name, and/or personal identification numbers. (PINs)
2 *Automated 'data telephony'.* This is typified by a combination of what, by necessity, has to be rather exaggerated speech by the consumer, or more commonly, tone entry push button dialling to give commands and receive computer-generated spoken responses. This 'voice response' technology utilizes spoken messages that have been pre-recorded, often with thousands of permutations.

Security is maintained with access codes, or account numbers and PINs, and consumers have the additional comfort of knowing that funds can only be transferred out of their accounts to known and pre-authorized beneficiaries. Consequently, if payment was made to a beneficiary who had not been pre-authorized, it is less likely that there would be difficulty in obtaining a refund.

Electronic banking

Again this is a term that is often mis-used and, to members of the general public, is probably somewhat perplexing. Perhaps a better description would be 'computer banking' or even 'paperless banking'?

The principle is quite simply, communication of messages between customers and banks, using computers with modems and telecommunications networks. In the early days, basic teletype equipment could be used in conjunction with very low-tech 'acoustic coupling' equipment, but standard 'kit' now consists of the archetypal 'compatible PC,' modem, printer and telephone.

One of the main features of electronic banking is the ability to convey large quantities of data over great distances, quickly and securely. Data transmission speeds continue to increase as rapidly as the development of PC equipment and one of the challenges for service providers is the ability to keep pace with not only the technology, but also the security implications and demands as a result of continuing upgrades.

Neither telephone banking, or electronic banking systems are inherently secure, but because both can and do incorporate appropriate security measures, potential problems are overcome. In the early days, security of EB systems was maintained with the use of identification codes and passwords. This was sufficient for the purpose of ensuring that banks were communicating with the correct counterparty, but it did little to prevent corruption of data by whatever means. As discussed later, EB systems now incorporate much more advanced security techniques.

Issues to consider when establishing a global cash management structure

Traditionally many corporates that are trading globally have accounts in a number of locations with a number of banks in order to satisfy local operating needs. To some extent it is only because of the local variations in banking services that this multi-banking need arises.

An issue that this presents for both the corporate treasurer and the banks is one of systems incompatibility. International standards only exist for a small number of computer applications so most bank applications are not compatible. Consequently, treasury staff often find themselves surrounded by PCs and software applications from a multitude of banks, all operating in different ways and requiring separate training and security measures.

As treasury functions reduce in size and staff numbers, there is increasing pressure on the banks to provide fully integrated, multibank functionality. A single system – through one gateway – will simplify the customer's management processes, and consequently has the potential to reduce their security concerns. However, each participating bank must ensure that its back-office systems retain the same level of security as if it were the only service provider.

The cash management principles of banking globally are the same as banking domestically, but their execution just becomes that much more complicated, necessitating a variety of security measures. Some important considerations are:

Different banking systems: It is often assumed that throughout the world, cheques and bank accounts operate in much the same way, but in fact this is not the case. Banking systems have evolved in each country to suit the local needs and customs and there are significant variations. The governing bodies and controls differ, as do the types of clearing systems employed and the operating cycles that they work to. Different banking systems are not just a risk consideration for banks, they also constitute a risk for account holders, and should constitute part of a risk analysis for a treasurer of a company operating overseas accounts.

Different payment instruments: Whilst cheques still account for the majority of all payments in the US, they are far less commonplace, or not used at all in some other countries. Alternative paper payment instruments, or electronic systems, are employed. Once again the rules, regulations and laws governing their use are all different.

Different currencies: Not all currencies are traded on a global basis, and exchange control regulations still apply in many countries.

Different banking regulations: Services which may be acceptable in one country may not be acceptable in others, e.g. notional pooling.

Different timezones: This is an obvious frustration for trading partners on opposite sides of the globe, but also an inherent risk for banks. Traditionally, international transfers have involved a complex web of correspondent banks, that move funds between each other, taking time and adding not insignificant cost. As technology develops, and banks adopt or create global banking networks, the speed and effectiveness of international funds transfer mechanisms will increase. Funds will be moved and used in financial markets on the other side of the world continually while we are asleep and, the greater the number of transactions that occur in the chain, the harder it will become to track or reverse those transactions in the event of a dispute. Clearly this is also an issue for the law enforcement agencies in respect of money laundering.

Different languages: Even where the same languages are spoken, terminology used can often mean quite different things and be the cause of subsequent dispute.

Different technologies: This can be a major complication when establishing electronic banking connections.

Different taxation laws: These are traditionally of more concern to the corporate treasurer than the banks which have tended to see themselves as the solution provider, rather than the tax adviser. This is not an unreasonable assertion on the basis that the banks are unlikely to know all of the corporate's tax circumstances.

Different legal jurisdictions: These will have major relevance in the event of a disputed transaction, where recovery of funds – or possibly data – is in question.

Different corporate security standards: Implementation of a cohesive system will require very close consultation and co-operation between all the group companies and other parties involved. Unless the group have a global audit and IT security function, agreement of all parties to the arrangements proposed is likely to be at best a time consuming exercise.

Potential cash management risks and security principles

As discussed in Chapter 8, a risk analysis may be required, the scope of which will depend on the complexity of the arrangements to be implemented. The analysis should include an assessment of the probability of each risk – individually, as well as any knock-on effect – the degree of risk (high, medium or low) and the potential impact on the business as a result.

The following risk categories should form part of an analysis:

Masquerade: A third party acting in such a way as to pretend to be one of the two legal entities within a transaction, e.g. where a third party sends to a bank a payment instruction purporting to come from a customer, in the hope of obtaining financial gain.

Alteration: A third party tampering with an instruction in such a way as to change key elements of it, e.g. payee details or amount.

Repudiation by sender/recipient: One or other party denying responsibility on the basis that they did not receive or send a payment.

Duplication, loss or replay: A payment instruction sent or processed more than once, or a payment lost in transit, or the instruction duplicated accidentally or for gain.

Loss of confidentiality: Confidential information falling into the wrong hands, either as a result of undue care or through inadequate security.

System failures/data loss: System failure causing non-delivery of a payment, resulting in loss of contract or an interest claim. Similarly data loss could result in an unsatisfactory audit trail and consequently little or no defence against a claim of repudiation.

Consequential loss: Exposure to unacceptably high/unquantifiable risks as a result of non performance, e.g. system failure resulting in a remittance being delayed 24 hours and the subsequent loss of a lucrative contract. The payee sues its bankers accordingly for the loss of business.

Reputational damage: Loss owing to fraud, error or negligence.

If risk analysis can identify a weak link in the chain, then so can someone else! A successful risk analysis will be one that is carefully and thoughtfully undertaken.

As long as there is an understanding of how the various systems function, the risks involved and the security principles or protective measures to be considered, then both the treasurer and the banks can employ the appropriate techniques to protect themselves. Of course the problems of incompatibility of systems, regulations, languages, laws and standards, etc, merely serve to complicate matters, emphasising the importance of paying even greater attention and taking greater care with the all important initial risk analysis.

What are the objectives? Protection from attack, failure or some other unwanted event, to minimise loss, theft, errors or any detrimental impact on reputation? The security measures employed must be commensurate with the value of what is being protected, as well as the possible impact of a security breach. A combination of measures should surround the process in order to cover the variety of risks involved.

Protective measures should include *physical security, logical security, organizational* and *procedural security*, as well as *personnel policy, management controls*, and *disaster recovery*.

Other chapters discuss the application of these and various other security measures in detail. It is however important that the security measures that are already in place, or are available when setting up your global cash management structure, must be understood.

Corporate security requirements and measures

It is the requirements of the corporate treasury that will continue to shape the security developments of the future. More specifically, it is not just the functionality that the security measures provide, but how the arrangements and their operation fit in with the day to day running of the office. A highly secure, but totally impractical arrangement will not meet with much enthusiasm from the user.

Chapter 7 discusses the basic elements of treasury security, but the following measures are relevant here, and are also common among many corporates:

Electronic banking: Many companies make it policy to use electronic banking whenever possible, as it can facilitate security measures that would otherwise not be possible, e.g. instantaneous encryption and transmission of data. There is no need to rely on handwriting, which is highly susceptible to forgery, and information can be conveyed accurately and, in theory at least, in 'real-time', thus facilitating potentially immediate detection of problems, but with the time to take evasive action. However, and conversely, whilst instantaneous processing of large volumes of data and transactions may be a huge benefit when compared with the manual alternatives, if inadequate care is taken in preparation and processing then, when errors do occur, there is the likelihood that they will take that much longer to put right. This in itself then becomes a risk factor for careful consideration.

Predetermined EFT: EFT systems usually offer the choice to make 'free format' or 'fixed format (library)' based payments. The latter are popular because they require a pre-signed mandate to pay a specific beneficiary, identical to any ordinary standing order, but with the date and amounts variable from one payment instruction to the next. The opportunities for collusion are largely confined to the process of establishing the database and consequently security risks are reduced. Another benefit is that they require fewer people to effect payments once the data has been established in a database, and they should therefore be that much quicker to prepare.

Security validation: Companies that do have stringent security guidelines will often wish to work closely with their system provider(s), requiring that they act in a quasi consultancy and/or security advisor capacity. They may even require the opportunity to thoroughly test the new systems and the inherent security before formal acceptance. If a security risk is identified, no matter how small it might seem, the system provider(s) will be equally keen to know about it and take remedial steps. Electronic banking systems often offer flexibility in available security and the banks will consider any developmental work, if the need is beneficial.

Automated cheque printing: Automatic cheque printing is commonplace in large companies and yet control over the equipment is often overlooked. Cheque book stocks should be stored under appropriate controls in a locked safe and should be used sequentially as a reconciliation aid. Signature plates should be kept in a safe but not the same one as that used for storing the cheques.

Outsourcing cheque payables: Despite the advent of electronic banking and its desirability, settlement by cheque is still a fact of life. This is particularly true in the US and parts of Europe where the cheque is still the most commonly used payment instrument. By outsourcing the cheque payables function to the bank and delivering the payables file electronically in a secure encrypted format the security risks associated with forged cheque signatures are removed, with responsibility for production placed with the agent.

Data protection: 'Information is power'. Companies have for many years been aware of the dangers of industrial espionage, but great care is needed when conveying all kinds of data which, although seemingly innocuous, may provide details of great interest to prospective thieves. Foreign trade import/export services would be a case in point with details about shipment arrivals, quantities and location.

Of significant importance is the consideration of microchip theft. Albeit hard to comprehend, the growing incidence of the modern crime known as 'ram raiding' can have disastrous, not to mention potentially fatal consequences. If computers with sensitive information are located on the ground floor, particular attention should be given to this risk.

It should also be remembered that, in the UK, the Data Protection Act 1984 does not govern corporate data (neither does the Data Protection Act 1998), although the same may not be true in some European countries, so it is important to review the position on a country specific basis.

Counterfeit protection: There is already a high incidence of cheque fraud and with the advance of technology in the form of laser printers this problem will predictably continue. Desktop publishing software, scanners, a reasonable laser printer and imagination, are all ingredients of a potential counterfeit fraud. Many companies are not prepared to take the risk, particularly as banks will require some form of indemnity if cheques are to be laser printed and consequently they insist on more traditional and secure printing methods.

Periodic reviews: Security reviews should occur as often as prudence suggests, and can be as informal or formal as is deemed appropriate.

Banking security requirements and measures

Banks generally give a high priority to security. Many years of experience have resulted in tried and tested measures applicable to most situations. As with almost any large company, banks invariably have to satisfy the requirements of their own internal and external auditors before and even after systems are offered to the public. Electronic banking is certainly no exception.

From a bank's perspective, there are three fundamental principles, with associated security requirements, that require particular attention – confidentiality, integrity and authenticity.

Confidentiality: Privacy is needed. The risk is one of potential damage to reputation as a result of transactions or messages in transit, or data held in a database, being read by unauthorized personnel. The potential counter-measures would include the techniques mentioned in Chapter 8, for example:

1 Encryption of the whole message.
2 Encryption of the database or sensitive fields within it.
3 Organizational, procedural and logical controls over access to the system.
4 Logical controls over access to the database.
5 Physical controls over access to the PC/network.

Integrity: Making sure that nothing is tampered with. The risk is one of financial loss and/or damage to reputation as a result of messages in transit being altered by unauthorized parties, data held on databases being altered by unauthorized personnel and/or software and missing, or replayed (duplicated) messages. Controls would potentially include, for example:

1 Digitally signed messages to ensure that a given individual – or organization – created or approved the message, and any change to data renders that signature invalid.
2 Control over access to the means to perform the addition of a digital signature to a message.
3 The use of message sequence numbers to be checked on receipt.

Authenticity: Whilst integrity is about ensuring that the data has not been corrupted by a fraudster, authenticity is about ensuring that the data originated from a valid organization/individual. The risk is one of financial loss through actioning a message which the sender denies creating and could occur, for example, as a result of cryptographic 'keys' becoming compromised.

The integrity of a message can be demonstrated to have been preserved by digitally signing the message. If the message has been tampered with, it will be apparent when checking the validity of the signature. It is possible to use this same principle (and the same technology) to identify which individual, or organization signed the data, and therefore to be sure not only that the message itself is unchanged since its creation, but that it has come from the person it purports to have come from, or even from someone, or some organization, empowered to send such a message

This is typically achieved using 'Public Key Infrastructure' schemes, in which the same ability to digitally sign messages is also used to sign a 'certificate' which can be used to confirm the individual or organization and, if required, their authority. Such schemes rely on cryptography to digitally sign messages, and require that the cryptographic keys are only available to those entitled to them.

For a full description of the terms used, see the Glossary at the end of this book.

Additional measures

In assessing the main areas of threat and applying the above mentioned principles, banks will also be concerned with the following:

Product development: The issue of integrity begins at the product's inception and with the software/hardware developers. Banks need to be completely confident and satisfied that vetting procedures are thorough and that software/hardware secrets are fully protected.

Resilience testing: If the stakes are high enough, there will always be someone trying to find a way of breaking down the security measures that are in place. Banks probably have more to lose than most if there is a security breach and consequently their own security arrangements are among the most stringent. Policies, standards and use of security consultants are all features of how bank security is implemented.

New products, particularly in electronic banking, undergo extensive testing to ensure that they not only perform their functions correctly, but also to ensure resilience and undefeatability. Banks have to account for the unpredictable and testing includes trying to make systems break and seeing what happens if they do.

Training, continuity and usability: No matter how much effort goes into data confidentiality, integrity and authenticity, there is always the problem that the security mechanisms provided are only as good as their weakest link – people. No matter how much effort the banks put into customer training, inevitably a high turnover of staff within a company can create the environment for a security breakdown. Banks have to place a certain amount of reliance on companies to provide the all important staff training and continuity that is needed, but pro-active support should be provided by the banks, to verify continually that the systems and their inherent security procedures are being followed properly.

Other considerations

Applications flexibility: No two companies are the same and no two treasurers have the same requirements. Apart from usability, what to some may be considered burdensome and unnecessary security, to others might appear quite lax. Banks and other system providers constantly strive (or should be doing so) to provide sufficient flexibility to ensure total security, but with the adaptability to meet a variety of circumstances.

Communication: Great care must always be taken in securing the four main components of electronic banking communication which are data, applications, systems and networks.

Cost of security: Security does have a price. Those seeking the very tightest and highest levels of security are perhaps those with the most to lose should security be breached; consequently they will be more able to justify any costs involved. The more companies are aware of the issues and the potential solutions, the easier it will be to determine the appropriate levels of security required for different types of transactions.

It is now quite common for banks and customers to work closely together to review particular requirements and to tailor the solution to meet specific needs. The big question is who should meet the cost? Customers expect electronic banking to be secure, this being an inherent requirement and a prerequisite of its acceptance. Ultimately, it will depend on the relationship and will usually be a subject for negotiation, depending on the wider applications and benefits to be derived by all concerned.

Availability and contingency: Systems and the best procedures, do break down, or can be interrupted, so the best systems available will incorporate full contingency backup. Banks pay particular attention to this requirement and the corporate treasurer needs to be satisfied that security cannot be breached if emergency procedures need to be implemented.

Legal agreements: As discussed in Chapter 5, conclusive legislation does not exist for electronic payments and so legal agreements are important for any service to protect both parties, setting out terms, conditions and responsibilities. The document should be signed to confirm that all parties accept and agree to the arrangements.

Encryption legislation: The subject of global cash management security is particularly relevant to the issue of import/exportability of encryption technology and encrypted information. In some countries, export/re-export of encryption software and hardware is generally allowed, but in some it may only be allowed subject to individual applications being submitted and, in others, it is not allowed. The impact of these regulations on a global cash management structure involving a country that has restrictions is self evident. It is not an insurmountable problem, but certainly one to be carefully researched.

Conclusions

With the continual advances in technology and communications, there is a continuous need to review and upgrade security measures to protect and keep safe our valuable resources. The technical security measures of today will be as outdated in the next decade, as they were revolutionary when they were first invented. Nevertheless, a great deal can be achieved through basic security principles and a partnership with the banks in striving for a common goal.

4

BACS: practical control issues

Tom Fallon and Brian Welch

Although Bankers' Automated Clearing System (BACS) in the UK offers an attractive electronic payments service for corporate customers which is secure in itself, this chapter takes a critical look at its security arrangements, to be used in conjunction with the BACS user manuals.

As described in Chapter 2, BACS was originally established as the Inter-Bank Computer Bureau in 1968 and operates as an electronic clearing house for bulk payments by the banks. BACS provides an electronic batch processing clearing service to the banks affiliated to APACS and any BACS user's contract is with its bank, described as the 'sponsoring bank'.

Potential perpetrators of a BACS fraud would need to have a reasonable understanding of computers and access to both hardware and software. Since 1968, a large number of people have become computer literate and, with the introduction of personal computers in the early 1980s and the Internet in the 1990s, many people have access to various different systems from their homes. In addition, many of the security arrangements rely on the corporate users' commitment to enforce that security, much of which is physical rather than computer related. Much of the security used in BACS was based on procedures which were developed in 1968, and subsequently updated. That security was designed to support the preparation and input of BACS payment instructions on ½ inch magnetic tape, 5¼ inch diskette or 3480 cartridge, which was delivered physically by courier or messenger. Whilst technical developments continued, the physical delivery methods inhibited the adoption of up to date security techniques although the introduction of BACSTEL and the phasing out of the physical methods by the end of 1998 has enabled BACS to improve the technical standard of its security. Nevertheless, part of the overall approach, which is still inherently secure, is still based on the earlier structure. BACS payments follow a three-day processing cycle as follows:

First day (input day) – the latest day for the receipt of the files at BACS if they are to be processed on the following bank working day.

Second day (processing day) – the day on which all records accepted on input day are passed to the banks.

Third day (entry day) – the day on which all debits and credits reach their destination accounts.

It is possible to submit payment instructions to BACS up to 30 days in advance of input day.

BACS only takes responsibility for the security of the instructions from the time that they have been received, in accordance with their requirements. BACSTEL is now the only method for transmitting transactions to BACS, and the principle which applies to other electronic banking products is also applicable in this instance. That is, that the security, both during and after transmission of data is so comprehensive, that any person or group with fraudulent intentions would turn to other, easier targets. As a result, the security when preparing the data for transmission needs to be as rigorous as the transmission itself.

An additional problem is that many companies now outsource different payment processes, such as salaries and accounts payable, which use BACS. The problem is that the process may be outsourced to more than one organization, possibly one for the preparation of the payments, and another for the data transmission. As a result more people are involved in the process, and in particular, the kind of people with the expertise and ability to tamper with the data before it is transmitted. BACS does monitor and approve the bureaux which prepare and transmit data but, given the growth of the volume of data processed by BACS, it is impossible to be confident that fraud, or fraudulent intent, is non-existent. In all instances, the organization should be checked for security and credit purposes. The contract documenting the agreement must clearly identify exactly at which point each organization becomes responsible for the security of the transactions. It should also specify the extent and value of the security which is provided, such as guarantees or insurance, and should include full responsibility for any fraud or negligence by its employees or agents.

BACS and the euro

The initial preparations for the introduction of the euro were focused on development of a wholesale payment mechanism using CHAPS, but BACS was also developed to process euro payments, although initially payments remain in sterling as they pass through the BACS infrastructure, with the final payment instruction to the recipient bank in euro.

BACS and year 2000 (Y2K) compliance

Security and control is not confined to the prevention of fraud, but extends to maintaining the integrity of a system in the light of external influences or events. The best example of this kind of event is the difficulties presented by the change from the calendar year 1999 to the year 2000. Computer programmers had traditionally identified dates with the last two digits to represent the year, such as 98 for 1998, and this meant that unless necessary steps were taken, computers would regard the digits 00 as representing 1900 rather than 2000, with serious consequences. In view of the importance of BACS in the national small payments infrastructure, all of the core systems in BACS were checked and tested before the end of 1998 to ensure that the payments software would continue to process payments correctly from 1 January 2000. BACSTEL itself in isolation was proved to be Y2K compliant, but the essential problem with Y2K existed with the data received and the interfaces used to receive the transactions. BACS required all users to test their BACSTEL links and all bureaux which act for individual users to complete a successful BACSTEL test before the end of 1998.

BACSTEL

All submissions to BACS are made online by 'BACSTEL'. Passwords are used for authentication instead of the former identification labels which are used for tapes and disks. A password is needed at the beginning of each transmission which BACS compares against its own records of passwords issued to each user.

BACSAFE devices which generate passwords are issued to users and computer bureaux through the sponsoring bankers. Users and computer bureaux must nominate at least one person who should act as a 'control point' to which BACSAFE devices can be issued. Each password is generated by an algorithm which ensures that the next password cannot be predicted. Once issued, it is identifiable with one user or bureau only, and any password can only be used once. A password is needed for each transmission and, if it has already been used, it is automatically rejected. This includes any transmission which is interrupted.

The call-back procedure for submissions by BACSTEL is to authenticate the Transaction Authenticating Number (TAN) number received in the on-line acceptance with the BACSAFE device issued to each control number.

There is no call back facility for BACSTEL to check the

authenticity of a transmission as long as the passwords used appear to be legitimate and data is transmitted without encryption, which is usually standard in other EFT systems. There is, however, an optional 'file authentication' facility.

BACS is also proposing to introduce Public Key Cryptology which is a very secure method of transmission (see Chapter 9).

File authentication

The BACS system, as it was originally developed, was not able to guarantee that specific accounts and amounts which the sender intended to be debited and credited, were processed as instructed. In the worst instance, the total value of the payments could be amended to be paid all to the same account, without the fraud being immediately obvious.

As a result, BACS introduced an optional authentication facility whereby the originators of instructions had the ability to record – in the trailer label on their file – a check total derived by the application of a standard algorithm to selected parts of each record (bank sort code, bank account number, amount and transaction code). The algorithm is applied with a private key distributed to the sender's control point in a secure manner and used, one per transmission. The sender states the header of each file, a 'key identifier' from which BACS can determine from its records the actual key used. Using the appropriate key, BACS performs a calculation to determine the check total for the file which should agree with that calculated by the sender. Any discrepancy indicates that the data has been altered during transmission and the entire instruction is rejected.

File authentication is a valuable addition to the controls provided by BACS and should be used for all types of instructions – tape, disk, cartridge or BACSTEL since it provides the means of detecting attempts to alter instructions between preparation and processing. It should be emphasized that file authentication is not a substitute for other controls but it does improve protection against external interference. The main risk is, however, from within and the measures which are now described aim to control that risk.

Control point

Each user is required to nominate a 'control point' to whom all identification labels and passwords are issued. The person nominated should be a senior authorized signatory who has no involvement with the preparation of the BACS submissions. The 'control point' will be required to sign and return a sequentially numbered acknowledgement for each batch of payments. Upon receipt by the sponsoring bank, signatures for acknowledgement are checked against the original identity label/password questionnaire. Failure to sign for receipt of the labels will cause a referral to BACS when labels are used. Any gap in the number sequence should be reported to the bank.

Validation

BACS validates all input instructions during transmission. When the instructions are received, they are checked to ensure that payments are addressed to valid bank accounts. Instructions will be rejected when:

1 There is unreadable data.

2 There are obvious defects.

3 They are exact duplicates of previous instructions.

4 There are discrepancies in control totals of numbers of records and value totals.

5 They fail authentication.

As well as rejecting instructions, BACS can amend certain errors, such as:

1 An incorrect bank destination sorting code, resulting from the merger or closure of branches, which BACS is able to redirect.

2 The appearance of non-numeric account numbers which BACS 'zeroizes'. This is designed to cover the accidental use

of the letter O instead of the number 0 during the preparation of instructions.

3 Invalid sort codes which BACS cannot forward (see section 9 of the BACS user manual).

If errors are spotted on file submissions, there are procedures which can be used to reverse or extract files, depending on what day of the cycle the error is detected. The details of amended, rejected and returned records are detailed on the input report.

Preparation of media

Tight controls should operate within the department responsible for the preparation of BACS submissions. There should be segregation of duties and thorough screening of new employees. It is essential that adequate procedures exist to ensure that the BACS submission is generated from authorized payment instructions, that all data entered is checked for accuracy and completeness at the earliest possible stage and that errors are quickly and accurately corrected.

Access by third parties, including software consultants and hardware suppliers, should be limited and restricted. Dial up or dedicated communications links to the equipment should be avoided and physical barriers created, where possible, restricting access to equipment, for example, the PC or terminal might be kept in a room with restricted access.

Beneficiaries' bank details

The company should maintain tight control over records of beneficiaries and their bank account details. Beneficiaries should be required to submit the initial advice of bank account details and any subsequent amendments only in writing. Access to computer records should be restricted and any input or updates should be independently reconciled.

Credit limits

The company may set a maximum amount for the aggregate value of submissions which the bank is authorized to debit to the company's account during a 'limit cycle'. BACS refers to this as the 'credit limit' (possibly because it was designed to protect the banks from customers of doubtful credit quality). It is advisable that this facility is used by the company to limit its exposure to fraud and error and that it is made clear to its bank that the limit is not to be increased without prior notice and that any fraudulent payments made in excess of that agreed limit will not be the liability of the company.

Limit cycle

Each BACS submission reduces the remaining credit limit available. At the end of the limit cycle, the credit limit resets. The limit cycle can be specified as: 1–99 days, weekly (Monday to Friday) or one calendar month. For a payroll application normally run on, say the 25th day of each month, the ideal time restriction would be to authorise the bank to make BACS payments only on the 25th day of each month or up to 7 days earlier (to allow for weekdays and bank holidays). However, BACS does not presently support this form of limit cycle because it requires limits to be in place continuously and the amount of the limit cannot be varied from period to period. As a result, the company which only uses BACS for its payroll should specify a limit cycle consisting of one month commencing 7 days before the usual salary payment date (or the earliest day of the month that the Christmas salary payment is made when that is usually made earlier). This means that the company is at risk to fraudulent submission up to the value of the credit limit each day until its own payroll is processed. Extreme care is therefore needed for what is often the largest single monthly payment.

Because BACS payments are usually the least expensive payment method, and companies are increasing the use of BACS for as many regular payments as possible, limit control and the management of the limit cycle has become increasingly important.

Transaction limit

BACS offers a facility for the company to specify what BACS refers to as a 'transaction limit'. It might reasonably be expected that payments exceeding the transaction limit are rejected by BACS, but this is not the case! Any transaction whether within the transaction limit or not is, in fact, paid. Transactions over limit are, however, listed on the 'input report' as an exception. If the limit exception is caused by fraudulent substitution of the company's payment instructions, any input report received by ordinary mail may arrive too late to prevent a loss.

If the company wants the input report to list *all* transactions rather than provide summary information *only* it could specify a transaction limit down to say £5. This would capture nearly all payments and cause them to be listed on the input report. (Depending on the size of the resultant input report, BACS might object to this approach, because the guide indicates that transaction limits should be realistic). In addition, this would only be worthwhile if the report were checked whenever it was received, although the problem with long routine reports is that they are rarely checked as closely as the people who originally specified them would wish. There are also now limits on debit files which, if not specified by the originator, default to £500 000. Originators can only set limits higher than £500 000.

Input report

BACS sends an 'input report' to the company, summarising the number and aggregate value of payments it will make on the payment day. The report does not ordinarily give any information regarding payments or beneficiaries. Since BACS submissions can be delivered up to 21.00 hours, two working days before the value date, it is possible that on occasions the report arrives on the day payments are being made to beneficiaries, too late to identify and stop any fraudulent transactions. The input report should be received on the processing day (second day). If this is not received, the BACS user may contact its sponsoring bank who will be able to provide a copy. It is possible to receive the report electronically by BACSMAIL one day before payment will be made.

Audit reports

BACS provides a facility to have 50 transactions chosen at random printed out on the input report. The procedure is described in the BACS User Manual. This could be considered an alternative to the process already described of setting a low transaction limit in order to have report details of individual transactions printed out on the input. However, a random sample of 50 records in some cases may be too small a sample to act as an effective deterrent.

Mandate

The company has no contract with BACS Limited which provides an electronic batch processing clearing service to the banks affiliated to APACS, although there is a very comprehensive set of rules by which direct debit originators must abide. However, the company's contract is with its bank and takes the form of a mandate. The standard mandates drafted by banks are sometimes widely drawn and may include clauses such as: 'The bank may debit to the company's account the value of any submission to BACS which *purports* to have originated from the company.' It is important that the company's mandate is tightly drawn and takes full advantage of the control restrictions which the BACS system facilitates.

The emphasis has been on the crediting functions of BACS, but it has also been developing direct debit capabilities. Although this chapter concentrates on the security aspects of BACS, it does need to be emphasized that relative to cheques, BACS security compares well with guaranteed delivery, known value dates, much lower transaction costs and simplified reconciliation for the user. Security concerns centre on organized and 'intelligent' fraud which, if successful, would prove to be more costly for the user than any occasional cheque theft or forgery. It is this risk which makes it important to make full use of all the security facilities provided by BACS.

Controls checklist

Procedures should be designed to help detect at the earliest possible moment a misdirection of BACS payments. The following checklist of controls will be helpful:

1 Do the controls prevent or detect:

(a) manipulation of data in the sender's own primary system;

(b) manipulation of data by the BACS conversion program;

(c) amendment of the BACS files on the sender's premises;

(d) amendment of BACS data during delivery;

(e) amendment of BACSTEL files during or prior to transmission?

2 Is there an audit trail which maintains control over transactions, individually and in total, from the primary system to the BACS input report?

3 Is there adequate segregation of responsibilities between those responsible for:

(a) development and maintenance of computer software for the primary and BACS conversion systems;

(b) running the computer programs which produce the BACS data file;

(c) examination of reports produced within the organization and from BACS and the custody of the identity labels and BACSAFE devices.

4 Before files are sent or transmitted to BACS, are they subject to preprocessing by independent interrogation?

5 Are BACS acceptance and input reports reconciled *before* the entry day? Are there procedures for non reconciliation or non receipt of the reports?

6 Have precautions been taken to protect the integrity of computer software? Is the interrogation program held independently?

7 Has insurance cover been reviewed as a consequence of using the BACS payments system?

8 If a computer bureau is used for BACS transmission, is it inspected and audited regularly and is it contractually responsible for any fraud or negligence by its employees and agents?

9 Is full advantage being taken of all verification facilities available from BACS as follows:

(a) file authentication;

(b) total limit check;

(c) individual limit check;

(d) sampling?

10 Are the total credit limit and transaction limit values set at reasonable levels and reviewed regularly by senior officers?

11 Has it been made clear to the bank that the agreed limit is not to be exceeded, and not to be used purely as an internal bank credit limit?

5

Electronic banking documentation

Brian Welch

This chapter represents a practical approach to the subject of electronic banking documentation. It does not constitute legal advice, although it has been reviewed professionally.

In the early 1980s, when electronic banking was being introduced into the UK by the US banks, separate documentation for the use of those services was fairly straightforward – in some cases non-existent and, in others, very simple, covering one or two pages. The treasurers who were offered such contracts, after referring them to their own lawyers, signed them quickly and since then have resisted attempts by their banks to replace them with anything more detailed.

When the UK clearing banks started to introduce their own electronic banking systems, the contracts which they tried to get their corporate customers to sign mushroomed. The corporate reaction fell into two categories, those companies which just signed anything the banks sent to them and those which referred the contract to either their 'in house' or external lawyers. In the second instance, the result was sometimes close to paralysis, with the company trying to chip away at the original agreement and the bank giving way here and there, but generally retaining a long and detailed contract.

The reason for such detailed documentation is that, even now, there is no legislation that specifically addresses electronic payments, nor is there any case law addressing any electronic banking issues which have needed to be clarified or resolved. The fact that, after nearly 20 years of electronic banking, there is no pressure for legislation, suggests that the contracts between the banks and their customers have covered most of the likely areas of dispute, although this may not necessarily mean that either party is completely satisfied. In the absence of a contract, the ordinary principles of law would apply which, whether there is any contract or not, in the event of any bankruptcy would be overridden by the mandatory provisions of the law.

The problem with the contracts offered by the UK clearing banks was that they seemed to be trying to restate the legal position covering banking practice which renders a bank liable if it pays a cheque with a forged signature, even if the forgery cannot be spotted. The view is that banks remain liable for paying away a customer's money if this is by 'conventional' means, on the basis of forgery, quite regardless of whether the forgery could be discovered because, if there were any other rule, nobody would use the banks. Although this is not unreasonable from the banks' point of view, their approach to electronic banking contracts appears to be an attempt to 'ring fence' electronic transactions from the traditional approach.

The trend of now offering Internet banking services to individuals seems to be following the same principle with certain undertakings being a condition of use which seems to distance the bank and the customer from the previous standard conditions. Once again, as Internet banking is a relatively new development, there is limited experience of fraud and even less experience of a successful prosecution following fraud.

The result has been that some companies have been reluctant to forego the protection provided by out of date legislation, perhaps providing a 'smokescreen' for technophobe companies (and their treasurers and finance directors) not to adopt electronic banking. The position taken by the banks is that it is a completely separate 'medium' with a different kind of transaction using an authorization code (the electronic signature) which they can check for correctness, but not for forgery. As a result, this redefinition of the responsibilities for electronic payments is one of the issues which is common to all of the UK clearing banks' documentation. This has now become accepted practice and is now unlikely to be reversed by an individual corporate.

Although the overall approach to documentation by the banks has been broadly similar, with several common themes, specific details do vary. The purpose of this chapter is not to discuss how best to bargain with each bank, but to identify common points of concern.

Negotiating with the bank

The attitude and position of the corporate user is also worth addressing. Many corporates are familiar with more than one electronic banking system and are aware of the critical issues. The very largest corporates sometimes use their relationships and positional strength to amend their contracts substantially, whilst the banks seem prepared to address proposed objections on a case by case basis. The problem is that this can be a time consuming process, whether the company uses in-house or external lawyers, the cost of which can far exceed any benefit of using electronic funds transfers in the first place. Those negotiations sometimes become a test of strength and principle when high minded corporates are involved. For less powerful companies however, it would appear to be sensible to confine proposed amendments to establishing an equitable contract.

The timing of contract negotiations varies from bank to bank, with some insisting that they will not supply the service before an agreement is signed, and others taking a more relaxed approach. There is some evidence of companies not signing any agreement at all, although this might prove to be particularly expensive in the event of a significant dispute which the bank concerned might decide to make into a test case. As a result, because of the absence of specific legislation, no documentation may be the most expensive and dangerous option of all.

In negotiating to supply its electronic banking service, a bank may sometimes present a contract covering all its electronic services even though the corporate's initial intention is only to take a part of the service, such as balance reporting. This may divert the corporate's attention from the potential liabilities and exclusions which it may be conceding, because they do not relate to the service to be taken immediately. However when the corporate is persuaded to extend its use of the services, no additional contract is needed and the clauses favouring or protecting the bank are not highlighted until a dispute between the bank and the corporate occurs.

The problem is that it is hard to envisage, for example, any consequential liability of a corporate to its bank when it is taking a balance reporting service. However, the potential liability which exists when it is giving instructions to transfer funds can be very substantial indeed. In view of the suspicion arising from this practice one approach is for the bank to offer a set of general terms and conditions to which are added separate agreements for each particular electronic banking service.

Specific points of concern

Specific issues which do come up regularly are as follows:

The authenticity of the payment instruction

Most EFT documentation incorporates a clause with a similar kind of phrase which states that 'the bank will treat as valid, any message or instruction which purports to come from the customer' or 'that the bank assumes no responsibility for the unauthorized use of the customer's password'. As mentioned earlier, this reverses previous banking practice which places the responsibility for the detection of forgery or fraud on the bank. Is there anything that the corporate can do to oppose the banks in an area on which all of them have remained intransigent? The answer is almost certainly 'no', so there is little to be gained by allowing this issue to become a matter of principle. This is an issue which has already been conceded by most major corporates, it is difficult to foresee any reversal by the banks in the face of objections by medium sized and small corporates which have less individual influence with their banks.

Equal treatment

Where possible, the contract should treat the corporate and the bank equally in regard to the following:

1 Confidentiality of software, passwords or other information.
2 Responsibility for security of the system.
3 Responsibility for maintaining the hardware and software.
4 Notification of any fraud or unauthorized use.
5 Losses, especially consequential losses.
6 Any breach of the agreement by either side.
7 Both sides should have the right to the same length of notice to cancel the agreement.

Ideally, the agreement, or any side letter, might incorporate a statement confirming equal treatment between the corporate and its banker.

Consequential loss

This might arise when a loss occurs as consequence of one of the parties taking action (or failing to take action) in response to an instruction from the other. An example might be an investment manager instructing its bank to make a payment to exercise an option, but the bank not doing so for technical reasons. The loss recognized by the bank might be the amount of the payment or lost interest on the payment, but the loss to the manager would be the lost value of the exercised option, which could be many times the amount of the payment. To add insult to potential injury, a bank will sometimes seek to hold the customer responsible for any consequential loss that it might suffer, whilst seeking to exempt itself from consequential losses suffered by the customer.

There is no hard and fast way of dealing with the issue which is a frequent reason for dissatisfaction with such agreements by corporates. Large companies, whose business is valued by the banks may succeed in eliminating all references to consequential loss, but smaller companies may be less successful and have to accept assurances that the banks have never used the consequential loss clause against its customers. Although this may be true, it is more likely that a bank might use it to put pressure on a smaller customer which is least well placed to bear any consequential loss claim presented by its banks.

A variant of consequential loss is 'third party loss' which banks seek to exclude. This is a loss or liability which might arise between the corporate and the recipient of a payment if it is inaccurate or incomplete when the recipient will have no direct connection with the bank.

It is notable that under Uniform Commercial Code 4A (UCC4A) in the US, banks cannot exclude consequential liability, but the current approach in the US is that banks are liable only for lost interest unless there is a special arrangement. This is, because of the very large number of payments which are carried out at high speed and at low cost, it is unrealistic to impose enormous liabilities for consequential damages if a payment did not reach its destination. It has been argued successfully in the US that if there was any especially sensitive payment, it was always open to the parties to come to some special arrangement in those instances. That is probably also the case in other countries where electronic banking techniques are applied. (See also Chapter 6). Whether or not corporates are able to satisfy their concerns about consequential loss it is most important that they are aware of this issue, and the associated risks.

Liability in general

The banks often seek to restrict their overall financial liability for fraud, wilful default or negligence *by the bank and its employees* to a ceiling of a specific amount, for example, £50 000 or other lesser amounts calculated by reference to a specific formula set out in the documentation. Although this limit may appear to be adequate for low volume users, it ignores the possibility of losses emanating from within the bank which could be for very large amounts. The limitation of the amount of any settlement suggests that compensation in those events is negotiable and the inclusion of any specific amount may well inhibit those negotiations.

A bank may offer to amend its documentation directly or by a side letter. The amendment of the main document is preferable but, if the best concession is by way of a side letter, it should be made clear to the bank that the corporate regards the side letter to be as binding as the main agreement. All correspondence relating to the negotiations should be retained separately and not archived in a manner which might lead to accidental destruction before the agreement is updated.

As explained by Tony de Caux in Chapter 6, if any part of an electronic banking transaction is routed through one of the states in the US which has adopted UCC4A, it is quite likely that it will be subject to the code and the particular circumstances are described in that chapter.

Electronic Data Interchange (EDI)

Although EDI transactions use the banks' EFT facilities, they are usually much more complex and part of a longer series of messages which are interdependent. Banks are therefore more involved in the entire process and some of the documentation which refers to EDI transactions reflects that deeper involvement.

As with the early EFT documentation however, the banks are following different routes in its development. Some are still treating EDI as if it were just a further extension of their existing electronic banking services, whilst others recognize the closer involvement of the bank in the overall transaction. As a result, some documentation accepts more responsibility for incorrect payments, providing equal treatment and mutual obligations between the corporate and the bank are a central part of some agreements. However, the issue of consequential loss remains! (Chapter 10 details EDI security.)

Agreements by subsidiaries or associates

It is important that, where possible, electronic banking agreements with banks should be negotiated and completed centrally. For instance, where the same bank is used in several countries, only one agreement should be necessary, that being the one between the company head office and the bank. Where additional agreements are required in other countries, they should be referred back to the head office to ensure that the subsidiary or associate has not conceded any additional issues which the head office has fought to retain with other banks. If any concessions are essential in particular countries, the head office should review, or at least be informed of, the agreement. In addition, agreements with local banks should also be subject to central approval so that individual subsidiaries do not expose the corporate to more risk than the agreements with its major banks. In any case, it is likely that a head office will have the ability and influence to be able to negotiate more beneficial agreements than subsidiaries or associates but, in the event of that not being the case, it is possible that a head office could benefit from additional concessions in contracts negotiated by subsidiaries or associates.

Electronic Funds Transfer Act 1978 (USA)

In the US the Electronic Funds Transfer Act was passed in 1978 to provide a basic framework establishing the rights, liabilities and responsibilities of participants in electronic funds transfer systems. Electronic funds transfers were defined as any transfer of funds, other than a transaction originated by check, draft or similar paper instrument, which is initiated through an electronic terminal, telephonic instrument or computer or magnetic tape, so as to order, instruct or authorize a financial institution to debit or credit an account. The act was aimed at retail transactions and wholesale banking transactions are covered under UCC4A which is described in detail in Chapter 6.

Computer Misuse Act 1990 (UK)

The Computer Misuse Act was introduced in 1990 to deal with the problem of unauthorized use of computers, which is usually described as 'hacking'. As the other chapters emphasise, the risk of genuine hacking into electronic banking can never be totally eliminated, but any attempt to do so is likely to be identified at a very early stage in view of the use of the security techniques including authentication, encryption, compression of messages and message sequencing.

The act introduced three criminal offences, namely:

1 Unauthorized access to computer material. (Maximum penalty – fine of £2000 and/or six months imprisonment.)

2 Unauthorized access with the intent to commit or facilitate commission of further offences. (Maximum penalty – unlimited fine and five years imprisonment.)

3 Unauthorized modification of computer material. (Maximum penalty – unlimited fine and five years imprisonment.)

The main offence which affects electronic banking or treasury systems is that of unauthorized access with intent to facilitate a further offence which might be theft or sabotage. To commit an offence, access must be deliberate and unauthorized and the person involved must know that their access is unauthorized. For these offences to be traced, it is necessary to have a full audit trail which records all access attempts, both successful and unsuccessful. Most electronic banking systems provide this facility and prevent access after a specified number of unsuccessful attempts. The audit trail should also record what action occurs after a successful access and it is important that the audit trail is always examined to look for unauthorized use of a system.

There have been various prosecutions under the Act. One technical ruling has said that access did not necessarily have to be unauthorized, to be covered by the act. This clarified the position where someone who was authorized to access a computer could be prosecuted if he or she used that access to commit an offence.

In another case, a printer, who was owed £2275 by a company, installed a pirate program which added a password to deny the company access to their own computer. The action cost the company £36 500 and they subsequently went out of business. Other prosecutions have concentrated on the offence of unauthorized modification, which is still a matter of debate, but there have been few prosecutions involving a major attempted theft.

The act does not clarify the responsibilities and liabilities between the bank and the corporate, which reinforces the reason for the detailed documentation on electronic banking. The main problem for the act is that, especially with the development of the Internet, electronic fraud has become international and, even apart from the difficulty of catching the criminal, any significant planned fraud is likely to be undertaken from outside countries which have tried to legislate against it.

Electronic banking documentation checklist

Corporate and individual users should ensure that they have considered the following:

1 *What does the contract cover*?: Does it only cover the services to used or does it extend to all the electronic banking services provided by the bank? Delete the references to unused services and review the agreement whenever a new service is to be used.

2 *UCC4A*: Does UCC4A apply and, if so, how does it affect the rest of the agreement?

3 *Equal treatment*: Where appropriate, ensure that there is equal treatment in the agreement for the customer and the bank on:

   (a) confidentiality;

   (b) responsibility for security;

   (c) responsibility for the hardware and software;

   (d) notification of any fraud or unauthorized use;

   (e) losses;

(f) any breach of the agreement;

(g) both sides having the same length of notice of cancellation;

(h) a statement confirming equal treatment for both parties.

4 *Consequential liability*: Resist documentation which excludes the bank from consequential liability and/or strongly resist any attempt to make the corporate liable for any of the bank's consequential losses. In the case of especially sensitive payments, it is therefore important to give the bank advance notice of that kind of payment to ensure that it is fully aware of the consequences. In the case of securities firms which regularly make sensitive payments, a separate agreement needs to be considered.

5 *Bank liability*: Request that the bank accepts liability for fraud, errors and negligence by its own staff. (If not, why not?)

6 *Insurance*: What kind of insurance cover exists? Fidelity cover to protect against theft and fraud by the corporate's own staff is essential. Insurance against external computer fraud is expensive because of the potential amounts involved. The corporate therefore needs to assess carefully the true risk, compared with the premium requested, and establish additional internal controls if insurance cover is not provided.

Conclusion

Although negotiations concerning documentation can be time consuming and, as long as external (or internal) lawyers do not get too involved in lengthy discussions, it is important that all electronic banking agreements should be reviewed carefully and any unsatisfactory aspects challenged. It may be surprising what a bank is prepared to concede and, even if it does not, the fact that the corporate raised it before taking the service may be useful in the event of any subsequent dispute.

6

Funds transfer laws

Tony de Caux

Over recent years, various bodies and authorities have drawn up codes of practice for handling funds transfers. Most have covered bank-to-bank relationships, such as SWIFT or bank-to-clearing system relationships. The relationship between the banks and the parties to funds transfers (the originator and the beneficiary) have largely been left to individual banks to negotiate and document with their customers. However, this is often a source of much wrangling between legal specialists at banks and corporates, often ending in an unsatisfactory position for either or both parties.

This unsatisfactory state of affairs has not remained unnoticed and three bodies have taken action:

1 The US Government.

2 The United Nations.

3 The European Commission.

The United Nations produced the UNCITRAL – a model law for international credit transfers which has been used in a substantially watered down version to draft the EC's cross border payments directive. The US has made most progress by developing a version of UNCITRAL and has incorporated this as an amendment to the existing Uniform Commercial Code which has been widely adopted by individual states and the main clearing systems – Clearing House Interbank Payments System (CHIPS), FedWire and the Automated Clearing House (ACH).

UCC4A funds transfer law

The Uniform Commercial Code, article 4, subsection A (better known as UCC4A) in the US has turned out to be a milestone in the development of US cash management services. The uniform commercial code is a federal code which, over the years, has been gradually accepted into state laws. Articles 3 and 4 of the code set out rules and common practices for issuing, processing and clearing cheques (checks) and other negotiable instruments. However, until amendment with section 4A, funds transfers were not covered.

Despite the maturity of the US market there has been much uncertainty about the law, rules, regulations and common practices in relation to funds transfer. With the development of EFT systems, another layer of complexity was added. Over the years, banks have sought to draw up agreements between themselves and their customers to clarify roles and responsibilities. In practice these have tended to be rather one-sided documents, very much in the banks' favour and have only dealt with the relationship between the sender of a funds transfer and his or her bank. Extensive areas and processes through which a funds transfer (and, more particularly, an electronic funds transfer) passes were not covered adequately or, in many cases, at all. Some companies refused to sign the banks' documentation or insisted on it being modified. On a nation-wide basis this meant that different banks worked to different rules in different states. The party liable for any problems that might occur in the payment process could therefore vary. As a result of a confusing body of law, those cases that did come to court had contradictory outcomes, providing little guidance to future cases. Both companies and banks realized that it was in nobody's interest for this situation to continue and work began on drawing up a legal code that could be applied on a national basis.

Input was gathered from interested parties. The Treasury Management Association (TMA) – formerly the National Corporate Cash Management Association (NCCMA) – represented the views of corporations in the process. The banks and other financial institutions engaged in money transfer activities were represented by bodies such as the National Automated Clearing House Association (NACHA) and the Federal Reserve Bank as the major providers of national funds transfer systems.

The purpose of UCC4A

UCC4A is a comprehensive law relating to wholesale funds transfers. It excludes consumer funds transfers which are covered by a separate law – the Electronic Funds Transfer Act. In effect it covers almost all corporate funds transfers that take place within the US, i.e. where an originator or payer instructs a bank to make a payment by wire transfer which will be cleared through a system such as CHIPS or Fed Wire. UCC4A was not meant to cover payment through the Automated Clearing House (ACH). However, most bank agreements cover all credit transfers and so, in signing a bank agreement drawn up under UCC4A, a corporate may agree to the same rules and regulations for its ACH payments. It sets out the obligations, responsibilities and relationships between the various parties to a payment, namely:

1 Originating bank.

2 Originator.

3 Intermediary bank.

4 Beneficiary.

5 Beneficiary bank.

These terms will be discussed in more detail below. *Direct debits* – where a beneficiary initiates the payment – are not covered. The law applies to any payment order passing through CHIPS or a bank that is located in a state that has adopted UCC4A into its laws. Additionally, any payment that passes through Fed Wire is governed by the law, even for those parts of the process that take part or pass through other systems or states that do not recognise the law. This is because Fed Wire payments are subject to regulation under federal reserve regulation J which has incorporated article 4A.

The law has now been adopted in roughly half of the states, the two major ones in terms of volume being New York and California, both of which brought the law into force in January 1991.

Terminology

The terms that the law uses are defined as follows:

Originator:
The party which initiates the instructions to make a payment.

Originating bank:
The bank which receives the originator's instruction.

Beneficiary:
The party that is due to receive the payment.

Beneficiary's bank:
The bank at which the payment is to be received.

Payment order:
The set of instructions issued by the originator.

Acceptance:
A bank accepts the payment order when it issues a payment in accordance with the originator's instructions.

Intermediary bank:
Where the originating bank is not able to make a direct payment to the beneficiary's bank, payment may be made through third party correspondent banks.

Completion:
The funds transfer is completed when the beneficiary's bank accepts the payment and pays the funds to the beneficiary.

The process

The originator issues a payment order to the originating bank, instructing it to make a payment to a beneficiary at the beneficiary's bank (see Fig. 6.1). On acceptance by the originating bank it is bound by the instructions in the payment order and must comply with them and issue a payment. Once accepted, the originating bank cannot later change its mind and decline to make the payment.

When there is not a direct banking relationship between the originating bank and the beneficiary's bank, one or more intermediary banks may be used by the originating bank (see Fig. 6.2). Any intermediary is similarly bound on receipt and acceptance of the instructions from its correspondent to carry out the transaction as instructed. The transaction is completed when the beneficiary bank advises receipt to the beneficiary and either credits funds to his account or pays out the required amount of cash.

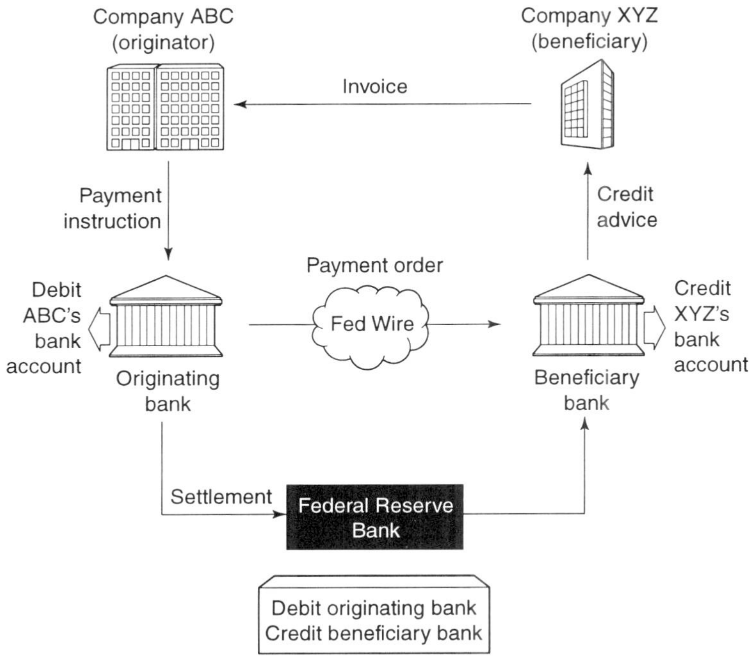

6.1 US domestic funds transfer

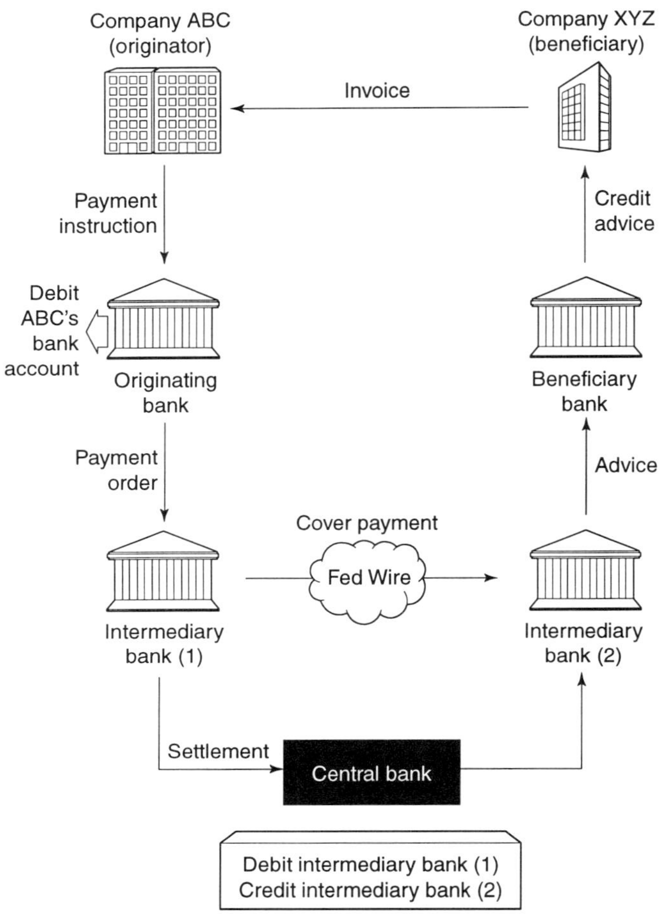

6.2 Domestic payment using intermediary banks

Cut-off times

Banks have the right to set cut-off times for payments or processes attending to payments such as cancellation and amendments. Such cut-off times may be different for different types of payment, different geographical locations or different types of originator. For example, cut-off times for CHIPS payments may be different to times for Fed Wire payments. Customers based in New York will have different cut-off times to those based in California and a government department or multinational corporation might be allowed different times to a middle market company.

Security

As a way of reducing potential funds transfer fraud, UCC4A lays down that the banks, clearing houses and systems used to process payments must have security to a standard that is 'commercially reasonable'. The article does not, however, say what 'commercially reasonable' means. The practical effects of this have been as follows. Banks have improved the security features of their products, particularly their computer-based EFT products. A de facto standard has emerged and all the banks' EFT products have to some extent become standardized as far as security is concerned. Features such as 'message authentication' and 'encryption' of, at least, passwords are now regarded as the norm.

Similarly, acceptance of telephone or faxed instructions to make payments has now become even more of a problem to banks and prices of such services are likely to reflect the banks' strategy to encourage customers to move to the more secure EFT method.

Originating banks have the right to debit their customer for a payment order that they receive, whether or not it was duly authorized by a responsible person working for the customer:

1. As long as 'commercially reasonable' security was in place, i.e. that it contains the necessary passwords or test keys and that it passes the authentication process.
2. In the event that the customer was offered, but rejected, some reasonable security device or procedures, and the customer had agreed to be bound by any payment order issued in its name.

If either of these situations has not occurred, and the bank accepts and processes an unauthorized payment, the bank will be liable and will not be able to enforce its customer to pay. It will also have no legal recourse to obtain a refund from the beneficiary although, in the instance of a mistake rather than a fraud, a request for return of the payment from the beneficiary might be a sensible first step.

What constitutes 'commercially reasonable' security is a subject of much debate. What might be deemed reasonable for a small company sending a batch of low-value pension payments may not be considered adequate for a multinational sending a batch of high-value payments issued to settle securities transactions.

When considering reasonableness, courts will also look at the security measures in place between similar customers and their banks for similar size transactions. The best security methods will not necessarily be deemed to be the most reasonable when applied to a particular company and a particular situation. Having to use SMART cards and several layers of signatories may be considered reasonable for a multinational, but unreasonable for a small company issuing only a handful of payments each month.

Generally 'reasonableness' will be determined on the basis of assessing whether the procedures put in place were sufficient to provide safeguards against possible fraud. For example, a bank has agreed to accept instructions over the telephone to make payments from named employees of a corporate customer on the basis that it telephones the company back and confirms the beneficiaries' details and amounts. Let us assume a recently dismissed employee telephoned a bank from his home and gave fraudulent instructions and asked the bank to call him back on 'his new office number' to confirm. Would the company be liable because it did not inform the bank that the employee had left, or is the bank liable because it was in breach of the arrangements, i.e. it did not call back to normal telephone number? An interesting dilemma and almost certainly the bank will be held responsible, despite the customer oversight in informing the bank of the employee's dismissal.

Errors

The general principle of UCC4A is that each party is responsible for its own errors. However, often banks will seek to shift responsibility to customers in their EFT agreements by using disclaimers. These need to be negotiated as they are not part of the 'non-variable' part of the article. The terms covering negligence need particular attention.

The issue of unauthorized payment orders

If a payment order was received by a bank and the person issuing the order was not authorized to do so, or a valid order was fraudulently altered prior to receipt by the bank, the liability for the payment will rest on the security procedures that were put in place and how they were used. The general rule is that where no 'commercially reasonable' security procedures are in place, the bank will be held to be liable. This will be the case unless the customer has rejected the bank's security procedures and there is an agreement between the bank and the customer that the customer will be liable for any payments issued in its name, whether or not they were properly authorized.

In circumstances where the bank provided reasonable security procedures, the liability for the payment will be with the customer, unless it can prove that the fraudster did not obtain information to enable him or her to commit the fraud from an internal source, such as a customer, employee, former employee or a source controlled by the customer. This means that a fraud committed by an unconnected third party (e.g. someone breaching the bank's security and breaking into the systems to trigger a payment from a customer's account) would be the bank's liability. Article 4A additionally allows liability to be altered by written agreement between the bank and the customer.

Liability for unauthorized payments does have some caveats. The customer must notify the bank of an unauthorized payment within a reasonable time. This will be deemed to be 90 days unless an agreement to a shorter period has been reached between the parties. If the bank is held liable, it must not only recredit its customer's account with the amount of the payment, but it must also pay interest to the customer. The liability for unauthorized payments covering most combinations of circumstances is given in Table 6.1.

Table 6.1 Liability of unauthorized payment order

Sender authorized payment	Y	N	N	N	N	N	N	N	N	N
Sender is bound by law of agency	↓	Y	N	N	N	N	N	N	N	N
Agreed security to verify authenticity	↓	↓	N	Y	Y	Y	Y	Y	Y	Y
Commercially reasonable security steps	↓	↓	↓	N	Y	Y	Y	Y	Y	Y
Bank accepted order in good faith	↓	↓	↓	↓	N	Y	Y	Y	Y	Y
Bank complied with security procedure	↓	↓	↓	↓	↓	N	Y	Y	Y	Y
Bank complied with written agreement	↓	↓	↓	↓	↓	↓	N	Y	Y	Y
Bank complied with written instructions	↓	↓	↓	↓	↓	↓	↓	N	Y	Y
Proof that sender is not responsible	↓	↓	↓	↓	↓	↓	↓	↓	Y	N
Who is liable? (S = sender; B = bank)	S	S	B	B	B	B	B	B	B	S

Source: Bank of America

Payments made in error

The following types of payment errors are covered:

1 Payment to the wrong beneficiary.

2 Payment of a larger amount.

3 Payments that were duplicated (but only if some security device or procedure was in place designed to detect duplicates).

Under Article 4A, banks' security procedures do not have to be able to detect such errors to be commercially reasonable. Security that is designed to confirm that a payment is from a specified customer will probably be held to be sufficient. However, if some procedure, process or device was in place to detect errors, and the customer complied with all aspects of these procedures, then the bank would be held liable and it will be the bank's responsibility to obtain a refund from the beneficiary. If the customer does not provide notification to the bank in a reasonable time and, in consequence, the bank suffers a loss, then the bank will be due compensation from its customer.

The liabilities of the parties may be altered under this section by mutual agreement. Table 6.2 summarizes the situations and liabilities relating to erroneous payments.

Table 6.2 Liability for sender's erroneous payment order

Agreed security procedures to detect errors	N	Y	Y	Y	Y
Sender complied with security procedures	↓	N	Y	Y	Y
Security procedure would have detected error	↓	↓	N	Y	Y
Sender exercised ordinary care to discover error and advise bank within a reasonable time	↓	↓	↓	N	Y
Who is liable? (S = sender; B = bank)	S	S	S	S	B

Source: Bank of America

Communication networks and clearing systems

When payments pass through a third party telecommunications network, such as General Electric Information Services (GEIS), BT Tymnet, or SWIFT, or through a clearing or settlement system such as CHIPS, the network or clearing system is regarded under 4A as acting as the agent for the originating bank. Even if that network or system is responsible for the mistake, the originating bank is held responsible for the payment error. In practice there will be a contract between the bank and the network or clearing system and compensation for payment errors resulting from the actions of the networks or clearing systems will be detailed in a contractual operating agreement.

Identification of the beneficiary

If, on receipt by the beneficiary bank, a payment order cannot be applied because the bank account number, account name, etc, does not exist, completion of the payment cannot occur. In such a case the beneficiary bank would be expected to return the payment to the originating bank.

If a payment order includes the beneficiary's name and account number and the two appear to refer to different beneficiaries, the bank can rely on the account number. As such payments are normally auto-processed this provision means that the bank is not liable to check that the account name and number correspond. However, if the bank is aware of the discrepancy, then, under the article, no one has a right to the funds and again the payment should be returned to the originating bank.

There are some grey areas in this section depending on whether the originator was a bank or a company. Originators, to be certain that payments are made correctly, should ensure that the beneficiary's correct account number is quoted, even if they are not completely certain of the account title in the beneficiary bank's books.

Identification of intermediaries and beneficiary bank

If a payment order merely quotes the name of the intermediary or beneficiary bank without its appropriate sort code, the receiving bank may act on that name. In cases where only a sort code or number is supplied, the receiving bank may rely on that number. The sender is obliged to compensate the receiving bank for loss or expenses incurred as a result of relying on the number in executing the payment. In the event that both the name and number of the intermediary or beneficiary bank are furnished and they apply to different organizations, the receiving bank may rely on the number.

Acceptance of payments

A bank receiving a payment order accepts it when it executes the payments unless the originating bank and beneficiary bank are the same, in which case the order cannot be considered to be accepted until the payment date on which the beneficiary or his account received the funds.

Acceptance by the beneficiary bank generally takes place when one of the following occurs:

1 The bank pays the funds to or notifies, the beneficiary that a payment has been received or credited to his account.
2 The bank receives settlement in full for the amount of the payment.
3 If, within one hour of the start of the next business day, the payment has not been rejected for any reason by the beneficiary bank or recalled by the originating bank.

In general, once settlement has been made by the banks involved in the process, acceptance will be deemed to have taken place. Once accepted, a payment may not later be rejected.

Rejection of payments

Payment orders may be rejected by a receiving bank by notifying the sender. Notification may be by telephone, by letter or through some electronic method. The method used to notify rejections must be 'reasonable' and any agreement that suits a bank and its customer will be deemed to be reasonable. Payment orders can be rejected because:

1 They contain ambiguous instructions.
2 There are insufficient funds in the originator's account.
3 There is some credit limitation on the receiving bank.
4 The receiving bank is operationally unable to carry out the instructions.

Cancellation or amendment of the payment order

The sender of a payment order may amend or cancel a payment and such an instruction can be notified by telephone, in writing or by electronic methods. In circumstances where security procedures are in pace, such procedures must be adhered to. A notification to amend or cancel a payment must reach the receiving bank prior to its published cut-off time and in a manner which gives the bank reasonable time to act on the instruction.

Once acceptance has occurred, an instruction to cancel or amend a payment will not be effective unless there is concurrence from the receiving bank and unless the funds transfer or clearing system used allows otherwise. Once a payment has been accepted by the beneficiary bank, cancellation or amendment can only occur if an error by the sender caused a duplicate payment or where the beneficiary is not entitled to the payment. An amended payment order effectively cancels the original order and is treated as a new payment. Generally, the sender of a payment is liable to the receiving bank for any expenses or any loss incurred in respect of an amendment or cancellation or any attempt to do either. A payment that has not been accepted within five days of the payment value date will be considered under the article as being cancelled. Unlike cheques, a payment order, once made, cannot be revoked if the originator dies, unless the receiving bank has received notice of the death prior to the receipt of the payment. This could occur in the case of a forward dated or ACH payment which may have entered the system prior to the originator's death.

The obligations of a receiving bank

A receiving bank, having accepted a payment order, is obliged to issue a payment on the day of receipt in accordance with the sender's order. Intermediary banks are similarly obliged to follow those instructions. Where the sender specified the use of a particular method of transmission (e.g. Fed Wire or ACH), it should be respected unless the bank knows of some good reason why another method might be better, such as a system failure. Where no method is specified, the receiving bank has to use the most efficient method of transmission and instruct any intermediary to do likewise. Where a value or payment date is specified, a method must be used that will get the payment to the beneficiary on the due date.

A receiving bank, unless specifically instructed to in the payment order, may not reimburse its expenses or charges by deducting them from the amount of the payment order. It will have to seek reimbursement from its (instructing) correspondent bank.

Late or improper execution

Where the payment is completed, but some delay occurs before payment is made to the beneficiary or credited to his account, the receiving bank is in breach of its obligation under article 4A. It will therefore be obliged to pay interest to the beneficiary or the sender in respect of the number of late days. Delays caused by a receiving bank that result in the payment not being made, being delayed, passing through an incorrect intermediary or not complying to any of the sender's instructions, will be the responsibility of the offending bank. It will have to bear any subsequent expenses and interest and it may also be liable for consequential damages resulting from losses or delays.

The obligations of a sender to a receiving bank

Apart from situations where a receiving bank makes errors in the execution of the payment, the sender is obliged to pay the receiving bank once the order has been accepted. If the payment is not accepted, the sender has no obligation to settle with the receiver. If the sender has already paid for a payment that is not accepted then he or she is entitled to a refund of the amount plus interest. In effect, this provides the originator with a money-back guarantee if the payment fails. The exception is in cases where a specified bank in the transaction could not complete the transfer for some reason, such as ceasing trading or insolvency, in which case the originator would have to pay the originating bank and the originating bank would have to pay any intermediaries specified in the transfer. The originator's remedy for reimbursement would have to be through the courts under the bankruptcy laws.

The sender is discharged from its obligations and payment is deemed to have occurred when:

1 The sender is a bank.

2 The receiving bank obtains settlement across its account (the account may be at the Federal Reserve Bank or at a correspondent bank) see Fig. 6.3.

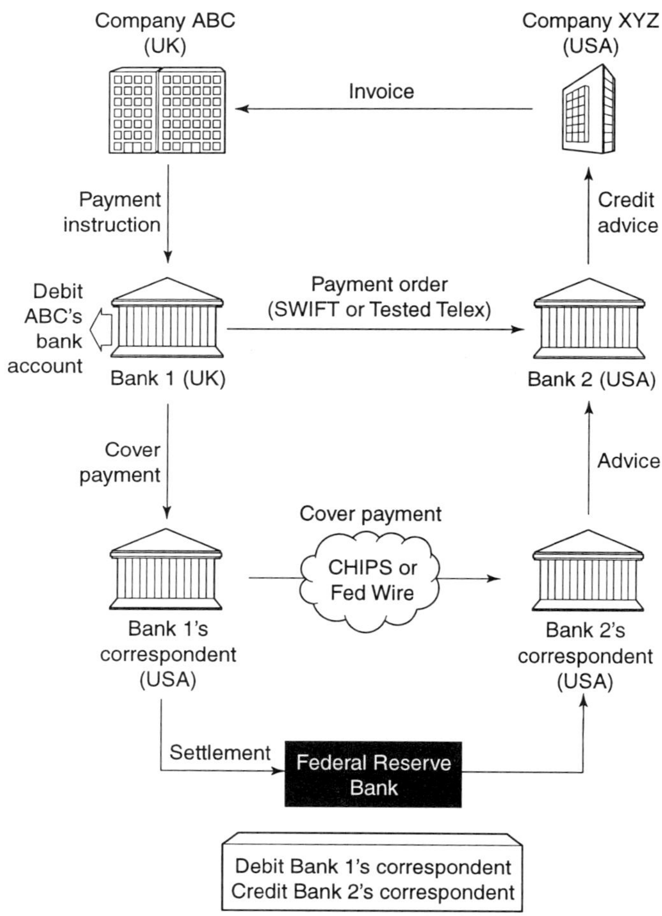

6.3 Cross-border payment into the USA using correspondent banks

3 The funds are withdrawn by the receiving bank at midnight on the day that the funds become available in its account.

In cases where the sender and receiver are both members of net settlement systems, payment of an individual payment order is deemed to have taken place when the two banks settle in accordance with the systems' rules. Where the sender is not a bank, payment occurs when the receiving bank debits the account of the sender in its books, provided that there are sufficient funds available to cover the payment order.

The obligations of the beneficiary bank to the beneficiary

When a beneficiary bank accepts a payment on behalf of a beneficiary, that bank is liable to pay the beneficiary on the payment date. If acceptance occurs after the bank's cut-off time, the funds should be available to the beneficiary the next working day. If the bank refuses to pay the beneficiary, it may be liable for consequential damages, unless it can prove that non-payment was due to some doubt on its part that the beneficiary had a right to the payment.

Notification to the beneficiary should be before midnight on the day following the payment date. If the bank fails to do this, it will be liable to pay the beneficiary interest from the payment date to the date on which he was made aware of the payment. The right to notification may be varied between the parties and, in some cases (e.g. ACH transactions), there is no obligation to advise beneficiaries of funds received for them (although in practice most banks will). Where the beneficiary bank credits the beneficiary's account in its books, payment occurs when:

1 The beneficiary is advised that the funds are available.
2 The beneficiary bank applies the credit in reduction of a debt in the beneficiary's name, such as a loan.
3 Actual cash or funds are made available to the beneficiary.

In circumstances where the beneficiary bank releases funds to the beneficiary before it receives settlement, such as CHIPS transactions prior to end-of-day settlement, it assumes the credit liability and the risk of non-settlement (unless it delays acceptance until settlement). A payment made to the beneficiary on a conditional basis or with recourse will not be allowed, unless the underlying funds transfer systems allow for it.

Variations by agreement

UCC4A enables some flexibility and certain provisions can be altered by agreement between parties. Variable areas include the following:

1. The time period for a customer to report an unauthorized payment.
2. The time period for a customer to report errors.
3. The obligation of a receiving bank to accept a payment order.
4. The obligation of the beneficiary bank to notify a payment receipt to the beneficiary.
5. The rate of interest to be paid for losses or late payment.

A number of areas of the article cannot be altered by agreement. These include the following:

1. The bank's obligation to provide and comply with adequate security procedures.
2. The bank's obligation to refund the originator for unauthorized payments initiated from outside the customer's area of control.
3. The bank's liability for late or improper execution of a payment.
4. The bank's obligation to refund the originator for payments made in error.
5. The sender's obligation to pay a receiving bank.

6 The obligation of the beneficiary's bank to pay the beneficiary.

7 The completion of a payment to a beneficiary by the beneficiary's bank.

Although the US funds transfer systems have amended their rules to bring them in line with UCC4A, in some cases the regulations of the Federal Reserve Bank and bank operating circulars may overrule UCC4A.

Bankruptcy proceedings

If a bank is served a notice of bankruptcy in respect of the account of a 'sender' of a payment prior to acceptance, the bank may debit the account if the staff responsible for accepting payments were not aware of the notice. If a beneficiary bank is served a notice of bankruptcy in respect of the account of a 'beneficiary', enabling a creditor to seize funds, it may not refuse to accept a payment to the account, unless there is a reason unrelated to the notice. In such a case, the beneficiary bank may also offset any incoming payment against and debit position it may have in its books in the name of the beneficiary.

Court intervention

A court can only intervene in the funds transfer process in a limited number of circumstances. The intervention can be:

1 To restrain a person making a funds transfer.

2 To restrain a bank from acting on an originator's payment order.

3 To restrain a beneficiary bank from releasing funds to the beneficiary.

4 To restrain a beneficiary from withdrawing the funds.

Order of application

On receipt of a payment order, or several payment orders or cheques, the bank may decide which it pays first and which it rejects if there are insufficient funds in the customer's account to cover them all.

The impact of UCC4A on US-based companies

Most companies making funds transfers domestically in the US have completed new funds transfer agreements with their banks within the last few years. These agreements will be in line with UCC4A but, generally, the banks are seeking to vary those clauses which can be altered in their favour. Therefore, corporations need to understand the article *and* the possible effect of alteration to variable clauses. Those customers that have not signed funds transfer agreements with their banks, or who refuse to sign the new forms, will be bound by the UCC4A as it stands.

The impact of UCC4A on companies based outside the US

UCC4A, although a US law, will affect any company based outside the US that makes US dollar payments whether they have an account in the US or not. For a company which has an account in the US and uses an electronic funds transfer system supplied in the UK, the chances are that the documentation is already subject to US law, in which case the company may be requested to complete a new agreement. If the system is taken from a non-US bank or a US bank that uses a UK-based agreement, once a payment enters the US jurisdiction it will be subject to US regulations and UCC4A is almost certain to apply to the payment because it is, in effect, a domestic transaction triggered through an international EFT system. When a UK company, banking with a UK clearing bank, requests that bank to make a dollar payment from its sterling account, the originator will only have a relationship with a UK bank and this will be subject to UK law. The bank, however, will need to use a US-based correspondent (or its own US branch) to effect the payment on its behalf. It will probably do this using SWIFT and, while in transit through that network, both the sending and receiving bank will be bound by SWIFT rules. On acceptance by the US correspondent or US branch (if situated in a state that had adopted it), Article 4A will start to apply.

The problem with a situation like this is how to determine which party was liable in the event of errors or mistakes, as three sets of rules apply to the transaction. The relationship between the originator and the originating bank will be subject to UK law and the signed agreement between the bank and its customer. The relationship between the bank and its US correspondent (or branch) will be governed by SWIFT rules and, from then on, all further relationships and obligations will be governed by UCC4A. Companies that send large volumes of payments to the US from offshore would do well to examine the funds transfer agreements that they have with their banks and examine how they would be affected by problems with large payments. Bankers, likewise, need to consider the implications of UCC4A, not just in terms of handling remittances for customers, but also with respect to the impact of the law on bank-to-bank transfers for transactions such as foreign exchange settlements. There could be unpleasant surprises for the unwary.

UNCITRAL model law on international credit transfers

The United Nations Commission on International Trade Law (UNCITRAL) has set about designing a law which will do for international funds transfers what UCC4A has done for US domestic funds transfer. In 1986, a study into electronic funds transfers resulted in the publication of a 'legal guide to EFT' and, between November 1987 and December 1990, the commission undertook the task of drafting a model law of international credit transfers. The model law contains 18 clauses and is designed to cope with all types of credit transfers, including cross-border electronic payments and will apply to banks and other institutions engaged in the funds transfer business. Some message carriers, such as SWIFT, may remain outside the jurisdiction of the law.

The law, when completed and agreed, may be adopted by any country and, at the same time, an adopting country would be expected to bring its domestic credit transfer regulations into line with it. Unlike UCC4A, it is designed to cover both wholesale and consumer payments. This may cause difficulties in some countries where the two sectors may use different payment networks or work to different standards.

The terminology used in the law is similar to that used in UCC4A – in fact, many of the clauses and areas of responsibility also bear a remarkable resemblance to the US article.

The model law recommends the use of message authentication to verify the authenticity of payments and has similar rules to its US cousin on acceptance and rejection.

The advantages of the law

The advantages to those companies making regular overseas transfers would be:

1. A reduction of uncertainty owing to the absence of statute law covering credit transfer.
2. Uniform rules for all countries adopting the law.
3. Comprehensive coverage of all aspects of the relationships and procedures in a funds transfer.
4. A framework of law in the event of there being no formal agreements between the parties to a transfer.

The disadvantages of the law

As it is produced by 36 countries and takes into account the views of banks, corporations and consumers, the law has, in some respects, been a series of compromises. Critics say that some of the provisions do not address the realities of the markets in some countries and areas such as high-volume automated payment systems where account numbers and figures are more important in straight-through processing than account names and amounts described in words. Unlike UCC4A, at present the draft law does not address these issues adequately. The law as it stands is a disincentive to automation and enables substantial damages to be claimed against automated banks that process payments against numbers alone.

The EC cross-border payments directive

This much hyped EC initiative has, during its discussion and drafting periods, been much reduced in substance and, whilst it will cover low value corporate payments, it has primarily been designed to cover payments made by and to individuals and small businesses cross border in Europe. The banking lobby in Europe is very strong and what started as an *all* payments directive has in fact ended up as a *small* payments directive. The size of payments to be covered by the directive has been subject to continued debate, but it has now been set at £50 000. It will only cover credit transfers, not direct debits, cheques or card-based transactions and only those in the currencies of member states of the EC (both those countries 'in' and 'out of' EMU). In response to this directive there have been a number of bank initiatives to provide small value cross border transfers in accordance with the provisions of early drafts of the directive including Eurogiro, Relay, Tipanet, etc.

In practice most corporates will have service levels which they can rely on. Unlike UCC4A and the UNCITRAL draft model law, the directive has been designed to protect the small man against the large banks. There is little in it about the originator's responsibilities. The essence of the directive is to speed up the movement of funds, to stop the old practice of double charging by the banks (originator and beneficiary banks) and, to some extent, quantify the responsibilities of the parties involved in the movement of funds.

The EC cross-border payment directive had still not been brought into law at the time this chapter was written. It will be enacted during

1999 to put an end to problems seen with cross-border payments over many years. These problems can be summarized as:

1 Lack of information available prior to a transaction being undertaken, particularly regarding charges.
2 The inefficiency of current practices using correspondent banks which leads to:
   (a) charges being taken by several banks and lack of price transparency;
   (b) double charging, where both the remitter and the beneficiary pay;
   (c) hidden charges being taken by value dating adjustments;
   (d) unreliability of the service in terms of time taken to move the funds between the remitter and the beneficiary;
   (e) lack of responsibility for errors and mistakes.

The directive will ensure that there is adequate information available to remitters prior to a transaction and that pricing is transparent, i.e. that there will be no hidden or double charges or significant losses of value.

The EC has intervened because it regards present cross border payment circuits as being an impediment to the completion of the European single market. Over the years, the commission has repeatedly sought to get the banks to put their own house in order with industry-lead initiatives. Unfortunately, despite a number of initiatives such as Eurogiro, Tipanet, the Inter-Bank Online System (IBOS), etc, many banks and some countries have generally had little interest in reviewing practices which for years have enabled them to make a good return for what they regard as nuisance transactions. The commission therefore decided to act.

Whilst designed to protect the man in the street and small businesses, the directive will cover all cross-border transactions made below the limit. This will therefore affect corporate transactions made using both manual and electronic banking methods. Many banks offer a special electronic service for low value cross-border payments and corporates need to ensure that the terms and conditions they sign up for will be at least as good a those in the directive. In practice, the terms of the directive are not particularly stringent and most large corporates are likely to be able to obtain far better terms from the major banks.

Given below is comment on the directive and, where appropriate, the latest thinking of the Commission and the European Parliament is discussed.

Article 1 sets out the scope of the directive in terms of the institutions involved, the types of payments covered and the currencies (as discussed above).

Article 2 sets out the definitions of the terminology used in the other articles.

Article 3 defines information that should be available to remitters prior to the payment being made. This should be a detailed description of the service, including timescales, pricing and other relevant details.

Article 4 relates to information that should be available to a remitter after a transaction has taken place. In particular, within a reasonable period, the remitter should be able to ascertain a reference number to be able to identify the payment, the exact amount of the transfer and charges to be paid by the remitter (and the beneficiary, if appropriate) and the expected date that the beneficiary will receive good value. The exchange rates used should also be available.

Article 5 sets out bank obligations to execute the payment in good time. This sets out the responsibilities of all banks involved in the transaction: originating, pay through or correspondents and beneficiary banks. The standard is that a bank must process an item received by the end of the business day following receipt. Additionally, the originating bank is held responsible for the whole end-to-end process completing within five business days, unless there is an agreement to the contrary. Beneficiary banks must make the payment proceeds available to the beneficiary within one day of receipt. Failure of a bank to meet these obligations will make it liable to pay compensation to the parties involved.

Article 6 is designed to ensure that all banks execute the payment in accordance with the payment order and covers the transparency of charging and effectively puts an end to the age-old process of double charging, i.e. the remitter paying on origination and the beneficiary paying by having amounts deducted from the principal amount by each bank handling the transfer.

Article 7 sets out the originating bank's obligation to refund funds to the remitter or to recredit his account if the payment is not received 20 days after the expected value date. The only way out for banks would be *force majeure*.

Complaints and redress are covered in Article 8. This sets out a timetable to enable companies' problems to be handled rapidly and specifies that each country should have a complaints body or ombudsman. Again, the banks are seeking to get any rulings by the complaints bodies or ombudsman 'not binding'.

Article 9 deals with implementation – originally expected to be December 1995. The cross-border directive is now approved and a consultation document on its implementation was issued in December 1997, with the directive being implemented by Member States by 14 August 1999, with those states in the first phase of Economic and Monetary Union implementing it on 1 January 1999.

Part 2

Treasury and systems security

7

Managing treasury security

Claire Goddard and Michael Deakin

A relatively small number of highly publicized events involving loss or near loss from fraud have created an impression that electronic payments are less secure than equivalent paper-based processing systems. In fact this impression is partly false and partly true.

It is false in that:

1. The physical risks inherent in electronic payments and in paper-based payment systems are virtually the same in principle.
2. Paper-based systems are sometimes judged to be secure owing to a misunderstanding of the risks in the system and reliance on 'tried and trusted' methods.

It is true in that:

1. A breach of control or security of an electronic payment tends to involve large values.
2. Electronic payments move funds more quickly than paper payments, giving management less time to react to problems.

3 Bank liability conditions for electronic payments tend to favour the bank more than cheque liability conditions.

'Computer error' or 'computer fraud' tends to be similar in kind to non-computer error or fraud, but uses the computer's inherent characteristics, such as speed or anonymity, to complete an illegal transaction. Unlike a human, a computer can be expected to run through the same set of tasks every time a process is completed, without changing its judgement and without forgetting any step. The computer will allocate exactly the same amount of freshness and attention to checking the millionth transaction as it did to checking the first.

The principles behind the design of a secure electronic system are the same as the principles behind the achievement of any secure treasury arrangement, manual or computerized. By identifying the requirements for adequate security, it should be possible to use the inherent discipline of computers to design and implement an electronic system which is secure at the time of its design; nevertheless, the perfect solution may be prohibitively expensive.

The basic criteria for adequate treasury security are as follows:

1 A planning and organizational framework.
2 Effective authorization procedures.
3 Adequate segregation of duties.
4 Practical dealing controls.
5 Accurate recording.
6 Secure settlement procedures.
7 Prompt reconciliation.
8 Independent valuation.
9 Timely management monitoring.

These nine elements can be combined to form a secure environment for processing. The important point is that the criteria should be met, individually *and* in total. The criteria may be met in different ways in different organizations; how they are met is not in itself important, whether they are met is critical. Nevertheless, some methods and techniques are better, more robust and more efficient than others and so managers should not only seek to meet the criteria but also to meet them in the most robust and efficient way.

Under statutory directors' legal obligations to shareholders of public companies, it is the responsibility of directors to maintain a secure environment and to be able to demonstrate why they believe that an adequate system of internal control is in place. They need to be satisfied that the control methods used achieve the criteria above.

Business owners may not have a statutory duty to meet the same obligation, but they are likely to be even more strongly motivated to maintain a secure environment because the cost of any irregularity will have to be met by them.

To help directors, owners and managers to identify how an appropriately secure environment should be set up and to assess their own treasury security, the rest of this chapter gives definitions, explanations and techniques which expand on the nine basic elements and show how they can be supported.

Planning and organizational framework

Adequate organizational control can be set up and demonstrated more easily when it is mandated by a clear policy framework approved by senior management. The framework should define the following:

1. The business objectives of the treasury which is to be controlled. These business objectives may be stated very precisely as financial targets, or more loosely in terms of support for an underlying business activity.
2. The policies approved by management. Policies may be general or very specific, but will normally define approved funding, liquidity and investment arrangements.
3. The responsibilities and accountabilities of those directly

involved in treasury activity. Such statements usually take the form of an organization chart, supported by job and sometimes personal quality descriptions for the principal positions on the chart.

4 Procedures for imposing control at the inception of each transaction, and for maintaining control throughout the transaction's lifetime. These procedures create the 'control environment' and should describe how security in treasury relates to and interfaces with security and control in other areas of the organization.

5 Where responsibility for setting and maintaining the policy framework lies, how the framework can be changed and how any changes are to be notified to interested parties.

Once the policy framework has been set, control methods need to be set up in practice to enforce practical controls in line with the policy.

Frequently, a computer system will have its own 'policy and organizational framework', imposed by parameters in the software. However, treasury computer systems and bank workstations should be operated within the company's own policy and organizational framework and should support the underlying control principles approved by management. Where possible, computer controls features embedded in the operating parameters of each system should be applied to reinforce the policy framework, for example, a system may be set up so that access to certain functions is restricted to the holders of certain positions on the organization chart.

Authorization procedures

In its simplest form, an authorization system makes it possible for a board of directors to delegate responsibility in whole, or in accordance with approved limits, to its individual members and to managers, acting together or separately. The ideal authorization procedure provides two clearly traceable paths:

1 *For the authority*: Starting at the board of directors, or owner,

and passing to the authorizer through a series of unmistakable instructions, limits and approval requirements.

2 *For the transaction*: Starting at the point at which each transaction is raised within the organization and maintained throughout the transaction's 'lifetime'.

Authorization procedures should govern access to and use of electronic payment systems by specific individuals. For electronic systems it is essential that continuity of control is maintained, especially if data is transferred from one system to another, as happens when a payment instruction is sent from a company's computer system or treasury terminal to a bank. A number of separate security risks must be overcome as follows:

1 The initial authorization must relate directly to the transaction. Access by password sign-on to the system as a whole does not imply authorization of each specific transaction during the sign-on period. Specific authorization (such as adding an authorization code) or release procedures are needed in addition to 'log-on' authority.

2 Control must be maintained throughout each transaction's lifetime. Payment files, in which transactions are created and aggregated prior to release and transmission, must be 'frozen' to ensure the transaction can only be changed before or during authorization on its journey between initiation, authorization and release.

3 Controls over amendment procedures must be at least as onerous as controls over original transactions. Current good practice indicates that a higher level of authority should be required to amend a transaction than the level which was required to initiate the transaction.

4 All communication channels must be physically secure. A message sent over a communication line could be interrupted and changed. Encryption and compression techniques can be used to reduce the ease with which a hacker can access messages in transmission and interpret the data.

5 The exchange of data between systems must confirm the

identity of sending and receiving systems and also check that the message has not been tampered with. Techniques include authentication messages, token exchange and random number authorization which attach message-specific codes to electronic messages which can be checked by the receiving system to detect unauthorized changes or tampering.

Where confidentiality of data is very important, access may be protected by SMART cards or by biometrics, such as finger prints, palm prints or optical retina scanning. Such access protection may prove that the original message was approved by an authorized person but does not alter the challenge of maintaining security throughout the life of the transaction after it has been authorized. Controls against interference with the message in transit must still be present.

Segregation of duties

In order to assure the security of any transaction, specific control should be established over the following processes:

1 *Initiation* – according to authorization to deal.

2 *Verification* – according to authorization to approve.

3 *Release* – according to authorization to settle.

The guiding principle should be to ensure that no single individual has control over all three activities.

In order to meet this requirement it is usual for 'dealing' to be physically separated from settlement and recording activities. In organizations which have small treasury departments – which is the case for most companies – the need for segregation comes into conflict with the justifiable demand that verification and, in particular, release should be carried out by someone with a sound understanding of the transaction in process. Most specifically, many organizations become temporarily vulnerable during holiday periods or at other times when key skilled staff are absent through illness or away on business trips.

Since separation of deal initiation and verification is an important control, errors found in the process should *not* be returned to the initiator. There is a great temptation to adopt a 'refer back' procedure that ensures corrections are subject to the same authorization process used to verify the original transaction. Surveys show that the typical initial reaction to fraud is for the discoverer to believe that there has been an error, rather than to suspect the initiator. Error processing procedures which refer an anomaly back to the initiator are, in practice, providing an efficient early warning of discovery and act more as a fail-safe device for the potential wrong-doer than as an effective control for management. While managers cannot act in the expectation of fraud all the time, it is vital for them to know accurately the risk from an internal control breach so that the true extent of exposure is known and accepted.

Computer systems achieve segregation by using sequential authorization techniques (such as password and numeric authentication) or by physical activity (such as the insertion of a SMART card and associated identification number). Such electronic segregation must be real and not apparent as follows:

1 If authorization requires the use of specific terminals, the authorizing terminals should not be accessible to transaction initiators. They should be physically separate, and authorizing functions should automatically 'log-off' if not actively in use.

2 Passwords, authenticating numbers and SMART cards should not be given to initiators for the convenience of the authorizer.

There is an interesting moral factor to be considered when using passwords and the like as 'electronic signatures'. Surveys show that few people will write someone else's signature on a document, yet most people will use someone else's password in a computer system. It appears that the depersonalizing effect of the computer removes the moral restraint associated with a signature.

Current good practice in using electronic banking systems reinforces segregation by separating authorization of counterparties from authorization of payment amount: one authority procedure approves the insertion of counterparty names and account details, for example into a library of standard settlement instructions, while another authority procedure confirms the amounts and timing of payments made to these counterparties. It is important to remember that computer systems use the numerical counterparty identity as the basis for processing a payment, but the numbers are typically meaningless to a human reviewer. The numbers are rarely checked, leaving the numbers open to tampering. It is important to impose specific controls over checking the target account numbers.

Access control techniques

The objective of modern technology is to move towards a paperless, 'hands-off' processing environment, while retaining security. Such a move requires management to assess the extent to which the computer system's electronic protection against unauthorized access can be relied on as manual checks are reduced. Once access (which may lead to loss of confidentiality, or amendment of data) has been protected, further techniques are used to apply and demonstrate authorization.

The scope of a review of access controls requires a review of the protection of data and transactions provided from the following various sources:

1. Hardware (computer) security such as access control systems on PCs or security set-up on AS400/mainframe, or even physical security devices such as keys.
2. Network access security, including networks dedicated to treasury or security packages on the treasury local area network (LAN).
3. Protection against 'computer buffs' or against programmers undertaking maintenance of programs.
4. Controls over specialist utility software, particularly on mainframe systems.
5. Internal reconciliations, for example, across interfaces between systems.

6 Protection of paper or electronic output from being viewed, suppressed or altered.

7 Regular comparison of data files, e.g. SSI libraries or report layouts against master versions.

8 Protection of master programs, spreadsheets or generated reports.

Dealing controls

Any activity which initiates a financial transaction between a corporate and a bank can be defined as a 'deal'. Computerized dealing controls should be designed to support the organization's dealing policies. Dealing controls, combined with an access control system, can be used to authorize the content of a transaction as well as to authorize the operator carrying out the transaction. Dealing controls, broadly, comprise:

1 An overall framework, or strategy, which defines the organization's willingness to enter into financial markets and risk positions.

2 'Counterparty limits' which define acceptable counterparties and the extent of exposure which is approved. For borrowings, the counterparty limit is usually the actual facility limit.

3 'Approved instruments', sometimes supported by instrument limits. The approval of instruments should also specify the use for which the instrument is approved.

4 'Position limits' which define the authorized level of exposure.

5 'Deal recording', which identifies the deal in the systems.

The main consideration in controlling dealing is the speed and sequence of activity. By custom, dealing is completed by telephone and the oral contract is binding. This market practice means that written confirmations and records establish control over dealing records and not over dealing activity. The principal control over dealing is exercised by the presence and integrity of the person who initiates the deal who becomes both the main defence and the main weakness in control.

Computer systems should establish control over the transaction as early as possible, especially if they are real-time systems, by comparing the deal done against computerized parameters which define the limits or contracts permitted and which report discrepancies. It is usual to use computer systems to record and highlight deals which breach approved limits rather than to prevent entry of out-of-limit transactions otherwise systems could refuse to record deals which have already occurred, thus failing to show a true position, or could inhibit the essential dealing needed to respond to exceptional market conditions.

Accurate recording

Computer records supported by accounting and book-keeping procedures usually establish control over the accuracy of recording. The book-keeper's discipline is carried through into computer systems by routines such as:

1 'Record counts' which identify the number of records offered, the number entered and the number processed.

2 'Aggregate values' at input and after processing.

3 'Before and after images' which show the state of the database before and after update.

4 'Audit trails' which list activity and demonstrate its effect.

In spite of their name, audit trails are in fact management trails. They are produced so that managers can confirm that control has been maintained throughout the processing lifetime of each transaction. It is important that audit trails are maintained in sufficient detail to allow managers to track back through *all* data changes so that, if an error occurs, they can identify the source. Audit trials may be electronic or paper, subject to audit agreement. If electronic trails need to be kept for a given period, it is important that a system which can use and access them is kept for the same period.

The circulation of control reports may need to be restricted because they could provide a failure warning to somebody who might be trying to defraud the company. Allowing free access to these reports is equivalent to referring anomalies back to the transaction initiators, thereby alerting perpetrators that their fraudulent activities have been discovered. In addition, the production mechanisms of control reports need to be protected so that control reports cannot be electronically suppressed or altered.

Settlement procedures

Settlement procedures provide the means by which value leaves the control of the organization, often in the form of a transfer of money. Settlements are often repetitive and may be made in large numbers which adds to the risks. Fortunately, the repetitive nature of settlements can be used to advantage by preformatting payment instructions to reduce the possibility of error.

Electronic payment systems can be an advantage in disciplining settlement, as long as practical details are controlled. For example:

1 Since it is a separate activity, settlement should be authorized at its initiation, verification and release. Authorization at the point of dealing is usually not sufficient to authorize settlement, but verification of dealing may also authorize the initiation of a settlement procedure.

2 Activities which release funds outside the organization's control are higher risk than those where value remains within the control of the organization. The repetitive element in payments does not reduce the risk and the delegation of repetitive detail to more junior staff should be commensurate with the inherent risk and not based on the apparent similarity and simplicity of the transactions.

Prompt reconciliation

Reconciliations confirm control by formally comparing internal records with externally-generated information. To be effective:

1 The external source must be genuinely independent of the internal source.

2 The channel of communication must be secure (e.g. confirmation to a fax machine located in the dealing room is not independent of the dealers). Indeed, faxes should be avoided unless stringent additional controls are applied.

3 The reconciliation must be soon enough after the event to give an opportunity for control action (e.g. significant bank accounts may require reconciliation daily before the start of the day's activity).

4 All significant elements must be checked (e.g. reconciliation of bank statements should confirm that value dates are reasonable. There have been instances where selective delay of payments has been caused by rerouting of the principal so as to misappropriate interest earnings).

5 Reconciliation items must be verified to actual events (e.g. causes of late entries, cancellations and amendments should be identified and verified and, if appropriate, authorization should be obtained for such items).

Electronic treasury systems provide many opportunities for rapid reconciliation, especially where data is transferred between systems. However, some apparent reconciliations can amount to comparisons of a transaction detail against its own source. Such checks confirm the integrity of processing but do not control the underlying activity and as such are not true reconciliations.

Independent valuation

Where mark-to-market valuations are relevant, the source of valuation should be provided or checked independently of the treasury. Such segregation may be very difficult in the corporate treasury and may be disguised by the intermediation of computer systems. For example, many computer systems require updating of a table of exchange rates and input is by a finance department from a list of rates provided by the treasury dealer. Although the resulting valuation of currency profits, losses and positions is calculated by the computer and given directly to the finance director, independent valuation has not been achieved. The rates should be verified independently of dealers from external sources such as newspapers, market-rate screens or bank dealing rooms.

Timely management monitoring

Ineffective management reaction to 'out-of-condition' reports has been a feature of a number of significant financial frauds and losses. In some cases, it has been reported that the loss could have been reduced significantly if management had responded wholeheartedly to the early signals, rather than being diverted by administrative or political difficulty. Unfortunately for senior management, confirming that response to concerns has been adequate tends to become much more difficult at the times when it is most important. Recent experience suggests that difficulties in obtaining management response may be a key indicator of serious underlying problems.

Control is established by management action in response to the messages received from control procedures. For example, authorization procedures become ineffective if management stops reviewing and enforcing policy. Management should monitor activity sufficiently frequently to allow corrective action to be timely and effective. It follows that the frequency of monitoring must be set according to the activity under review: bank reconciliations for accounts with high-value traffic may require daily review, whereas less significant accounts may be reconciled and reviewed monthly.

The monitoring system itself should enable hierarchical progression to be achieved. This should do the following:

1 Report low-value and low-risk activities frequently for review at appropriate levels of the management hierarchy.

2 Escalate higher value, high-risk or long-outstanding exceptions to be dealt with at higher management levels.

3 Summarize the result of low-level monitoring, and action taken, for higher management review.

4 Include adequate feedback arrangements to review the result of management action.

The aim of this chapter has been to show some of the ways in which electronic control features can be used to strengthen the control environment. An adequate control environment will depend on the harmonious operation of personal integrity, manual or paper-based procedures and computer techniques. The precise arrangements needed will depend on the policy and activities of each organization. There is no one right answer and it is necessary to apply carefully considered standards to each control and combination of controls before deciding appropriateness in any specific case.

Treasury security checklist

The basic elements of treasury security and control should include the following:

1 An appropriate planning and organizational framework which incorporates:

   (a) specific business objectives, approved by the board and regularly reviewed;

   (b) corporate financial objectives, which serve the approved business objectives;

   (c) approved treasury policies for;

      (i) funding;

      (ii) liquidity management;

      (iii) investment management;

   (d) a procedure for setting and maintaining the security and control framework which allocates responsibility clearly and is approved by the board;

   (e) procedures which capture control at the point of inception of each transaction and maintain that control unbroken for the whole transaction lifetime;

(f) a formal hierarchy for delegation of treasury activity which holds executives accountable for the consequences of decisions and action.

2 Effective authorization procedures, which include:

(a) a clear definition of what activities and decisions are delegated;

(b) financial limits for the powers delegated;

(c) a specific description of how delegated authority applies to each part of the transaction.

3 Segregation of duties appropriate for the complexity and value of the transactions processed which include:

(a) separate responsibility for:

(i) initiation;

(ii) verification;

(iii) release;

(b) transactions confirmed away from responsibility for deal initiation;

(c) approved and tested error discovery/correction procedures, which are independent of the transaction initiator;

(d) reconciliations completed by knowledgeable staff soon after transaction completion and independently of the treasury function;

(e) frequent review of reconciliations by more senior management.

4 Practical dealing controls such as:

(a) an overall framework which defines the organization's current attitude to market trends and acceptance of risk;

(b) appropriate limits for exposure to:

(i) counter-parties;

(ii) instruments, including approved uses;

   (iii) positions;

(c) approved procedures and authorities for changing limits;

(d) procedures for monitoring performance against limits and reporting breaches.

5 Accurate recording such as:

(a) audit trails revealing:

   (i) number of records processed;

   (ii) aggregate values processed;

   (iii) before and after images of records updated;

(b) procedures for reviewing and following up audit trail reports;

(c) procedures for retaining, protecting and accessing audit trials.

6 Secure settlement procedures such as:

(a) settlement authorized at initiation, verification and release;

(b) last point of authorization appropriately close to the point of release;

(c) protection of message after authorization;

(d) procedures for changing standard settlement instructions.

7 Prompt and effective reconciliation which include:

(a) reconciliation to a genuinely external data source;

(b) data received through a secure and independent channel;

(c) reconciliation completed quickly after the event to provide an opportunity to take remedial action (e.g. daily reconciliation of significant bank accounts);

(d) all items of significant value checked;

(e) reconciliation items checked to confirm they were completed;

(f) reconciler is knowledgeable and authoritative.

8 Independent valuation which includes:

(a) source of valuation independent of responsibility for the performance measured.

9 Timely monitoring by management which entails:

(a) policy is reviewed periodically;

(b) activity is reported frequently;

(c) the review process escalates for higher values and increased risk;

(d) more senior management receives summaries of the aggregate impact of lower risk items;

(e) 'out of condition' reports show the impact of breaches of limits, including items corrected later;

(f) management responds regularly and constructively to reports;

(g) adequate feedback arrangements follow up on management response.

10 Electronic elements to check and control such as:

(a) access to:

(i) software;

(ii) computers;

(iii) networks;

(iv) utilities;

(v) report formats;

(vi) spreadsheets;

(vii) electronic output and print queues;

(viii) master files of programs and logic.

(b) protection from:
  (i) viruses;
  (ii) program amendments.
(c) use of master file comparisons.

8

Security and control of treasury systems

Brian Welch

If the first ten years of the development of treasury management systems was from 1983 to 1993 dynamic, in the five years to 1998 development has been explosive. It is hard to say what came first, the pressure from treasurers to do more, the innovative nature of banks, or systems suppliers offering increasingly sophisticated products and opportunities to treasurers but, one way or the other, systems capabilities have changed beyond all recognition from the first workstations which were offered to treasurers on IBM XTs and ATs.

Definition

The basic functions and the security requirements have not changed much so it is probably helpful at the outset to suggest the following overall definition: Originally, the definition was limited to being 'A database of treasury transactions and additional facilities for recording information for analyzing and reporting the transactions'. Additionally, treasury systems are now able to collect bank account information – balances and transactions – to provide the capability to manipulate that data and to make investment decisions based on that information.

Description

The cash management functions handled include the manipulation of the cash balances to take account of expected transactions to make investment decisions based on that and any other information. However, the original role of early systems has remained, namely the recording of money market, foreign exchange and debt related transactions. With this information the treasurer can track the company's treasury related asset and liability position, including a running position of the company's exposure to counterparties, such as banks with which deposits have been placed or borrowings arranged, and outstanding foreign exchange transactions and derivative transactions. The system should produce confirmation letters or messages to the banks in respect of those various transactions and may initiate payment instructions. Treasury systems often incorporate facilities to track the overall exposure of a corporate user which is using derivative products, such as options, futures and future rate agreements (FRAs), and they can also incorporate a capability to develop future strategies, to measure performance and to measure risk using Value at Risk (VaR) techniques.

Increasingly, systems provide a direct interface to the main company accounting system which eliminates the need for the details of treasury transactions to be input twice, once in the treasury system and separately into the accounting system. It may also be possible to import information from the accounts payable and the accounts receivable parts of the company accounting system.

Early treasury systems development was linked directly to the availability of processing capability, especially that provided by the PC. Advanced treasury management techniques have developed in line with the growth of systems which could support and analyze the complex treasury techniques which are used to develop risk management skills and instruments. Systems therefore developed in different directions in different countries. For instance, treasuries which were operating in a mainly single currency environment, such as the US, had little need for high volume foreign exchange dealing support. Similarly, companies in countries where interest rates were stable had only a passing interest in instruments and methods which were designed to manage highly variable and volatile rates. Local confirmation and settlement practices also gave rise to the incorporation of special facilities.

This resulted in an uneven development of systems, with the more complex ones emerging in countries like the UK where treasurers had to learn to manage a volatile range of economic variables. However, treasury systems developed in the majority of commercial centres now cover most treasury requirements as suppliers are now selling throughout the world and their products have generally become competitive in most respects.

Early treasury systems

Initially, treasury systems were based on software which had been written to manage bank treasury operations and ran on mainframe or minicomputers which were kept in a secure, clean and temperature controlled environment. Only specialist computer operators (and well trained treasury support staff) could hope to follow the routines needed to run those systems which meant that the risk of outside interference was limited. However, as previously stressed, the greatest threat to security comes from within a company, not from the outside.

Thereafter, systems were designed and introduced specifically for corporate treasury use. The first PC-based treasury systems (which emerged around 1983) used the then 'state of the art' PCs which would probably have had 286K of RAM and two 360K floppy disk drives. (The 1998 equivalent has a minimum of 32MB of RAM, a 4GB hard disk, a 1.44MB floppy disk drive and a CD-ROM.) They were limited by the original structure of the hardware, a problem which, in some cases, has carried over into the present day in spite of the introduction of the hard disks and local area networks, both of which have made security issues more complex.

Some systems were based on larger systems such as UNIX processors to gain access to sufficient processing capacity to cover complex functionality, although subsequent PC development and especially the Windows NT technology are now matching the original capacity advantage offered by the UNIX-based systems. The PC-based systems took advantage of the flexibility offered by their size and cost offering smaller treasuries the ability to achieve the same degree of control as their larger counterparts.

Basic security considerations

There are three basic security considerations: firstly, it is important to control access to a system to prevent it being used by unauthorized people for dishonest, disruptive or commercial purposes. Secondly, there is the system-based risk of inadvertent incorrect input, omission or editing of data, or inaccurate reporting of data, which could result in a treasurer either failing to take the actions needed to manage a risk or acting unnecessarily. An audit facility, usually described as an audit trail, identifies who has accessed the system and what they have then done. Thirdly there is the concern of physical damage to the system or loss of the data held on it. This can be covered by regular and controlled back-up of the data on the system.

One problem is that, as systems have become more complex and have ceased to stand alone, they now receive and export data, becoming integrated into the overall corporate data structure. This can include incoming data feeds, such as exchange rate information and cash flow forecasts, and the exporting of data to other departments, such as financial accounting. Typically, those functions will wish to access and draw on the data at a time of their choosing, rather than receiving it from the treasury system. As a result, systems security needs to control all these different types of access, whereupon a trade-off arises between the appropriate level of security and accessibility.

A security issue which a system can help to monitor is dealer input of transactions. It is clearly more cost effective if the dealers are able to input their transactions, but it does become more important for a second person to verify the input and to check for subsequent unauthorized editing. Modern systems can, however, immediately update credit limits and portfolio listings so that the dealer will be warned if a credit limit has been exceeded, an event which should be listed on the audit trail report.

Security and access

Typically, access in early systems was hierarchical, meaning that there would be various levels of access with the highest level having access to all the functions of the system and lower levels having access to progressively fewer and fewer functions. Each level would usually have had access to all the functions available to the levels below. The kind of functions involved would be input of transactions, any editing of those transactions, production of payment instructions and confirmation letters, and access to reports. The disadvantage of this structure is that functions allowed by the lower access levels may not be appropriate for higher access level users. The most serious issue was that, in some systems, access to each level was controlled by the level of access above and not by a separate security function.

Access in modern systems provides for more flexible control, typically with one function being designated to control all other user access, limiting the functions to the ones each particular user requires. This enables the system to help enforce the segregation of functions which is essential to a well controlled treasury. Access can now be controlled by user identification and passwords which need to be changed at regular intervals and cannot be recycled, although the degree of access security necessary will depend on which functions the system provides. This might include allowing certain users access, for reporting purposes only, without the ability to change the data in any way. The increased flexibility of access enables a system to control input and verification of input into the system more closely. In particular, it can specify who is able to verify input depending on who was responsible for the original entry.

Clearly, a system which interfaces with electronic banking or accounting systems needs a higher degree of access control than one which is just recording transactions where too much access security merely makes the system less 'user friendly'. However, many more people are now interested in accessing treasury information because of the integration of its data with other company systems, making access control a critical function in itself.

Access control can be further improved by the use of SMART cards which are encoded with information unique to the holder. Where they are used access is dependent on the use of a password in conjunction with the card. Biometric techniques using physical characteristics, such as fingerprints or even voiceprints, may be used to identify users in future systems. Again, this degree of security may not be necessary for all treasury systems.

Early systems, once accessed, remained live until logged off. The danger of this is that unattended, logged-on terminals could be used by unauthorized personnel. Modern systems usually provide a 'time-out' facility which automatically logs out a terminal if it is unused for a certain time which is determined by the systems administrator. Although this can be inconvenient for treasury personnel, it is a useful feature to prevent unauthorized use of a 'live' terminal.

Password abuse

Chapter 7 – Managing treasury security – comments on the fact that people are often prepared to use colleagues' passwords, even though this might be regarded as the systems equivalent of forging a signature. This practice, sometimes described as password sharing, is one example of password abuse. Another is to keep a password in an obvious place, such as taped to the side of the PC, or noting it in the front of the user's diary which may be kept close to the terminal. Other examples of abuse include trying to gain access with the wrong password or attempting to use facilities which are not assigned to that user's function.

Most systems users will not be more disciplined about the use of their passwords than a system demands. It therefore needs to be designed to enforce regular password changes and to require the user to employ passwords which meet certain conditions to prevent them from being derived or discovered by unauthorized users. The latest systems can require passwords to be of a minimum length and to include the use of numbers or other characters. They can require regular changes and prevent the reuse of passwords. This is more a feature of electronic systems and is most important where the treasury system gateway may be reached by unauthorized users over a company-wide, or local area, network. A similar risk exists where the system can be accessed from outside the company by modem, by outsiders intent on gaining access to the system for competitive, fraudulent or disruptive purposes (hackers).

Audit trail

The glossary of computing terms of the British Computing Society defines an audit trail as 'a record of the file updating which takes place during a specific transaction'. In theory an audit trail should enable each entry or transaction on a system to be traced back to its source of input, but this becomes difficult where high volumes are involved, both in recording each entry and in tracking a particular entry after the event.

Treasury system suppliers have nearly always claimed to provide a full or comprehensive audit trail and, indeed, with some effort, the trail of a particular entry can probably be traced. That is rather different from the printed audit trail which most systems provide, which report certain key information relating to actual transactions. This normally includes who input a deal into the system, the date and time of that input and similar details of any subsequent editing or deletion. Additional key information includes access or attempted access by unauthorized personnel and attempted unauthorized transactions and password abuse. This information is usually produced and printed daily, but such an audit trail is of little use if it is not reviewed on a regular basis and the knowledge that such a review takes place deters potential internal fraud and system or password violations. It is also the review itself which identifies any external attempts to gain access which need to be picked up at the earliest possible opportunity.

Back-up and recovery

In a wider sense, the system hardware needs to be protected from theft or physical damage, and, similarly, the original system code needs to be kept physically separate, yet readily available, together with the data on it, to enable it to be recovered in the event of a systems failure. This involves the regular discipline of backing up all information at regular intervals; it should be done at least once a week and preferably on a daily basis.

Measures to prevent a system failure can include maintaining an 'uninterruptible power supply' (UPS). This will enable a system to continue to operate in the event of a power failure for long enough for it to be closed down without any damage to the database. These techniques are important for the management of all types of systems and treasury systems are no exception. The latest systems can assist the good practice needed by enabling back-up routines to be run overnight and even reminding the operators when back-up is needed. Now that most PC-based systems are run on a local area network, with a server and several terminals, some of them provide a disk-mirroring facility which ensures that the database on the server is copied simultaneously to another hard disk elsewhere. A variant of this is to have two hard disks on the server, one of which acts as the back-up to the other, whilst some software can automatically be recovered to its last recorded transaction and will manage its back ups between servers in totally different locations.

System upgrades

Once installed, early treasury systems changed very little but, as the pace of change in treasury has accelerated, so have the systems improvements so that upgrades will often occur at least annually. These may include additional reporting facilities, the capability to operate on new and higher capacity hardware, the ability to handle new instruments and other general improvements to remain competitive with other systems. Some users may prefer not to take upgrades but it is sometimes the case that, whilst software suppliers are prepared to support several earlier versions, eventually they will give notice that they will no longer be supporting a version of their software, whereupon some users may be left 'on their own'.

Two key events which represent major events for most software suppliers are the introduction of the euro, and the treatment of the year 2000. As an entirely new currency, ultimately replacing individual currencies for each participating European Union country, the euro has inevitably given rise to the introduction of system upgrades to handle it. Similarly, the systems implications of the new millennium have, at least, given rise to tests to ensure that a system would perform as expected from the year 2000 onwards and would offer an upgraded version of existing systems more often.

Documentation

All systems should have full and comprehensive documentation which will form the basis of all security procedures and techniques. This should include how to prepare to install (as the preparation is as important as the installation itself) as well as installation and setting up, even though that will often be handled by personnel from the software supplier. They may not be available when something goes wrong and someone different wants to see how the system was, or at least should have been, installed.

The main documentation should cover the core functions of the system, the various enquiries which can be made and how to use them. This will include the reports which are available, when they should be run and other routines which have to be undertaken regularly, including the security structures. Increasingly, systems are supplied with specialist tools (such as report writers), interfaces and accounting functions which sound easy to use, but are much more difficult without instruction or a very comprehensive manual.

The documentation should be produced by the system suppliers and, in the event of upgrades, should also be updated as appropriate. As systems develop further, they will be supplied with documentation accessed using the 'Help' facility on the Windows toolbar, but for the traditionalists, there is nothing to beat the reassurance apparently offered by a set of manuals.

The unthinkable

It is not unknown for software houses to fail, or for suppliers of systems to decide to 'pull out of certain markets'. Fortunately, treasury systems suppliers have a good, but not totally unblemished, record in this respect and the commitment to this market by some banks is reassuring, but this does not mean that the users should cease to be vigilant. Where the software has been provided by a small supplier, the user should require it to deposit a copy of the source code for the system with their bank or other custodian, with the instruction that the title passes to the user in the event of failure of the supplier.

In-house systems

In spite of the availability of a wide range of very comprehensive and competitively priced treasury systems, a significant number of companies still use treasury systems which have been developed in-house. These systems range from those created for small company treasury departments, based on spreadsheets, to very comprehensive systems developed by the systems departments of very large companies. Every one of those systems will be unique in its structure and undoubtedly many are first class which has prompted some corporates to sell their systems to other companies. Notwithstanding the particular arguments in favour of developing in-house systems, the security aspects are especially difficult to compare with 'off the shelf' systems. Password structures and access controls may be replaced by particularly rigorous manual supervision, but a serious concern may exist with the system code.

Where the system has been developed in-house, the system code will be accessible to the systems department programmer who, for legitimate maintenance purposes, may leave uncontrolled access structures in the system which could be used for less legitimate purposes. Where systems are supplied by commercial software houses, the user should have a right of action against that company for fraudulent access to the system by their employees. This cannot be the case for systems department employees, and although, in many cases, the systems developed are ideal for the company's purposes, the potential risk of non-treasury employees (or ex-employees) being able to access the system should be given special consideration by companies which have adopted this solution. The company should also check its fidelity insurance cover to see to what extent that risk is covered.

Security in treasury systems is not just system based and does not only cover the obvious. If a treasury is aware of the risks which need to be managed, as well as their potential cost, there is no reason why a first generation or in-house system cannot meet minimum control standards. Higher levels of security are clearly required if the system is accessible from outside the immediate treasury area, or if it is used to generate EFT or other payment instructions. In those cases, unless an in-house system has received special security screening, it may be preferable to use an up-to-date system specially developed for treasury management.

In-house systems are rarely documented as well as commercially produced systems and they are less likely to be kept up to date as improvements and enhancements to handle new hardware or new instruments are frequently handled on an ad hoc basis. This illustrates another aspect of the increased risks which arise when using treasury systems developed in-house.

Security and audit checklist

1 Functions handled.

(a) recording;

(i) foreign exchange transactions;

(ii) money market deposits;

(iii) non-bank short-term investments (commercial paper);

(iv) medium-term investments (gilt-edged stocks and certificates of deposit);

(v) borrowings (bilateral facilities – drawings or acceptances, syndicated facilities – drawings or acceptances);

(vi) derivatives (options, futures, FRAs).

(b) maintaining;

(i) credit limit control.

(c) producing;

(i) confirmation letters for all transactions;

(ii) settlement instructions for all transactions.

2 Controls required.

(a) integrity of input and verification;

(b) segregation of functions (dealing, confirmation and settlement).

3 Access control.

(a) hierarchical or flexible?

(b) record of all authorized users and their level of access;

(c) what can be accessed?

(i) ability to input, edit or delete information;

(ii) settlement or payment instructions (EFT);

(iii) confirmation information;

(iv) data reading;

(v) accounting output.

(d) is there a time out facility?

(e) is there access by modem? Can it be accessed overnight?

4 Password control.

(a) password abuse (sharing);

(b) insecure use or maintenance of the password.

(c) Does the system:

(i) enforce regular password changes?

(ii) require minimum length passwords?

(iii) prevent recycling of passwords?

(iv) identify password abuse in the audit trail?

5 Audit trail.

(a) who receives it and checks it?

(b) what does it include?

(c) input:

(i) who did it?

(ii) when was it done (date and time)?

(iii) full details of transaction.

(d) editing of input:

(i) who did it?

(ii) when was it done (date and time)?

(iii) full details of changes.

(e) deletion of input:

(i) who did it?

(ii) when was it done (date and time)?

(iii) full details of deletion.

(f) limit violations:

(i) who was responsible?

(g) attempted access:

(i) who tried it?

(ii) when did it happen?

(h) attempted unauthorized actions on authorized access:

(i) who tried it?

(ii) when did it happen?

(i) password violation – what was the nature of the violation?

(j) is there an error checking capability and are errors identified on the audit trail?

6 Back-up and recovery.

(a) how frequently is the system backed up?

(b) where is the back-up kept?

(c) where is the source code?

(d) is there an alternative or uninterruptable power supply?

(e) is the system physically secure?

7 Documentation.

Check that the documentation includes:

(a) how to prepare to install;

(b) installation and setting up;

(c) core functions and enquiries and how to use them;

(d) what reports are available, when they should be run and other routines;

(e) how to use specialist tools like report writers;

(f) how to operate the security structures;

(g) how to set up and manage the interfaces and accounting functions;

(h) system upgrades.

8 In-house systems.

(a) who developed the system?

(b) where is the source code and who controls it?

(c) is it fully documented?

(d) are there upgrades for new instruments and requirements?

(e) is it year 2000 compliant?

(f) is the documentation kept up to date?

(g) is all access controlled? Are you sure?

(h) does your fidelity insurance cover fraud arising from treasury systems developed in-house?

9

Security on the Internet

Roger Gate and Tony Palmer

Introduction

Use of the Internet for World Wide Web (WWW) communication is a growing method of not only gathering information but also carrying out electronic commerce activities. As with any computer system there are inherent security risks to manage when conducting business transactions over a public network, many of which are identified and amply covered in other chapters of this book. The Internet's innate accessibility to people world-wide, a small proportion of whom are computer literate with dubious intentions, magnifies these risks. An evaluation of security threats must, therefore, be addressed in a more rigorous way than has been the case in the past. The safety of a closed business network gave the required protection but businesses progressively need to interact electronically to remain cost effective.

Businesses using the Internet must assess the value of data they are exchanging and the impact upon their business should it be compromised, both in financial and reputational terms. This analysis will determine the level of confidentiality, authentication and integrity that must be applied. In addition, businesses must understand the vulnerabilities of their systems and the threats posed. It should also be noted that attacks by staff are far more common than those by the headline grabbing hacker. Nevertheless, by joining the corporate systems and networks to open public networks there is potential for attack from sophisticated computer-literate hackers. Therefore the appropriate level of defences must be put in place. This often means that for internal use businesses will operate their own closed network or intranet that uses Internet/WWW technology and protocols. Counterparties in different businesses that require a high degree of electronic interaction protect their networks within a trusted network environment where the corporate intranets are joined to form an extranet.

Internet/World Wide Web (WWW)

The Internet (INTERnational NETwork) is an open network of some 10 million computers in more than 100 countries. All these networks use a suite of common communication protocols TCP/IP (Transmission Control Protocol over Internet Protocol). TCP/IP provides a communication base upon which a range of different system application services enable computer systems to inter-operate in various ways. These services range from (Telnet), a remote terminal access service giving the appearance of permanent direct interaction with a host, to HTTP that manages the transmission of files and information pages to a remote user. The WWW is based on the HTTP service where Hypertext, containing pages of information in text, graphics, moving images and sound are interpreted by a browser application running on the user's computer. This means that the user's computer is able to request and receive various data content in real time from a distant host or server.

The Internet was built deliberately using information broken down into data packets for routing purposes, however in such a large and disparate network these can become lost and not arrive at their intended destination. Therefore 100% reliance cannot be placed upon the Internet as a delivery mechanism. It was not designed for performance or as a secure communication medium. Internet transmissions may be intercepted and, with the right computer equipment and knowledge, hackers can view, change or create bogus (spoof) data packets. The vast potential of the Internet for business and its risks must be counterbalanced by robust security protection backed by proactive risk management. The risks are established by identifying the vulnerabilities and the potential threats.

In assessing the security vulnerabilities the first thing to understand is the main way in which access to WWW data content from your network and computer systems can be configured.

Direct Internet access

The corporate network is permanently linked through a managed gateway to the Internet and is protected by filtering out unwanted data traffic. This applies to information going in and out of the corporate, with filtering rules configured to match the business needs and the security requirements. This type of link enables all the corporate employees to have high performance response from the Internet. Access controls are managed by systems and network administrators using bespoke firewall filtering devices (see later) and software tools.

This method can also allow network administrators to predetermine which WWW sites and types of data should be allowed into the corporate environment. These gateways can also be configured to handle email and even permit access to the corporate's own server giving access for staff and/or business partners to marketing information and support services. Many businesses are enhancing the use of these servers or 'sites' as a sales channel, shifting greater emphasis to their electronic commerce initiatives.

Internet Service Provider (ISP)

The majority of users, whether corporate employees or private individuals, do not set their computers as an actual server on the

WWW or Internet. This is mainly because they require transitory access and a permanent link would be costly in relation to the value gained. Managing the security technicalities may also be beyond their capabilities or interest.

Users temporarily gain access using a dial-up connection to an ISP's network node using a modem browser and software client for dialling the specific network chosen. ISPs are often the indigenous telecommunications companies or medium sized enterprises offering these core services. Once the connection has been authenticated to the node, a server then gives users a gateway to the Internet and access to all the other sites that are available. This server may also act as a mailbox for storing and forwarding email messages.

From a security perspective this does limit access to the end user's own system but data gathered from the WWW may be malicious. Virus contamination of files is a growing problem and internal computer systems may be compromised in this scenario. It is strongly recommended that a corporate network workstation should never use an ISP directly because the user will have navigated around the protection of an isolated network and, where present, the firewalled network gateway.

Commercial Service Provider (CSP)

Media and telecommunications companies such as CompuServe, America Online (AOL), Microsoft Network (MSN) and BT offer a commercial service.

The vast majority of personal users and a large number of business users subscribe to one of these popular commercial concerns. They offer bespoke software to connect to their communications network and through this out into the WWW. Effectively they offer additional content and services without the user needing to become a direct participant of the WWW. CSPs do, nevertheless, offer access to the WWW as an additional user selected option. CSPs, within their own network do separate the user from some of the risks of the Internet, but data, messages and instructions will be exchanged and are vulnerable to attack.

Intranets and extranets

The underlying technology that has made the Internet/WWW possible can also be used within a closed user group intranet environment. This means that the corporate's network is either physically isolated, uses dedicated communication lines or is logically separated from the Internet.

The latter is achieved using the same switching and routing devices of the Internet but the communication is protected within a secure encrypted telecommunications tunnel. This is often known as a virtual private network. Many companies have adopted an isolated approach to give them ease of use and accessibility to their own data without the risks inherent in connecting to the Internet. This type of configuration has many advantages as it limits access to a known set of users and for those users to a controlled set of data and services. The approach has also been used by a number of third party suppliers who offer a specific range of services or information only to registered users.

As stated above, most intranets are used and set up within an individual company. However, additional benefits can be gained by adding business trading partners to the network, e.g. suppliers, customers or other third parties. By connecting separate intranets these form what is increasingly being understood to be an extranet. In extending the reach of the internal network the security and administration requirements are increased, particularly in firewalling between the separate corporate or departmental entities. This configuration, however, can still be considered as being within a controlled environment as it does not involve direct connections to the Internet.

Clearly, reducing the accessibility of our data and systems and increasing the degree of control improves the effectiveness of the security. By limiting access and the possibility of attack by hackers we are minimizing the threat of theft or corruption of data and applications. Also, it is increasingly difficult for hackers to enter our systems and act as a user, for instance to arrange payments or delivery of goods to themselves. Again it should be noted that the majority of system security incidents originate from deliberate or erroneous misuse by internal staff rather than from an external hacker.

Therefore, in any assessment of risk the first area to be decided and set out is how the whole system is used and configured and the threats posed by potential intruders, external and internal. However, these levels of access are themselves often used in combination, with each element protected from the next by a 'firewall' or 'gateway' to control access and corresponding privileges.

Firewalls

A firewall is a security device which controls communication between networks. Firewalls are commonly used to protect a private corporate network from external networks (the Internet or the networks of suppliers and business partners).

The basic approach is to allow connection between specified network addresses and services (WWW, mail, etc) by explicit permission, known as configuration rules. Modern firewalls offer additional features such as user authentication, encryption and, in some cases, virus control.

Firewalls are far from being a total security solution and should therefore be used as part of a wider approach to security. Network security is a dynamic challenge, so on-going operational management is key to their continued effectiveness.

Cryptography

Cryptography is a way of safeguarding the confidentiality of data but it can also provide a means of authenticating users and remote systems, protecting data integrity and a facility for proving non-repudiation claims.

There are a number of cryptographic tools that assist the corporate in minimizing the risks of using the open 'public' Internet to conduct electronic commerce. These consist of symmetric and asymmetric encryption algorithms, hashing, message authentication codes and digital signatures. They are used to provide different levels of protection to data and applications.

Encryption is based upon the use of an encipher key to transform plain-text data into enciphered code and a decipher key to decrypt it back into plain-text. The encipher key and the decipher key may be exactly the same, or different but mathematically linked. When the same key is used it is known as symmetric and when separate keys are used they are termed asymmetric. When linked to certificates identifying the user they can also ensure authentication and non-repudiation.

The keys must be used appropriately in the business environment with the design, implementation and deployment being equally as important as the popular and contentious debate over key lengths. On the one hand, governments want to control the use and strength of these keys in the interests of national security, whereas many individuals see it as an issue surrounding free speech and confidentiality. Businesses want a secure environment to conduct electronic commerce and, therefore, key recovery or escrow arrangements (where keys are deposited with third parties) have been developed to allow access for government/police against appropriate court orders. Most of the cryptographic functions described below use publicly available algorithms whose strength is in their design and not the secrecy of their existence.

Symmetric encryption (secret keys)

Each user or system is allocated a symmetric key that is used to encrypt and authenticate each file, message or session. An identical key is held on and used by the host server to decrypt the communication. The main drawback is that once the keys have been generated they must be distributed to users and systems in a secure way. Therefore any method used to distribute keys whether it is by phone, secure post or some form of computer link has to be in itself very secure at every stage. This makes logistical administration very cumbersome. Secondly, in many cases maintaining all the keys in one place on a system gives hackers an obvious target. Finally, if two people want to share the same data they first of all have to exchange keys with all the attendant time, administration and security risks. However, secret keys remain a very effective security mechanism between two parties. Secret keys are mainly used to protect confidentiality between two trusted entities.

The Data Encryption Standard (DES) has been around for over 20 years and is still the most commonly used symmetric encryption algorithm that uses an effective 56-bit key to encrypt blocks of data, giving trillions of possible permutations. IDEA is another popular symmetric algorithm that uses 128-bit length keys.

The rapidly increasing speed of computer processing power enables cryptoanalysis to ascertain (crack) the single length DES key values relatively quickly. Therefore, in the near future businesses should look at either using triple DES (encrypting data three times using two separate single length keys) or utilizing different algorithms that have longer keys.

Symmetric encryption is also employed to protect transmissions across networks where error rates are low. Typical uses of this are cellular networks and GSM mobile telephones. This could in the future provide some protection to interception risks as mobile computers or intelligent telephones become commercially available to gain access to the Internet.

It is also important to consider where the encryption happens. If the encryption is done at the application level then each packet will contain encrypted data packets and therefore be protected if intercepted. However the delivery information will be in clear data and therefore open to scrutiny by anyone monitoring traffic on the network. Hackers have been known to take the packet's envelope details so that they can mimic them and get into the host system (spoofing). In another scenario, hackers can take out envelopes that look interesting, remove the contents and add new data of their own thus 'hijacking' the packet to get past the system or firewalls defences. Alternatively, they may simply just view the data packets as they pass through the network routers, which is known as 'sniffing'.

For this reason many firewalls now encrypt at the communication or network level, creating a virtual private network. They add an additional security envelope that is discarded at the other end in favour of the encrypted envelope that can be thoroughly checked.

It is easy, however, to over secure data, creating a slow down in the speed of the encryption thus making the overall system slower. Therefore it is important to look at the value, risk rating and useful life of the data when applying an appropriate key structure. For instance, if a piece of data is only of use to anyone else for a short period of time, then a 56-bit key is still considered adequate.

Asymmetric encryption (public/private key pairs)

Asymmetric encryption uses two different but asymmetric 'public and private' keys which means that, whilst mathematically linked, one cannot be derived from the other. The user's private key must be held securely by the owner either password protected on the computer's hard disk or on a smartcard, if available. The public key is published in publicly available directories; this will be described in further detail in the section on trusted third parties and certification, below.

Public/private key pairs are used in producing digital signatures and encryption. Remember that the private key is always under the owner's sole control. Digital signatures provide authentication, integrity and non-repudiation evidence for the recipient. Additionally, by using the recipient's public key this method also provides an encryption option to safeguard confidentiality. This needs explanation.

If we look at an exchange of data where user A wants to send a secure message to user B, then user A first looks up user B's public key and uses that key to encipher the message. At the other end, user B employs his/her private key to decipher the message. Only user B has the private key so he/she will be the only person able to decipher the encoded message. To reply, the procedure is reversed and thus the private keys themselves have never been exchanged but the messages are encrypted. In fact, public/private key services are often used to distribute secret keys where there are logistical and geographic problems.

Message authentication codes (MACs)

MACs are used to provide data authentication and integrity during transmission and storage. The user has a secret key, and putting a message through the MAC algorithm produces an appended encoded output.

If the body of the message were to be amended then the recipient with same secret key would recognize that the MAC value was incorrect. By inference, if the MAC value matches the message and the sender has the other secret key then the recipient must assume that it is a genuine message originating from the sender. MACs traditionally have been used in the financial services industry within closed networks and digital signatures offer a more flexible solution in an open and untrusted environment such as the Internet.

Trusted third parties and certification

Giving away public keys sounds unusual and perhaps complex but it does eliminate the need for both users to have to exchange a secret key which increases the risks during distribution. Public/private keys are useful if the communicating parties do not have a trusted relationship established and a third party who issues the keys resolves the trust requirement.

Public key systems are being further enhanced by the use of 'certificates' – information that identifies users – that can be thought of as being resident on a server sitting on the network. Here user A wants to sends an encrypted message to user B and he/she does so, signing it with his/her private key and encrypting it with user B's public key. User B then decrypts it with his/her private key but also goes to the certification authority to get user A's public key, thereby confirming the origination of the message. In this way certification authorities add a layer of additional security. There are a number of providers of this certification service, the main ones currently being RSA and Verisign.

Challenge and response

A number of companies use challenge and response to authenticate users seeking access to internal services. Each user is issued with a credit card sized token and a private key. When initiating a session, the user sends the private key to the server which uses that key to retrieve a second key that it encrypts and sends back to the user (the challenge). The user then enters the challenge into the token via a small keypad where it is decrypted and a response is displayed. The user enters the response and, if accepted by the server, the session is set up.

As can be seen there are many different types of security methods evolving and there are moves to try and develop international standards. A good example of this is the Secure Electronic Transaction Protocol.

Secure Electronic Transaction (SET) Protocol

Secure Electronic Transaction (SET) is a message protocol designed to verify the authenticity and legitimacy of credit card transactions for cardholders, merchants and acquirers over open networks, such as the Internet. This protocol is being jointly developed by Visa and MasterCard, with contributions from major software vendors, to address the security issues of engaging the cards payment method or similar transaction solutions in settling electronic commerce trading.

There is strong consumer demand for secure methods of purchasing goods from the electronic 'shopping malls' multiplying on the Internet and the merchants equally require simple, cost effective ways of conducting business electronically. Financial institutions are also seeking open and secure standards to safeguard their integrity and to promote further competition without compromising the rights of the parties involved.

SET uses a combination of symmetric (private key) and asymmetric (public key) encryption techniques plus certificates of authority to facilitate:

1 Confidentiality of the trading data between supplier and customer.

2 Authentication of the trading entities' legitimacy.

3 The integrity of the financial data settling the trade.

SET has been tested and piloted by a number of companies and financial institutions and commercial software supporting it is now starting to become available.

Summary

As with most other systems, the first requirement when assessing risk is to understand the value of the data being transmitted, be it from a need for confidentiality as in sensitive company information, integrity where data is used for ordering or fulfilment of orders or authentication where the message is an instruction to pay funds away.

Once this and the system configuration are understood we can go on to choose the most appropriate security method allowing for what is available from any service provider's own system. Because of the inherent accessibility of full WWW sites, it is also very important to consider the protection of any internal systems from any form of hacking attack.

This chapter has only given a brief overview of the issues and security methodologies in what is a developing and changing environment. The use of certification authorities to create 'trusted third' status and new security protocols for financial institutions and corporates will facilitate the growth of electronic commerce. Change and the pace of development will be rapid and therefore treasurers will constantly need to assess the security mechanisms available to ensure their security policies and implementations are effective. Indeed, by the time this book is published, new software services and protocols will have been developed as change continues endlessly.

10

EDI security

John Sherwood

Electronic Data Interchange (EDI) which offers a secure interchange of information in a united Europe will provide the means by which major companies conduct their business as we move forward into the twenty-first century. It replaces the traditional paper transactions with their well accepted mechanisms for proving origin, preventing repudiation and maintaining confidentiality. This chapter looks at how these security features can be replicated in the environment and discusses how the security must reflect the nature of the business relationship between the parties. It also examines the security mechanisms defined in current international standards and discusses their appropriateness for EDI.

What is EDI?

EDI is a technique which enables computer-to-computer transfer of structured information, usually between companies who are 'trading partners'. An EDI message has a formal syntax structure which can be generated by one computer and interpreted on its receipt by another computer. The message has a header which contains various control fields and a body which contains the main content of the message. This entire data structure is carried across the network by being put into an 'envelope' which is provided by a messaging system such as X.400. Fig. 10.1 shows this outline structure.

The technique is used to exchange documents of all types which are involved in the trading partner relationship. Orders, invoices, specifications, parts lists, catalogues and many other documents are transferred between the computers of the trading partners to facilitate paperless trading. EDI often embraces the exchange of computer aided design/computer aided manufacturing (CAD/CAM) product design data and also includes the use of electronic funds transfer (EFT) for settlement of invoices. As well as the trading partners themselves, there are many other parties who get involved in a trade, including the banks. Figure 10.2 shows some of the parties who might become involved in an international trade where the goods are shipped by sea from an exporter to an importer.

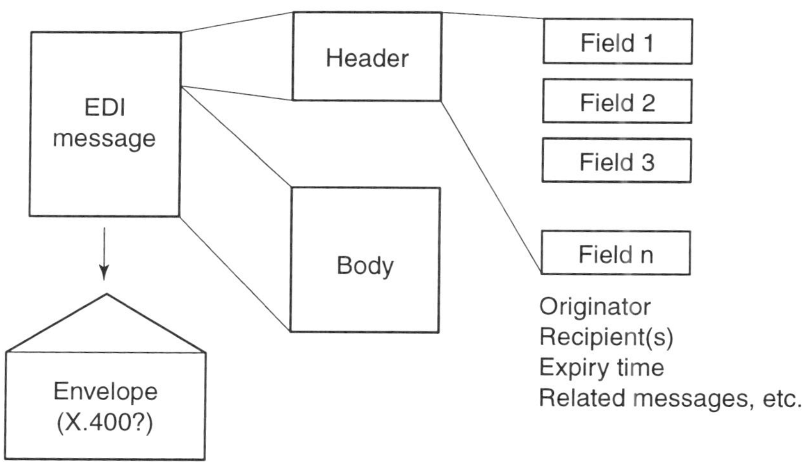

10.1 Outline structure of EDI messages

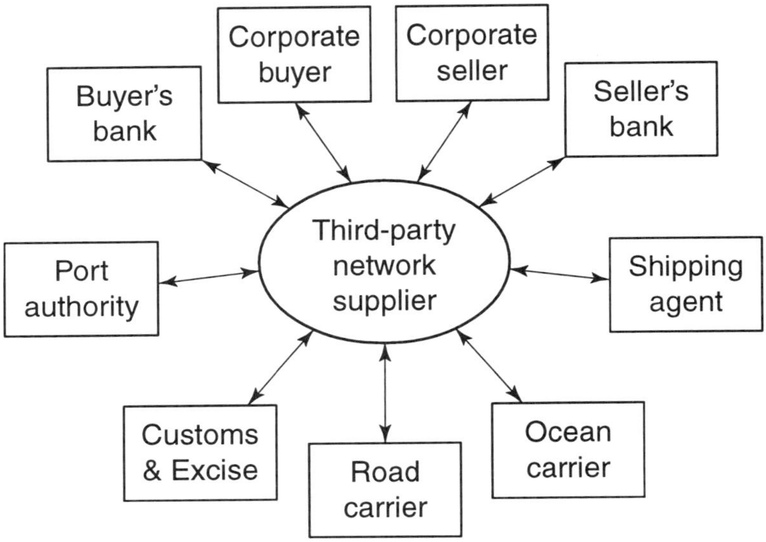

10.2 Parties involved in an international EDI trade

EDI will be a major feature of business in the twenty-first century. Already some of the largest operators are unwilling to trade with suppliers who do not use EDI. It is seen by many as one of the most important factors, together with the development of the European economic union, which will have an impact on the way that business is conducted in the European Union. Those companies which make a commitment to EDI are expected to gain competitive advantage through the range of benefits which should result.

The benefits of EDI are as follows:

1 The reductions that it gives in lead times, thus speeding up the trading cycle.

2 The improvement that it gives in customer service.

3 The savings that it makes in the cost of printing and mailing documents.

4 The improvements that it makes in cash flow by releasing capital traditionally tied up in high stock levels.

5 The improved trust that it engenders in trading relationships which are based on 'just-in-time' manufacturing strategies.

6 The improved 'supply chain management' that it provides, offering better control over the business.

The technical basis of EDI is the wide range of data communications technology now available and commonly in use. Networks of computers have been with us for some time and, in recent years, we have heard much about 'open systems interconnection' (OSI). Because of the newer transmission technologies, bandwidth is becoming almost a commodity, available in huge quantities at low cost. It is this range of technological solutions which have made EDI possible. However, the application of these techniques in EDI is an emergent field of technology which yet deserves a great deal of attention in its further development, refinement and standardization. In particular, the security of EDI systems will become a more and more pressing issue as EDI matures and becomes totally integrated into almost all major trading relationships.

Why does EDI need security?

Providing 'security' is all about creating an environment in which we can use our business systems with confidence, knowing that we have protected adequately against the unexpected, unwanted, disruptive and damaging events which are frequently referred to as 'risks', but which are more accurately called 'threats'.

What, then, are the threats which potentially confront us if we use EDI? Will any of our trading partners attempt to defraud us to benefit their business at the expense of ours? Will individuals who work either for our company or for a trading partner attempt to defraud us for their personal benefit? Will third parties attempt to intercept our electronic trading to divert goods or other valuables fraudulently to themselves instead of to a genuine trading partner? Will they masquerade as a genuine partner to achieve this or will they simply change the details of instructions issued by a genuine partner? Will any of these people use the EDI system as a means to get access to confidential information to which they are not authorized and will they then use this information against us in some way? Will they simply disrupt the EDI service to sabotage our business operations? These are some of the possibilities that immediately spring to mind.

There is nothing particularly new in any of the risks mentioned above. We have simply identified some of the ways in which fraud and malicious damage have been committed for many centuries and history tells us that, wherever there are opportunities to commit fraud, there is usually someone with criminal tendencies close at hand who will take advantage of the opportunity. What is different about EDI is that it is a completely new environment in which to conduct trade and we therefore have limited experience of how large or small the risks may be. It is also very easy to be seduced by the glamour of the new technology and forget about the dirty deeds that may be done by society's criminals.

Every trading organization suffers a certain level of theft which it is prepared to tolerate because it would cost more to prevent the losses than to sustain them. Fraud has been defined as 'theft by lying' and so one can assume that all organizations also have a tolerance to a certain level of fraud. It seems unlikely, however, that organizations would be prepared to tolerate the levels of fraud that could be executed in an EDI environment. Computerized systems provide the potential both for very high-value fraud (the 'big job') and for systematic, long-term milking of small amounts which in time add up to a very large sum of money (the 'salami fraud').

An additional factor which must be addressed in EDI environments is that processing is done by machines rather than by people. The opportunity is lost for a human operator to question the validity of what he or she recognizes as an unusual transaction. If we look to history it is this human curiosity which has often led to the foiling of frauds which would otherwise have been successful.

It seems then that, when considering fraud, EDI may provide a higher risk environment than the more traditional methods of trading. This should not discourage its use but should prompt us to incorporate mechanisms to protect sufficiently against the potential frauds in order to provide the right level of business confidence. In particular, it should be recognized that EDI provides a tempting target for organized crime which is only ever interested in large-scale projects where there is sufficient opportunity. Our security arrangements for EDI must therefore make such organized fraud economically unattractive.

Another equally important reason for providing security is to ensure that nothing gets lost, that records of business transactions are complete and that, at the end of the day, all trading partners can reconcile their accounting information and agree on the financial transactions requiring settlement. The risks attributable to errors can be significant and, in many cases, they outweigh the risks from fraud. The security that we build into an EDI system must therefore protect against these risks. EDI should intrinsically reduce the risks in this area because it greatly reduces the amount of 'rekeying' of information by human operators, itself a major source of error in some computing systems. On the other hand, transactions are carried out more quickly and with a great deal less human intervention so it becomes a matter of primary importance to prevent errors occurring, since there is little opportunity to correct them.

Additionally, there is the issue of availability. It is fatal to move business operations on to a computer-based system which cannot be relied on to be up and running when it is required. Many of the benefits of EDI are related to an improved ability to turn business around quickly and to implement 'just-in-time' management of stock levels. This increases the vulnerability to the threats of system failure; hence the systems used for EDI must be able to guarantee high levels of availability and must be able to offer fast and accurate recovery in the case of any temporary failures.

What are the security requirements for EDI?

EDI involves communications between trading partners. There is often a network service provider who links these partners together and who provides the technology and equipment by which the messages are transmitted and switched in the network. It is certainly the job of network providers to build their networks so as to protect their own network resources and hence to ensure continuity and quality of network service to their customers. They also want to be able to charge correctly for services delivered to authorized users and to prevent fraudulent use of the network services by unauthorized users.

It is tempting to imagine that EDI message security should also be the responsibility of these service providers and many commentators on EDI have written along such lines. However, EDI message security is incorporated so as to protect the business activity of the trading partners. It must be selected for its appropriate reflection of the business relationship which exists between them and it must be under their operational control. For these reasons it is not the role of the network service provider to address security issues such as message confidentiality and message integrity protection.

EDI message security is an 'end-to-end' issue which must be the concern of the trading partners. Solutions must be sought which give the trading partners the same full control over their own security that they would expect in other areas of their business management. This means that the systems must not require complete trust in other parties, whether they be service providers or trading partners. It ought to be possible to do business with organizations whose integrity is not necessarily fully known or trusted, otherwise the opportunities for doing business will be restricted.

One thing that should be understood from the beginning is that 'message security' does not necessarily imply 'message confidentiality'. For most EDI users, message security is more likely to be concerned with 'message integrity' (has it been altered?), 'message origin authentication' (does it come from an authentic source?) and 'non-repudiation of a message' (can I prove that it came from you, even though you now deny that it did?).

Clearly there is a need to protect the integrity of EDI messages to prevent them from being altered without the alteration being detected. Proving the origin of a message is also important and providing restricted delivery with authentic acknowledgement closes the loop and assures both parties that they are genuinely doing business with one another and not with a fraudster. Furthermore, non-repudiation is needed to prevent either party from later claiming that they were not the originator of either the message or its acknowledgement.

Confidentiality is perhaps more debatable. Many companies would argue that it is not necessary to prevent outsiders from knowing how many widgets they are buying. However, it is very common for highly confidential proprietary information to be sent back and forth during the negotiation of trading terms. This would be particularly true of a manufacturer bringing a new product to market where sub-assemblies are to be purchased from other suppliers. Potential suppliers are given information 'commercially in confidence' to enable them to design and quote for the supply of components. Such information would probably be of the CAD/CAM variety in an EDI environment.

Another reason for not dismissing confidentiality is that its existence makes the job of the fraudster so much more difficult. The criminal who commits fraud takes time to research your business and to look for the opportunities. If you make everything easy for him to read you are helping him a great deal. If you encrypt your EDI messages you will probably cause him to look elsewhere because suddenly it is all too much hard work for him and hard work rarely appeals to the serious criminal.

Confidentiality in EDI may also be important where the business transactions themselves need to be confidential. To determine whether this is the case, it is essential to be aware of the potential business impacts that can be suffered if certain types of information are intercepted and read by an eavesdropping opponent. Consider the following examples:

1 A major clothing manufacturer begins exchanging EDI messages with the Ministry of Defence in the UK. The messages reveal that the MoD is ordering 100 000 sets of combat clothing of a particular type (desert camouflage/jungle camouflage/snow-scape camouflage?). Could this information be useful to an eavesdropper? Should it be kept confidential?

2 A major chemical company supplies commercial explosives to quarries and civil engineering operators who have legitimate uses for these materials. The details of lorry shipments, including shipping dates, depot addresses and delivery addresses are sent in EDI messages. Would you be concerned

about criminals and terrorists having this information? Should it be kept confidential?

3 EDI messages are used in the UK to coordinate hospital treatment, GP treatment, out-patient clinic treatment and pharmacy prescriptions used in patient health care. Details of patient health records are sent in the messages. Would it matter if these details were intercepted? What would happen if they were published? What would happen if the press found out that they could be published, even if publication were withheld for ethical editorial reasons? Could these details be used to blackmail some patients?

These examples are of limited applicability but they show that there are many different ways in which business impacts can arise from the disclosure of information. A careful analysis of potential business impacts is always required to ensure that all possible impacts have been identified and understood before a decision is made on the business requirements for providing confidentiality of EDI messages.

With regard to service availability, systems must be built with intrinsic resilience to single component failures. They must also be built and operated so that back-up systems are available and so that business continuity plans exist for dealing with emergencies caused by system failure. To avoid the chaos that could result from loss of synchronization between the computers owned by trading partners, the EDI application-layer protocols must be capable of recovering from failure of the system when a transaction is partially completed.

Other requirements are concerned with the manageability of the security sub-system. It must be possible to log selected message attributes for audit purposes, both on incoming and outgoing messages. It must also be possible to correlate the authentic acknowledgements with the appropriate outgoing messages. Since EDI is always performed in association with other parties, interoperability of security mechanisms is of the utmost importance and, since third parties will frequently be involved in providing network services, the routing and delivery of EDI messages must be

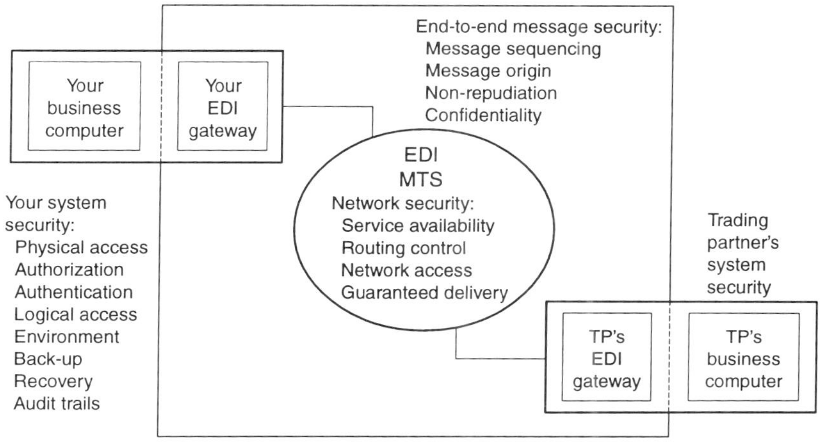

10.3 Domains of responsibility for EDI security and the associated security services

completely independent of any message content which will be subject to security treatment.

Figure 10.3 shows a summary of the overlapping domains of responsibility and liability with regard to EDI security and lists the security services to be provided in each one.

How does EDI compare with traditional systems?

When a document is sent through the conventional postal system, it arrives in a sealed envelope. This fact provides us with a degree of confidentiality for we know that, although the document may have been handled by a variety of people on its journey, it has been protected from prying eyes. Sometimes, as an additional security factor, and especially in the case of registered mail, sealing wax is applied to the envelope. Such seals often carry a personal or company imprint such as a coat of arms or a company logo. This makes it extremely difficult for the envelope to be opened without detection, since the third party will be unable to reproduce the authentic seal.

Once the envelope has been opened there are additional security checks that can be made. Does the document or accompanying literature carry the company's normal printed headings? Is the written signature familiar to you? If the document is of a particularly sensitive nature, have there been any alterations and have such alterations been signed or initialled? Sometimes a signature is used to authorize a particular action and this signature constitutes proof that the originator did, indeed, issue such authority, for example, the signature attached to a purchase order for goods or services. If there is eventually a denial that authorization was ever given, the signature becomes the item of proof.

These features of traditional mailing systems have been used for many hundreds of years, evolving and being refined to a point where we take them for granted. In moving to EDI, similar protection must be provided. However the problems associated with securing digital information are much greater than those associated with paper-based mail. Digital information is open to almost infinite manipulation without any detriment to its quality. It can be copied, deleted, extended, stored and transmitted with ease. Indeed these are the very qualities that make digital computers such powerful tools for information technology applications.

Most existing EDI systems provide little protection against fraud or espionage. Some access control mechanisms may be implemented on host computers to prevent unauthorized access but messages may still be transmitted over public networks using formats and protocols that conform to insecure published standards. If someone intercepts communications or circumvents the access controls, there will be no way of detecting loss of privacy, integrity and authenticity. We therefore need some additional digital techniques to protect these aspects, particularly if we wish to use EDI for financial transactions, highly sensitive company data transmissions and the like.

What international standards are available?

The issue of inter-operability immediately suggests that whatever we adopt must be internationally standardized. For this reason the ITU (International Telecommunications Union which has taken over the work of CCITT) X.400 and X.500 standards for digital communication systems are of particular interest, since they jointly contain much that is relevant to the security problems of EDI. X.400 is the series number of a group of ITU standards relating to message handling and electronic mail. One of the series, X.435, deals especially with EDI messaging. The standards define both the system architecture and the communication protocols that are required to implement two distinct types of system. These are called the message handling system (MHS), used for applications such as EDI, and the interpersonal messaging service (IPMS), used for electronic mail. Figure 10.4 shows the main architectural components for an EDI system as described in X.435.

The entire system shown in Fig. 10.4 is known as an MHS. The architectural definition of the MHS contains elements such as the user agent (UA), message transfer system (MTS), physical delivery access unit (PDAU for printing messages for physical delivery, as in EDI Post, and message store (MS). The MTS is itself made up of a network of message transfer agents (MTAs) and the standards also describe the protocol definitions to cover layers four, five and seven of the open systems interconnection (OSI) model for communication between these various elements. X.400 was the first comprehensive set of standards which defined protocols at the 'application layer' of the OSI seven-layer model.

What is most important about X.400 is that it provided the first real hope of vendor-independent system architectures with the ability to implement systems in a multi-vendor environment. The release of X.400 in 1988 also addressed many of the issues of secure system management. (For those with a specific interest in the detail, refer to Section 10, Security Model, of X.402, 1988.)

X.500 is the series number of another set of standards from ITU which complement X.400 and which define the structure and management of an 'international directory'. This directory holds

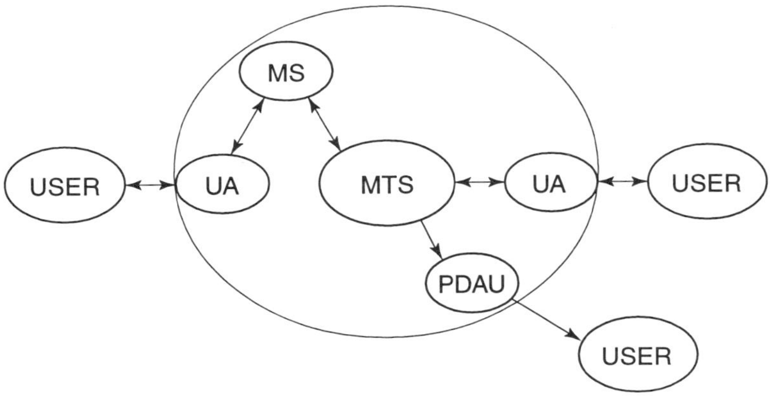

10.4 The overall architecture of an X.435 EDI system

information on users, such as their addresses and other routing information required to deliver electronic messages to them. It also stores security-related attributes such as the certified RSA public key of the user. The specific standard which deals with security matters is X.509, The Authentication Framework. Annex C of X.509 describes the RSA public key crypto-system in detail.

The MHS architecture of X.400, combined with the directory services of X.500, is seen by many as the solution to providing the basic service for EDI. On top of that can be implemented specific EDI application protocols such as the United Nations EDI for Administration, Commerce and Transport (UN/EDIFACT) standard. This latter standard is also published as ISO 9735. EDIFACT provides the syntax for the actual EDI messages to be constructed by one computer and interpreted by another, whereas X.400 MHS provides the means by which these messages can be put into 'logical envelopes', addressed, moved around and delivered.

What are the security features of EDIFACT?

Parts 5 and 6 of ISO 9735 provide some special EDIFACT syntax segments for carrying security information inside an EDIFACT message. ISO 9735, Part 5, describes 'integrated message security' in which the security fields relating to a given message are carried inside that message, whereas Part 6 describes 'separate message security' in which a special EDIFACT message type called the 'secure authentication and acknowledgement message (or AUTACK message) is defined to carry the security fields relating to a separate batch of messages.

Figure 10.5 shows the hierarchical structure of an EDIFACT 'interchange' – the term which describes a large file of many messages. At each level of the hierarchy (interchange, message group and individual message) the element is delimited by a pair of header and trailer segments, respectively UNA/UNZ, UNG/UNE and UNH/UNT. Inside an individual message is the option to include up to nine nested security header/trailer pairs (USH/UST, see Fig. 10.6), each of which can carry a different digital signature. This allows for multiple authorizations on messages and for historical authorizations to be preserved when new ones are applied.

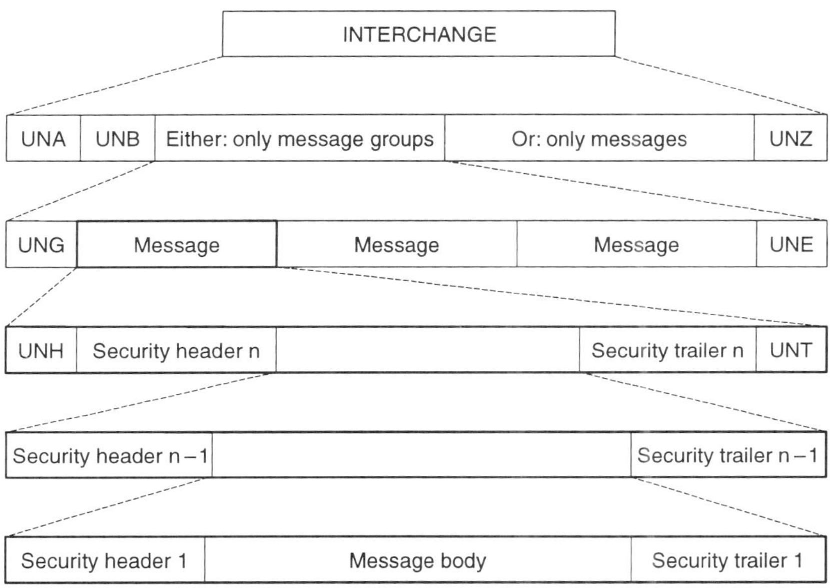

10.5 The hierarchical structure of an EDIFACT interchange with integrated message security

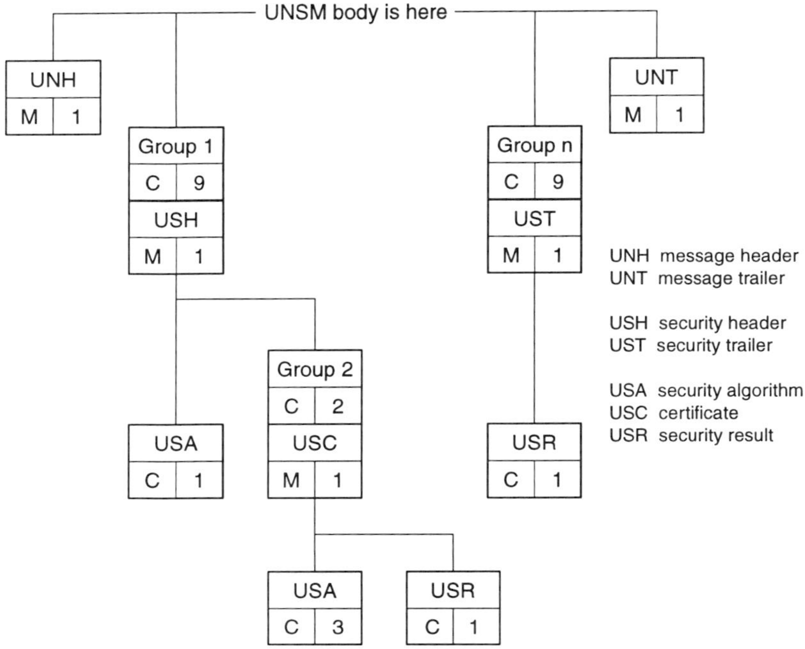

10.6 The syntax scheme for integrated EDIFACT message security

The syntax segment diagram for a message with integrated security in standard EDIFACT format is shown in Figure 10.6. (UNSM is the UN/EDIFACT standard message.) Unless public key techniques are used, segment group 2 is omitted. The USA segment in group 1 is related to the actual security on the message, for example, the hashing algorithm. When public keys are used at least one segment of group 2 must be present, triggered by the USC. In the USC the three USA segments are: the certified user public key algorithm, the certification authority (CA) public key algorithm and the CA hash function used to calculate the certificate. A digital signature, whether it be part of the certificate or appended to the EDI message, is carried in a 'security result' segment (USR). The actual syntax rules for the cryptographic variables carried inside these EDIFACT security fields (such as certificate syntax, digital signature syntax, etc) are provided

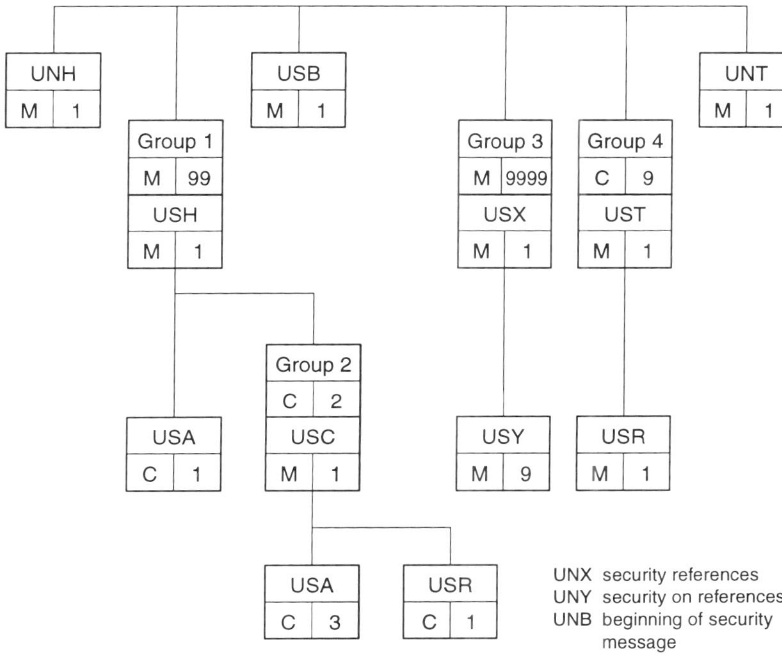

10.7 The syntax scheme for the AUTACK message for separated EDIFACT message security

by suitable supporting standards such as X.509 which lays out ASN.1 definitions for these types of item.

In Fig. 10.7 we see the syntax scheme for the AUTACK message, which carries the security information when 'separated message security' is in use. Most of the segment types are the same, but there are extra 'security references' which point to the actual messages to which these security fields apply.

An AUTACK message can be used by another party on behalf of the originator or by the originator, giving greater flexibility than is possible with integrated message security. AUTACK provides message origin authenticity, validation of message content integrity, validation of completeness and non-repudiation of origin. When used with an acknowledgement message, it also provides confirmation of receipt, validation of integrity of content, validation of completeness and non-repudiation of receipt.

What cryptographic techniques are available?

Encipherment and decipherment

Encipherment is the conversion of a 'plaintext' message into a 'ciphertext' message by applying an encryption algorithm and a secret encryption key. The converse process, decipherment, recovers the plaintext from the ciphertext, again using a decryption algorithm and a decryption key. Only the authorized sender and receiver know the secret key and so an opponent listening in on the transmission path sees only the ciphertext and cannot decrypt the message to obtain the plaintext since he does not possess the key.

If the keys used for encipherment and decipherment are identical, then the algorithm is known as a symmetric encryption algorithm. If these keys are different from one another, the algorithm is asymmetric. Asymmetric algorithms are also known as public key algorithms because the encryption key can be published whilst the decryption key is kept private (provided that knowledge of the public key does not allow the private key to be calculated).

Encipherment can be applied to whole messages as they are prepared by the business application program before they are packaged in EDIFACT syntax for transmission. However, this would hide the message structure and so ordinary EDIFACT translation would not now be possible. To support this approach, a special EDIFACT message type called CIPHER is being developed. It will transport the results of enciphering an application message but that message must be compatible with the receiving application, otherwise there is no way to interpret its contents.

Encipherment can also be applied to whole EDIFACT messages after their EDIFACT translation. In this case the normal translation process is used and the enciphered message must be deciphered at the receiving end before it can be submitted to the receiving translator. This approach can be implemented either as post-processing at the EDIFACT translation module or preprocessing at the data communication module (such as an X.400 UA in a mail gateway). However, in either case, consideration must be given to how the network addressing and routing will be achieved since the internal addressing information in the EDIFACT message has been obscured by the encipherment process.

Encipherment can also be applied within the network infrastructure in the form of stream encryption of point-to-point network links or in the form of protocol-sensitive encryption schemes which encipher only the information fields of the protocol data units (PDUs) and leave alone the headers in which routing and other network control information is located.

Finally, it may only be certain information items within the message which are confidential, in which case encipherment can be applied on a selective field basis within the business application and those enciphered fields can be loaded into the relevant EDIFACT segments as enciphered data items.

One can see from these various approaches that encryption of EDI messages can be a complex task, requiring the resolution of many problems. There are still more to consider: the communicating parties must be able to inter-operate the encryption scheme in use. This means they must agree on how the encryption will be applied. At which of the levels described above will data be encrypted? Using which algorithm? What will be the key length? What will be the key management scheme? What will be the syntax for key blocks?

There are yet more considerations because encryption of data produces output which has a random appearance. Thus all possible binary strings are produced, some of which may not be handled transparently by the intervening network. For example, any network which uses asynchronous transmission will crash if it is subjected to spurious control characters. Thus, for transmitting binary data across such networks (such as the Internet), some suitable encoding and decoding scheme must be used to ensure that only permissible (usually printable) characters are contained in the messages. EDIFACT data automatically complies with this requirement – until it is encrypted! Even within EDIFACT itself data transparency is an issue because, if the selective field approach is used, data will no longer contain only EDIFACT alphabet characters and it will need to be re-encoded to comply with these rules.

Message authentication

An encryption algorithm can be used to generate a check sum (called a message authentication code or MAC). The check sum is calculated from the entire message and, if any single bit (or more) is changed, the check sum will be different (with very high probability). A message is sent along with its MAC and the receiver generates the MAC again and compares the received MAC with the computed one. If they are the same there is a very high level of assurance that the message has not been altered during transmission. The message itself is not enciphered but is sent as plaintext. Because the process is cryptographic, and involves the use of a secret key known only to the sender and receiver, an opponent who intercepts and alters the message cannot compute a MAC value that will be verified by the receiver. Hence all such interception attempts will be detected.

Digital signature

This is similar to the MAC generation and verification process except that it utilizes an asymmetric algorithm such that the signature generation key and the signature verification key are different. Thus the sender generates the signature using a private key and the recipient can verify the signature using a public key (as can anyone else), but no one can forge the signature because only the authorized signatory possesses the correct private key. Each party who wishes to be signatory has their own private signature key and their public keys are made available to everyone who might need to verify their signatures. These algorithms have the disadvantage that they are very demanding of computational power, making it unrealistic to apply them directly to very large messages or files.

Hashing

Hashing is used as stage one of a two-stage digital signature process to solve the performance problem mentioned above with respect to digital signature algorithms. A hashing algorithm is fast, efficient and produces a brief check sum of fixed length (say, 128 bits) which can then be used as the target for a digital signature, thus limiting the signature process to short data blocks and hence maintaining acceptable throughput performance. The hashing algorithm must be ‘collision-free’ to avoid alternative messages being constructed which hash to the same value as the target message, but hashing algorithms do not need to have a secret key (although some do have).

Certification

Public key techniques are only secure if the public keys have been ‘certified’ as being authentic. A certified public key with other credentials of the owner is known as a certificate. In order to produce certificates, a trusted third party must act as the certification authority (CA). The CA has a special private signature key which is used to ‘sign’ or ‘certify’ all other public keys in the community. Everyone has the CA public key and can verify the signature which proves the authenticity of the certificate.

The setting up of CAs is an organizational and political issue, rather than a technical one. Someone must be selected who is trusted by all parties in the community that is to be served, who is acceptable to all those parties and who is willing to take on the job.

In general there is a vacuum at the present time with regard to CAs. Countries and industries that wish to promote secure EDI messaging must address this issue and must set up a suitable organizational infrastructure. There are several technical products on the market to equip such an organization to carry out the duties of CA. An example of an initiative of this type is that currently under discussion within the Health Information Systems across Europe. There is also a current programme run by the UK government to licence trusted third parties (TTPs) for this and TTP service provision.

How is encryption technology used to provide message security?

Encryption technology has many useful applications in the provision of message security in EDI. Used in appropriate ways, it can provide the following:

Message confidentiality: protecting a message containing confidential information from being disclosed to an unauthorized party.

Message origin authentication: proving that the originating source declared in a message is the actual source of that message.

Message contents authentication: proving that the contents of a message remain unaltered between despatch from the authentic source and receipt at the destination.

Non-repudiation of origin and contents: preventing an authentic sender of a message from later repudiating that the message did in fact originate from that source and that the message contents on despatch were as received at the destination.

By combining the message content authentication technique with timestamps and sequence numbers, these benefits can be extended to provide the following:

Timeliness authentication: proving that there has been no unauthorized delay in delivering the message.

Completeness authentication: proving that no messages have been deleted.

Sequencing authentication: proving the order in which messages were despatched.

Replay detection: ensuring that any attempt to replay a previous message will be detected.

By using the non-repudiable message origin authentication technique with acknowledgement messages, the benefits can be further extended to provide the following:

> *Proof of delivery*: showing that a non-repudiable acknowledgement has been received, indicating that delivery of the original message occurred.

The EDIFACT syntax has been extended to provide security segments which can be used to support these various techniques (see above). However, EDIFACT is merely a delivery mechanism and, in order to make use of its security facilities, one still needs to select a suitable cryptographic algorithm for use in each of these instances. In fact, several algorithms may be required because different algorithms have different characteristics which are suited to these different techniques with varying degrees of suitability.

In addition, cryptographic keys will need to be managed and exchanged between trading partners using these techniques and this may imply the use of different algorithms again. Another on-going development in EDIFACT is the special KEYMAN message to be used in this key management process.

What special purpose does X.435 fulfil?

For EDI messages that are to be carried end-to-end in an X.400 MHS, the contents of the message are completely transparent to the messaging service. The envelope is closed when the message is taken into the MHS by the sender's UA. It is not opened again, nor does any process look inside it, until it arrives at the recipient's UA where it is delivered out of the MHS environment.

However, some value-added network services (VANS) suppliers wish to offer additional services to EDI customers. X.400 is a store-and-forward technology and hence messages reside for some time inside the MHS in one or more message stores (MS). For the VANS suppliers who wish to offer value-added EDI services, these are usually based around some extra processing at the MS. For example, rather than simply deliver all EDI messages in transparent end-to-end fashion, the VANS supplier may offer the service of retrieving all invoices, or all orders, leaving behind other message types in the MS. VANS customers may be able to interrogate the MS to find out the number and nature of all the EDI messages awaiting delivery. To execute these services, the VANS internal process must look inside the X.400 envelopes and read the EDIFACT messages. The MHS is no longer end-to-end transparent.

This non-transparent service poses a problem. EDIFACT (and also ANSI X.12, its American equivalent) is a syntax based upon character strings with special delimiter characters separating the fields, rather like the traditional communications protocols such as bi-synchronous communications (BSC) and high-level data-link control (HDLC). However, X.400, in common with all modern OSI protocols, uses an abstract notation form of defining syntax structures called Abstract Syntax Notation No 1 (ASN.1). This separates the definition of the form and content of messages from their actual encoding. Thus, in order to achieve compatibility between these two syntax forms, they must be reconciled. That is the job of the X.435 standard.

To enable the special VAN services, special EDI UAs are used, creating a special version of the MHS. This is called the EDI messaging system (EDIMS). A message in this system is called an EDI message (EDIM). A special protocol is also used between these EDI UAs and the MTA, in place of usual one which is known as P2. This special protocol is called P35 (originally known as Pedi). P35 is the X.400 syntax definition for EDIMs. (An X.400 EDIM 'message' submitted via P35 contains an EDIFACT 'interchange' which contains many EDI messages. Be careful of the words 'EDI message' in this context.) The MS is also special so that it can interpret the special P35 protocol. The enhanced version is called an EDI MS (not to be confused with EDIMS – see above).

The P35 protocol is defined in X.435. The X.435 EDIM header contains both X.435 control fields *and* copies of the UNA, UNB and UNG fields copied from the EDIFACT interchange and translated into ANS.1 to facilitate full X.435 functionality at the MS. The service elements of this special EDIMS are described in a related ITU standard, called F.435, which defines services such as:

1 EDI forwarding.
2 EDI message.
3 EDI notification.
4 EDI user.
5 EDIM responsibility.

One of the sections of F.435 contains a description of the security services required for EDI. It repeats all the good things that are said in other places where EDI security is discussed, listing the types of security service required and describing each one. The P35 protocol includes a number of features to implement these security services on an (almost) end-to-end basis. The 'almost' qualifier is because the security can only be from EDI UA to EDI UA. Such a concept of end-to-end assumes that the EDI application to EDI UA interface is a trusted one.

Some of the P35 security features are merely restatements of standard X.402 security features. Others are special EDI-related security features, much like those provided in EDIFACT security. The security features are optional and, if present, are indicated in the EDIM header by the EDI Application Security Elements Field. There is certainly an overlap between EDIFACT security and X.435 security. They are attempting to achieve the same thing, that is the end-to-end security of EDI messages. Hence there seems to be a choice: EDIFACT or X.435, but not both together.

EDIFACT security or X.435 security?

The main issue is concerned with making the security as completely 'end-to-end' as is possible. If X.435 security services are implemented, they must be positioned at the EDI UA, since this is the furthest outboard point in the X.400 MHS domain (see Fig. 10.8). If the UA is integrated into the computer on which the EDIFACT messages are translated, then there is no great difference between this and a message security system which is associated with the EDIFACT translator module. However, in many organizations the X.400

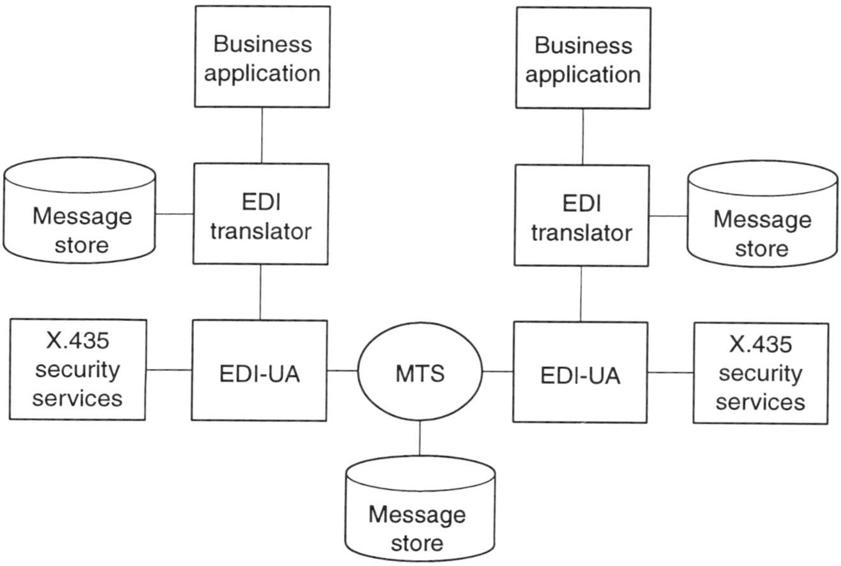

10.8 The architecture of an EDI system using X.435 security

gateway is a separate computer which provides an interface between the internal corporate computing domain and the external world. Thus the gap between EDIFACT translation and X.400 encapsulation could be enormous, with messages passing across many internal networks before reaching the X.400 UA. If this is the case, then the messages are insecure during that journey to the gateway and this will expose them to unacceptable business risks.

By far the best way to achieve 'end-to-end' message security in EDIFACT is to incorporate a security sub-system which provides security services to the EDIFACT translator, such that EDIFACT security syntax is created or interpreted during the translation process. The overall architecture of this approach, including the other security-related components, is shown in Fig. 10.9.

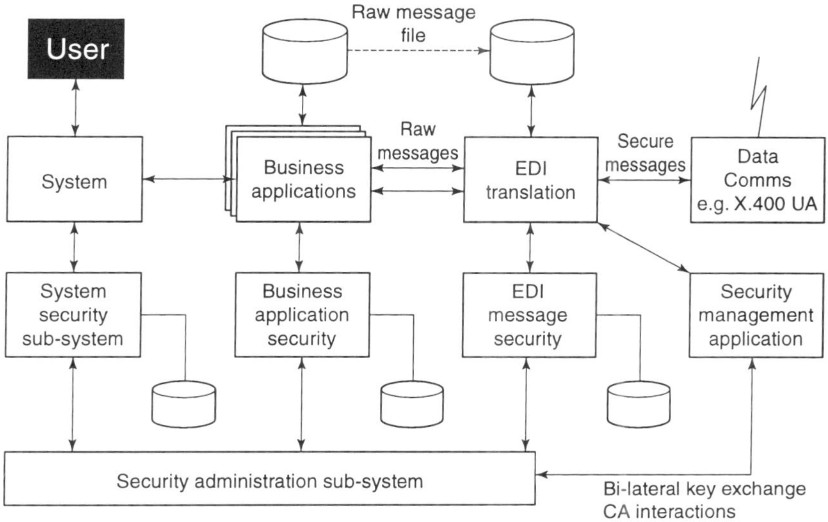

10.9 The architecture of an EDI system using EDIFACT security

What are the legal issues affecting EDI security?

There are potential problems associated with using new techniques and technologies to support legal transactions and contractual arrangements where the legal status of electronic documents and digital signatures is not clear. The lack of clarity arises from a number of sources: insufficient case law in this area, lack of statute law covering this area and inexperience and lack of knowledge amongst the judiciary and the legal profession in general when dealing with litigation in this area. In order to avoid some of these risks it is therefore regarded as good practice to set up an interchange agreement (IA) between trading partners to agree upon the issues of responsibility, liability and legal status of techniques, such as digital signature and admissibility of computer-based evidence. An IA sets out the full range of terms and conditions for conducting business on an EDI basis and is quite separate from the commercial contract which deals with the core business transaction (prices, volumes, schedules, etc).

Other legal issues which arise are those concerned with corporate record keeping to meet the requirements of finance acts, banking and financial services acts, companies acts and other relevant legislation that may be industry-specific (e.g. hazardous cargo notifications). There is also the whole issue of audit procedures and the event logging that is required to make audits possible.

Technical security solutions, as described, will assist with the implementation of an EDI security policy which meets the business requirements of the organization and protects against the perceived business risks. However, such solutions will always need to be set in a framework of legal and contractual controls to ensure that the technical controls really do deliver what the business requires.

EDI security checklist

1 Interchange agreement.
   (a) scope and terms definition;
   (b) liabilities and responsibilities;
   (c) protecting integrity of messages;
   (d) protecting confidentiality of messages;
   (e) procedures on receipt of an instruction for:
      (i) verification;
      (ii) acknowledgement;
      (iii) confirmation;
      (iv) actions to be taken;
   (f) storage, archiving and evidence;
   (g) relationships with third parties (e.g. VANS);
   (h) dispute resolution procedures.

2 Network services contract.

(a) responsibilities and obligations with regard to VANS;
(b) defines the service;
(c) defines user obligations;
(d) security in the VANS;
(e) liabilities and warranties;
(f) remedies;
(g) audit;
(h) network inter-working with multiple suppliers.

3 Evidential issues.
(a) legal status of some messages (e.g. VAT invoices);
(b) record keeping for compliance with some laws;
(c) admissibility of computer-based evidence;
(d) legal status of digital signatures;
(e) audit procedures (security and financial).

4 Security requirements definition.
(a) business impact analysis to determine message sensitivity;
(b) EDI security policy statement.

5 End-system security.
(a) system security policy;
(b) system security standards;
(c) personnel security procedures;
(d) physical security;
(e) environmental security;
(f) data back-up and recovery;
(g) change control;
(h) virus control;

- (i) user authorization;
- (j) user authentication;
- (k) functional access control;
- (l) data access control;
- (m) event logging and audit trails;
- (n) data validation;
- (o) message authorization and release procedures;
- (p) message sequence control;
- (q) message time-stamp control;
- (r) post-authorization message integrity protection in storage;
- (s) specification of end-to-end message security procedures;

6 EDI message security architecture.

- (a) message security at the point of translation;
- (b) international standards for inter-operability;
- (c) cryptographic syntax definitions;
- (d) security management and administration interface;
- (e) trusted third party certification services.

7 End-to-end message security services.

- (a) message confidentiality;
- (b) message origin authentication;
- (c) message contents authentication;
- (d) non-repudiation of origin;
- (e) non-repudiation of contents;
- (f) timeliness authentication;
- (g) completeness authentication;
- (h) sequencing authentication;

  (i) replay detection;
  (j) proof of delivery.

8 Network security.

  (a) service availability;
  (b) routing control;
  (c) network user authentication;
  (d) network access control;
  (e) integrity of call logging and billing;
  (f) guaranteed delivery.

Part 3

The future

11

Future developments

Michael Deakin and Claire Goddard

Electronic banking technology has come a long way since its beginnings at the centre of bank clearing systems. Analysis of past trends leads us to conclude that electronic banking applications will continue to broaden in scope, to reach more bank customers directly and to carry more services. But the future will be more than an extrapolation of past trends. Electronic technology is moving through revolutionary change and the pace of change is accelerating.

The success of companies like Microsoft and IBM in creating 'standards' which whole industries adopt suggests that standardization will increase rapidly and that electronic banking systems will become more compatible across banks and between banks and corporates. The resulting ability to share services will change the way in which banks use electronic banking as a competitive weapon – just as ATMs developed as a shared service, rather than as an area of interbank competition. For example, in 1996 15 North American banks and IBM announced plans to join together to set up a common private banking service using an 'open interconnectivity' standard which will be published for others to adopt.

In the past, banks have been early users of developments largely paid for by other research/developments. There is no reason for this trend to change. Another new development direction for the banks to watch closely is the combination of the falling cost of computer power and the growth of multimedia. Communications companies (telephone and television) are developing exciting new products such as 'set top' modules which use cable television or telephone lines to bring electronic messaging capability into the home. The major communications providers are actively seeking and marketing new products for transmission across their networks and they will seek to work closely with the banks to include financial services early in the development cycle.

The Internet is a another agent of rapid change which is making electronic services accessible to an ever-widening population of users. The first banking systems designed for operation through the Internet were being written and marketed in 1996 and the first Internet bank has been set up in the United States. Developments in security arrangements for the Internet – such as 'certification' of Internet sites to give active confirmation of their integrity and tamper-proof message elements – still need to be proved to be providing the sound base required for electronic business transaction but the opportunity is clear.

These developments offer banks the opportunity to become gateways to a number of networks and bank services could focus on assisting banks' clients to use the networks effectively. For example, major banks could use the strength of their reputation and name to provide 'stakeholder' or trustee services for businesses which wish to encourage their customers to make payments across the Internet. We predict that many new applications will be created as banks and businesses realize the capabilities of open access services.

As in the past, cost will be a significant element in identifying the priorities for development. Most banks have proved reluctant to lead development in technology; they still have very significant 'sunk costs' in existing technology and systems and will have to consider very carefully the size and justification of the investment which would be needed to expand some forms of electronic banking further. Even though the cost of hardware, software and communications will continue to drop, the write-off costs of abandoning past investment could prove to be a severe constraint, except in cases of immediate and direct benefit. For example, banks may prefer to connect their existing electronic banking platform to one of the new delivery channels, rather than appear to scrap a significant sunk cost. Nevertheless, banks will continue to seek to use technology to make their services more attractive to customers.

It follows that customer needs will continue to be one of the drivers of the direction of further development. Both domestic retail banking and corporate treasury needs put pressure on bank developments. But customer needs will not be the only driver. Open access will change the parameters of electronic service delivery as fundamentally as the Walkman changed the world of audio reproduction. We should look out for new services which appear to be impossible until new technology makes them possible and we should expect to see new applications which are more than a simple substitute for traditional delivery routes.

Retail banking services

In retail banking, use of technology to provide extra service or extra quality has been seen in developments such as First Direct, the UK's first non-branch, 24-hour electronic banking service and the NatWest ActionLine and PrimeLine services. These services remove the need for customers to visit bank branches and, using ATMs for cash deposits and withdrawals, lengthen the banking business day to provide services at any time convenient to the customer.

Throughout Europe, the adoption of the debit card and developments such as the 'electronic purse' are likely to have the effect of gradually separating retail banking from bank notes and coins. As a result, retail customers can be expected to demand more home-based banking, based on the telephone or computer terminal (which could be incorporated in the television receiver, many traditional 'boundaries' will disappear in the technology revolution).

Expansion of these and similar services, combined with the newer capabilities of multimedia, will provide a further generation of private banking activity incorporating the following:

1 Voice recognition will reduce the need for operator intervention, reducing the cost to the banks of providing the service and increasing the speed and efficiency of delivery. (This implies a further significant reduction in the need for bank branches.)

2 Further financial products will be added to retail electronic banking, such as insurance products, share dealing and so on.

3 Further shopping products may be added, linking credit sales or direct debits to televised or computerized retail sales catalogues.

4 Data manipulation services may be added, such as domestic accounts analysis.

Corporate treasury services

As electronic banking services progress, we are seeing a clearer separation of 'basic' bank transaction processing from other forms of banking, such as corporate financing and financial structuring. At present, corporate treasurers are displaying the behaviour patterns similar to those of personal bank customers when ATMs were identified – that is, they prefer automated delivery of low value or straightforward transactions but want to deal with a person for transactions which they consider to be high value or complex.

For transaction processing, corporate treasurers want cheaper and more efficient computerized services from banks which give rapid access to funds. Further, they are spreading their demands to include:

1 The co-ordination of services from more than one bank, delivered through one single electronic access point.

2 The integration of electronic bank services with corporate computer systems to create the paperless treasury.

The provision of single point, multi-service delivery, drawing data from multiple banks, has been technically possible for some years but delivery of this service in practice has been held back by the unequal capabilities of underlying banking systems. No matter how technically advanced the delivery system is, the full benefits of automated processing and 'instant' access to information cannot be achieved if the bank's back office processes are paper based, requiring manual intervention to create the electronic data for transmission. Corporate treasurers now know that the technology is available and the pressure will increase on the banks to provide the good quality, timely data needed to turn the technical possibility into reality.

Already, major corporations are quantifying the benefits available from expanding the scope of EDI systems to include payment messages. EDI systems were introduced by corporations to improve the efficiency of their own order processing cycles. By linking suppliers and/or customers directly with manufacturing, planning and order processing systems, corporations have gained significant reductions in working capital tied up in stock and in administration costs by creating efficient throughput times. Now that EDI can be extended to convey payment and text messages together, it is possible to automate the last link in the whole business and banking cycle and to cut down human intervention. Clerical checking and re-keying will be removed, making it possible to discontinue the manual verification and reconciliation checks which have to be completed whenever human processing is involved. Error rates will therefore drop, giving further cost savings.

At this point we meet resistance from corporates for the same reasons that there is resistance in banks – sunk cost of legacy systems. If existing accounts payable or accounts receivable software has to be replaced in order to interface with electronic banking systems, then the new efficiencies may have to wait until replacing legacy systems is cost justified or is essential for some other reason (such as the year 2000 with its associated date algorithm challenge).

Although EDI and paperless treasury operations will remove many of the sources of manual error, the security demands discussed in earlier chapters still need to be satisfied, but by electronic rather than clerical means. Because the topic is still young, many security issues are the subject of hot debate with solutions still experiencing teething troubles and with legal interpretation still evolving.

The following are some particularly hot issues:

1 EDI standards: absence of a single data standard is still a major inhibitor of the spread of financial EDI.

2 European legal development.

3 Confidentiality during transmission through commercial networks.

4 Detection of fraudulent or duplicate messages.

5 Reconciliations.

6 Message failure arrangements.

Banks will not have a monopoly hold on the EDI/EFT (often known as Financial EDI or FEDI link) or on the transmission of payment messages. EDI networks could be extended to accommodate electronic funds transfers by direct communication between companies. The indications are that banks are trying to retain customers by adding value from their own EDI network carriers and database arrangements.

When data about corporate business transactions and financial transactions are combined on bank databases and can be accessed through an EDI/EFT network, it will become possible for banks to expand the services supplied electronically. Companies may be able to access bank services such as:

1 *Modelling software*, loaded automatically with the company's actual data and fed with up-to-date market rates, to provide a facility for manipulating data collected in the normal course of banking business.

2 *Risk management services*, such as currency exposure and sensitivity analysis, interest rate sensitivity, liquidity statements and balance sheet structures based on actual cash flows and exposures.

3 *Bench-marking comparisons*, giving 'league table' comparison with anonymous data about other organizations or with the average for all customers in an industrial sector.

These risk management and bench-marking services have the potential to benefit both banks and their corporate customers.

Improved currency and interest rate risk management by companies should improve their stability and creditworthiness, as well as provide fee opportunities for the banks which sell the treasury risk management products used for hedging or smoothing exposures.

An increasingly close partnership between companies and banks will be generated by the joint use of data collected in the course of banking transactions. Traditional boundaries between banks and corporates may be challenged constructively if all parties have equal access to data. The bank/corporate partnership will achieve additional efficiency levels and cost benefits if electronic banking services are extended to the point at which companies can use banking services as an outsourced alternative to replace their own in-house administration. An extension of bank provision of EDI/EFT networks could permit banks to provide accounts payable and accounts receivable records for corporate customers, and we may see banks becoming major outsource service operators. Overall savings would be generated by discontinuing the present duplication of financial records by banks and companies.

The effect of continuous progress

Recent surveys have revealed that the cost of computer hardware is falling at 30% per annum. At the same time, improvements in computer technology mean that the size of computer hardware is shrinking rapidly. History has shown that electronic banking develops rapidly when cheap and convenient automation is available and so it is likely that we will see some revolutionary changes in the early years of the new millennium. Creative use of the imagination allows us to picture a future in which individuals carry pocketbook (or even wrist-watch) size computers which hold details of bank accounts and which are tendered to EFTPOS stations in place of money. Indeed, development of the portable telephone/computer could remove the need for separate EFTPOS stations. Companies may come to transact business directly into customer and supplier computers. In this scenario, the transaction processing bank becomes entirely the 'electronic bank', maintaining and administering the software, networks and databases which drive seamless payment and receipt systems. The world of electronic banking will be complete. Will it be a security dream – or a nightmare?

Appendices

Appendix 1

Selecting a new treasury system

Brian Welch

Selecting a treasury system is an important event in the life of a treasury department. If it is handled correctly, there will be little recognition outside of the treasury itself, apart from the cost, but if the selection, installation and final product is unsatisfactory, it gains a much higher profile in a company, and the reputation of the treasury can suffer.

The risks of developing a treasury system in house are covered in Chapter 8, and the selection process is not an exact science, but the aim of this appendix is to cover the issues which should be addressed when selecting from one of the various packages which are available.

If the company is replacing an existing system, there will already be a clear understanding of what treasury systems can do, the shortcomings of the existing system, and the expectations of the new one. Sometimes treasurers who are new to a company will want to replace an existing system with one with which they are already familiar, and some searches may be undertaken with the preferred choice already known, although this hardly gives the other candidates an opportunity to be treated impartially. New systems may be chosen in the wake of a major corporate treasury loss, part of which may be attributed to lack of information, in which case cost may not be as significant as selecting a system which can ensure that the same problem does not occur again.

If the company is selecting a treasury system for the first time, the initial stage of the selection process needs to be managed carefully to identify company requirements and expectations.

Establishing the need for a treasury system

At the very basic level, treasury departments can manage without a treasury system, relying on a combination of bank balance reporting, spreadsheets and word processing packages, and indeed when linked together, these can provide functionality which might exceed some of the earliest treasury system packages. What such *ad hoc* combinations are *unlikely* to provide is:

1 The pro-active functionality which can highlight and initiate actions, such as maturing transactions.

2 The security which surrounds a discrete system.

3 Documentation which a treasury system supplier provides, can mean more continuity and less reliance on individuals.

4 The audit trail which can identify and prove all of the transactions handled by the system.

5 The overall re-assurance that all transactions are processed *securely* and *correctly*.

6 System updates and upgrades to cover environmental changes.

Nevertheless, a treasury with a small number of daily bank account movements and transactions may still not justify the cost of a treasury system, even compared with the potential costs of treasury related transactions being missed.

However, as soon as the number and complexity of transactions increases, a treasury system becomes essential to:

1 Ensure that all transactions are properly recorded.

2 Ensure that maturing transactions are not missed.

3 Provide reporting to ensure that more than one person can be informed of the transactions, to segregate responsibilities and improve the underlying security

4 Provide reporting to the accounting function, for the transactions to be correctly recorded.

5 Provide reporting to senior management, to ensure that they understand the level of activities being undertaken by the treasury functions.

6 Assist analysis of the transactions for them to be correctly managed.

An example of where a treasury system was needed was in the London Borough of Hammersmith and Fulham which became overexposed to interest rate swaps during the 1980s, and ran a portfolio of over 400 transactions, using just a desk diary to keep a note of the various transactions and their maturities.

Budget and pricing

Approval of the principle should also include an agreed budget. It should be clear what this budget covers – software, hardware, installation, training, maintenance, personnel to operate the system. Prices for the software range from £10 000 to £5 million, and it should be understood that the buyer gets what it pays for. Systems might be cheaper because they are getting old and they may not compare favourably with the newer competitors. However new systems seeking to get a foothold in the market may also be good value, although the corporate which purchases a system which is not already in use elsewhere should recognise the particular risks involved in doing so.

The suppliers may not regard their pricing as including hidden extras, but so that there are no misunderstandings, the corporate should give an indication of its attitude to price levels at the outset. There is, of course, a place for negotiation on price, but it is important that the corporate understands the general range of prices, and that the supplier is likely to be within that range, to avoid unnecessary meetings and demonstrations of systems which were always going to be too expensive.

Defining the requirements

As soon as the principle of the need for a treasury system has been accepted, it is important to define exactly what functions it is expected to cover, and the likely volumes and currencies such as:

1 Bank balance reporting.
2 Recording of transactions – identifying the different instruments used and which may be used in the future.
3 Security standards (see chapters 7 and 8).
4 Counterparties and control of counterparty exposures.
5 Confirmations.
6 Settlements and payments.
7 Accounting.
8 Statutory reporting.
9 Reporting including standard reports and the use of report writers.
10 Analysis (for example Value at Risk).
11 Valuation.
12 Forecasting.
13 Decision support .
14 Hardware and network constraints.

In addition, at this stage, it is important to identify the various non-treasury parties who are likely to be affected by the system, and who may specify certain additional requirements. These will include:

1 The IT Department:

   (a) Do they want to participate in the search?

   (b) Does the company standardise its hardware requirements on a particular manufacturer or certain type of system?

   (c) If it is to run on a PC network, have decisions been taken on PCs or networks which will affect the selection?

   (d) Is the company committed to a particular operating or software strategy or database?

2 Financial Accounting:

   (a) What interfaces will be required to the main accounting system?

   (b) Would treasury like to have access to accounts payable and accounts receivable and longer term forecasts to assist treasury cashflow forecasting?

3 Internal Audit:

   (a) How closely does Internal Audit want to be involved with the search?

   (b) Will that department pay particularly close attention to the structure of the security (and do they understand the nature of treasury security standards)?

4 External Auditors:

   (a) If the company does not have a separate internal audit group, should the auditors be informed of the search?

   (b) Do you want the auditors to get involved in the search? They will have expertise and knowledge of the various systems, but they will be expensive.

5 Overseas Subsidiaries or Divisions:

(a) Will the company be aiming to extend the system to overseas operations, building a worldwide treasury network?

Preparation

A project team should be formed, with participation from treasury at least and some of the other various parties already mentioned.

It is not unusual for 'non-treasury' interested parties to want to be actively involved in the search, in particular, the IT department. However, if possible, it is important to keep control of the project in the hands of a person who understands treasury, and if the treasury department is small, it might be better to use a consultant. The consultancy divisions of the auditors will have the expertise to manage such a search, although they can be quite expensive compared with some of the independent specialist consultants which are also available.

A consultant could eliminate the need to attend conferences or to assemble other information on the systems which are available, but even if a consultant is used, it is still worthwhile attending one of the specialist conferences, such as that run by the ACT, to see the various systems being exhibited. These conferences provide good background material, and will often include systems demonstrations and presentations from treasurers who have recently selected and installed new systems. They may also draw attention to current trends, developments and issues, relating to the systems market, which may not be immediately known.

There is also a useful listing of systems suppliers published by the ACT in *The Treasurer's Handbook* and there are directories published by magazines and by specialist consultants which cover the treasury market. The Internet is also a useful source of information, and some specialist websites are listed on the ACT website (www.corporate-treasurers.co.uk) and in the *Handbook*. Using these sources it is possible to contact potential suppliers to obtain enough basic information about the various systems to compile a list of likely contacts.

A word of warning. Treasury software suppliers often appear to be quite secretive. Some never exhibit at conferences and some only advertise in certain magazines and do not have websites, so a little detective work is sometimes needed to find them!

Approaching the suppliers

There are two kinds of documents which are prepared at this stage, the Request for Information (RFI) and the Request for a Proposal (RFP) (or Invitation To Tender) (ITT). A detailed RFI enables a short list to be prepared to which an RFP is then sent. However the preparation and analysis of the RFI responses can be very time consuming, and as the preparation stage can produce a slightly longer list of potential suppliers, it is probably just as easy to send the RFP to the longer list (a draft RFP is shown at the end of the appendix).

The RFP is a description of the company's requirements accompanied by a long list of functions in detail for the supplier to indicate how its system meets those requirements. Sometimes each item on the list is classified by priority to the potential purchaser, such as:

1 Essential.

2 Normal requirement.

3 Nice to have, but not essential.

Some RFPs may also indicate other codes to help classify answers as follows:

1 Y. Yes – The software fully supports this function without any modification.

2 P. Partial – The software partially supports this function.

3 F. Future – The software does not support this function, but it will be covered by a future release which will be available on...

4 C. Customization – The software does not support this function, but it can be customized to do so.

5 D. Develop – The software does not support this function, but the supplier is prepared to develop the required functionality in conjunction with the prospective purchaser.

6 N. No – The software does not and will not support this function.

The suppliers receiving the RFP should be told the timetable for the search and given a deadline for their reply. They nearly always reply close to the deadline, but for those who miss it, unless they have a particularly good excuse, if they cannot meet the first deadline, what is the likelihood of installation being completed on time, if they are selected?

The compilation and the completion of RFIs and RFPs is like a game of poker between the corporate and the software supplier. The corporate tries to phrase the questions in the RFP as unambiguously as possible, whilst the supplier will bend over backwards to have as few 'Ns' as possible in its response. There is even a suspicion that some suppliers ignore the questions and answer 'Y' to all of them with the objective of being invited to demonstrate their system, in the belief that the corporate can then be seduced by the quality of their demonstration and the look of its screens. In practice, nothing could be further from the truth, with corporates giving short shrift to suppliers who have been misleading in their RFP responses.

There should also be a space in the RFP for the supplier to add comments explanations and clarifications, but the use of codes enables the responses to be analysed more easily.

Some corporates ask for a trial version of the software, but although this might seem like a good idea, very few suppliers will release any of their software, and it is unlikely that the corporate will see the system at its best without sufficient training.

The responses to the RFP need to be evaluated carefully, probably on a spreadsheet extended from the basic questionnaire. Some systems will rule themselves out by failing to provide, or meet the 'essential' and 'normal requirement' criteria, whilst others can be eliminated on the basis on their overall response, and cost. From that analysis it is usually possible to draw up a short list which the corporate would like to see demonstrated.

The demonstration

There should be a full demonstration of the system, at either the supplier's or the corporate's offices. Both alternatives have their own advantages, but it is valuable to visit the supplier's offices to gain an impression of its size and approach. It is in the interests of the corporate that the system should be viewed to its advantage, and the demonstration should, where possible, cover all aspects of the functionality. The corporate should draw up its own list of what it wants to see, and to give the supplier an agenda and timetable into which the demonstration can be reasonably made. Demonstrations will normally last for the most of a day and any attempt to fit more than one into a day should be avoided as unrealistic. Particular care should be taken with functions which are skipped over by the supplier, or said not to be easily demonstrable.

At this stage, security aspects may be glossed over in the excitement of viewing the latest optional features. This must not be allowed to happen. It is essential to have a separate agenda item on security and to have the features fully demonstrated.

Where systems are expected to be demonstrated in the corporate's offices, there may be technical or communications difficulties which may detract from a comprehensive demonstration compared with a cut down version of a system on a portable PC which might therefore seem to be better. On the other hand, it is easier to compare systems under the same demonstration conditions.

After the first demonstration it should be possible to select a short list or a preferred system, after which a second meeting is normally organized to handle each system. It is important, especially where the corporate uses the full range of treasury instruments, that it should insist on running its own data over a system with a realistic volume of transactions to ensure that the system can perform in the manner as claimed by the supplier. It is also essential to speak to, and preferably visit, an existing user of the system. The supplier will, of course, have selected a satisfied user for a site visit, and will usually expect to accompany the corporate to 'make the introduction'. In such instances, the corporate should ask to speak to the existing user unaccompanied, and if this is not possible, to contact them separately to enquire if the user has had any problems with the system, or the supplier. Treasurers are normally honest about their experiences with a system, but that shouldn't be taken for granted. If a system is trying to break into the market, an existing user could well be keen to get other users to buy it so that its future is more secure.

Although at this stage there will probably be a preferred candidate, it is important to maintain contact with at least one other possible supplier in case either the first choice cannot deliver within the corporate's requirements, or there are problems about agreeing on the price, in which case there is a reference point for comparison, and competition at the point of negotiation.

The subject of the financial stability and commitment of the supplier to the treasury systems market was referred to in Chapter 8, and there is little which can be added, other than the observation that each kind of supplier carries its own particular risks. The small focused system supplier is more of a financial risk, whilst the larger systems supplier or bank may not have the same level of commitment, and may exit from the market if higher returns can be secured elsewhere. The market is supplied by numerous small specialist suppliers, and this has made it very competitive.

Implementation

As with the other stages, implementation varies widely. No system is likely to be installed in a matter of weeks, but some of the larger ones have taken up to two years. (Can you wait that long?) The normal course of events is for:

1 Hardware and network to be installed and configured.

2 Software to be installed, plus any customisation which has been agreed.

3 Security structures to be established.

4 Standing data to be inputbasic operating units, counterparties, accounting structures and interfaces

5 Checking and customization of reports to be carried out to

ensure that when the system goes 'live' the output is as expected.

6 Transaction datapast transactions, existing unmatured transactions and current data – to run in parallel with any existing system. Parallel running is essential, but migration to the new system should be undertaken as quickly as possible in view of the additional pressure placed on treasury personnel by running two systems at the same time.

7 Training to be undertaken at various levels. Dealer, Back Office, System Administrator, Auditor.

8 Live running!

The security of the corporate user is based on sound systems selection as much as on secure working practices. Diligent selection will add to the overall security of a concern in the long run.

Appendix 1

Draft request for a proposal (RFP)

OUTLINE OF THE CORPORATE TREASURY

Description of the company, its operating locations and treasury structure, functions and locations			
Operations			
Cash management	A/Cs		Types of services used
Currencies USD			(Transactions, Balance Reporting, EFT, etc)
Euro			
Euro currencies B Fr			
DMk			
DFl			
Esc			
FFr			
FM			
IRP			
Lit			
LFr			
Pta			
Sch			
Non Euro EU currencies			
DKr			
Dr			
GBP			
SKr			

Non EU currencies			
NKr			
SFr			
Other major international currencies JPY			
etc			
Banks used			
Domestic			
National Westminster			
etc			
International			

Appendix 1

Function	Priority	Response	Comment
	1 / 2 / 3	Y/P/F/C/D/N	
SYSTEM OPERATING REQUIREMENTS			
Operating system(s) Windows NT, UNIX etc			
Database used: Oracle, Sybase etc			
Ability to utilize security of the underlying database			
Client/Server architecture – Relationship between the data on the server and the PC workstations			
Client /Server architecture – The residency of application and database on multiple servers and synchronization of selected data elements that require replication?			
Client application running on a LAN?			
Client software Windows 3.1 compatible?			
Client software runs on Windows NT?			
Context sensitive help?			
System based tutorial?			
End user documentation			
Administrator documentation			
Network – multi user version			

Function	Priority	Response	Comment
API (published/standard)			
Security architecture and functionality			
Different levels of access for various types of user			
Log on restrictions – passwords and enforced changes at intervals			
Restricted access to data – users only to have access to the data they require			
Restricted access to individual screens, inquiries and reports			
Control of functions within individual screens			
System Administrator responsible for security			
Ability to monitor usage (who is using the application and database and how often)			
Capability to recover data in the event of a system failure – manual or automatic			
Full audit trail to identify access, attempted access, input, amendments and deletions			

Appendix 1

Function	Priority	Response	Comment
	1 / 2 / 3	Y/P/F/C/D/N	
CASH MANAGEMENT			
Cash Flow forecast: settlements by date, currency, entity, bank account			
Download/Import bank transactions and balances			
Import accounts receivable and accounts payable data from internal sources			
Consolidated daily liquidity position forecast by currency, forecast, entity etc			
Consolidated forward liquidity position forecast by currency, forecast, entity etc			
Grouping of Current Accounts for pooling			
Ability to warehouse expected transactions			
Ability to calculate variance of forecast against actual			
Export of transactions and payments to bank from cash position worksheet			
Automated update of system balances after payments are transmitted			
Daily cash analysis – calculate cash position per Currency, Entity and Bank			

CASH MANAGEMENT (continued)

Function	Priority	Response	Comment
	1 / 2 / 3	Y/P/F/C/D/N	
Average balances per day (value) for pool and account performance			
Automated reconciliation of known and expected transactions; other transactions get flagged for review			
Ability to warehouse known transactions			
Automated transfer for targeted balances			
ACH capability			
Full balance history retained for interest calculation			
Cheques issued			
Non-cash settlement/ Settlement on balance			

DEBIT/INVESTMENT MANAGEMENT ST/LT

All instruments funds, bonds, cp, etc			
Borrowing (third party and inter-company)			
Loans third party – Facility amounts			
Loans Inter company – Facility amounts			

DEBIT/INVESTMENT MANAGEMENT ST/LT (continued)

Ability to track interest payments on a monthly or daily (variable) basis			
Early repayment			
Reference rate for analysis (debt/borrowing)			
Bank balance interest calculated for each entity and bank balance			
Generate confirmations for investment/debt on selected transactions (optional)			
Manual adjustment to repayment amounts by specified maximum			
Calculating improved return on intercompany loans against reference rates			
Include interest income/ expense forecast (Profit & Loss)			
Security held or given			

INTEREST RATE / RISK MANAGEMENT

Exposure tracking by location, entity, type of debt, etc			
Physical debt link with hedges			
Physical debt payment generation			
Authorization limits – Trade entry			
Swaps			
Futures			
Deferred Forwards			
Options			
Exotic Options			
User defined Derivatives			
Forward Rate Agreements (FRAs)			
Generate payments for debt/hedges			
Broker reconciliations for futures			
Generate confirmations			
Generate invoices			
Individual tax structures by entity			
Benchmarks			
Interest rate histories			

Appendix 1

FOREIGN EXCHANGE

FX deal processing			
Spot			
Forward			
Swap			
OTC Options bought/sold			
Exchange Traded Options			
European Options			
Barrier Options			
Options strategies/Linking of options (e.g. collar, barrier, contingent options etc)			
Option valuation; Mark-to-Market Options, etc; individually and for a portfolio, strategy and/or programme			
Futures			
Mark-to-Market traditional instruments			
Reference rate – compare options against forward			
Note field relating to deal			
Identification inter-company/ Bank for internal deals			
For inter-company contracts, generate deals for both companies			
Identification of trader executing the deal			

FOREIGN EXCHANGE (continued)

Ability to segregate Treasury settlements across companies (Shared application that can separate settlements)			
Ability to correct errors			
Control of FX rate input vs market rate from Reuters; ability to flag differences based on tolerance			
Ability to handle multiple currencies; accounting transactions should have transaction currency and functional currencies			
Facility to do a historic rollover without generating a settlement instruction or create a new deal			
Generate grouped confirmations automatically			
Generate confirmations FX-Match			
Generate confirmations facsimile			
Netting of settlements (optional)			
Ability to note and track confirmations for banks not on FX-Match			
Ability to group internal entities			

FOREIGN EXCHANGE (continued)

Trading limits – direct lending limit, daily settlement limit, global limit to a counterparty; daily settlement is a subset of the global limit			
Exposure identification			
Transaction exposures (firm cashflows/transactions)			
Anticipated exposures (economic cashflows/ transactions)			
Identify exposures by subsidiary, business unit etc			
Transaction exposures by order/invoice			
Permit input of multi-year exposures (minimum 3 years)			
FX, Int Rate, Debt, Inv Exposure Analysis			
What if? analysis			
Decision Support, Modelling, Monte Carlo Simulations			
Options pricing model			
FX exposure management			
Ability to track and monitor selective hedge positions			
Identify ultimate maturity on specific hedges; account for gain or loss on actual maturity date			

STATIC DATA MAINTAINED BY THE SYSTEM

Counterparty details			
Bank account details			
Counterparty addresses			
Contact methods (phone/ fax/e-mail)			
Contact names			
Standard Payment Instructions (correspondents, etc);			
Location profiles			
Overall exposure per third party (FX, IRR, per bank)			
Internal static data			
Division/Subsidiary details			
Bank account details			
Contact methods (phone/fax/ e-mail)			
Contact names			
Operating/base currency			
Tax details			
Facility amounts			
Dealing			
Borrowing			
Lending			
Credit risk limits			

STATIC DATA MAINTAINED BY THE SYSTEM (continued)

Settlement risk limits			
360/365 days as required			
Holidays to be accommodated			

INTERFACES

Collect balance and transaction data electronically from other locations and banks			
Ability to transmit EFT instructions electronically to banks			
EDI interfaces			
Interface with commercial database systems (e.g. Reuters, Bloomberg, BRIDGE)			
Automatic download valid rates (from Reuters, Bloomberg etc)			
Interface to accounting systems			
Link to A/P and A/R systems			
Link to electronic FX transaction confirmation matching			
Interface with commercial paper dealers for automated download of CP rates			

REPORTING

Standard reports – number and examples including:			
Maturing contracts by subs/ currency/ maturity			
FX volume by entity or counterparty (amount, no of deals)			
FX volume by currency			
Mark-to-market valuations			
Commercial paper performance by dealer against reference rates			
Credit Exposure by counterparty			
Exposure Reports by currency, entity, maturity, firm, forecast			
Exposure by type, (transaction: firm vs forecast/ translation/economic)			
Retrospective balance adjustment by value date			
By legal entity, the ability to provide mark-to-market values on the net of the receivables/ payables; system needs to distinguish between contracts deferred and contracts which are marked-to-market (in aggregate)			
Communicate sales order rates and forward rates internally			

REPORTING (continued)

Communicate closing rates internally			
Exposures into base currency by subsidiary view			
Cross-currency exposures			
Bank Balance per value date per company and currency			
Report writer for customised reporting			
Ability to fax reports			
Ability to e-mail reports internally and externally			
Ability to automatically schedule faxes and mailed reports			
Ability to evaluate competitiveness of bank quotes (rating different banks/spreads/successful quote linked to multiple failed quote)			

ACCOUNTING

Provides audit trails			
Provides General Ledger			
Accrual, Deferral and Mark-to-Market accounting entries			
Accounting Exchange Rate field			

ACCOUNTING (continued)

Ability to generate accounting entries related to type of transaction by default to accounts			
Holds dummy counterparty portfolios			
Holds separate profit centres			
Ability to generate entries to all cash accounts			

SUPPLIER INFORMATION

Financial strength			
Customer references available			
Purchase or lease available			
System sold on modular basis?			
Typical system cost?			
Willingness to provide trial copy of software			
Training costs			
Strategic relationships			

INTER-COMPANY/NETTING

Interface with main accounting system for payables and receivables			
Manual receipt of data			

INTER-COMPANY/NETTING (continued)

Identification of inter-company and third party payments			
Identification of inter-company transaction requests			
Automated netting settlement			
Automated inter-company payments			

DECISION SUPPORT

What-if? modelling			
Risk analysis			
Analysis on hedge possibilities			

LETTERS OF CREDIT

Ability to track all issued letters of credit with different banks			
Ability to calculate and reconcile bank invoices for L/Cs			
Ability to input L/C information and fax to bank			
Interface to bank L/C and payment system			

BANK ACCOUNTS

Track signatories for all bank accounts			
Ability to issue letters to bank for changes, open, close			
Reporting capability of open, closed and changed accounts			
Other mandate details			

BANK RELATIONSHIP MANAGEMENT

Details of bank addresses updates for all the system			
Details of bank contacts			
Database for bank facilities			
Database of charges tariff			
Calculate bank charges			

SUPPORT

Vendor has international support available			
Technical hotline support			
Availability of consultation/ customization support			
Training support			
Maintenance support			

Appendix 2

The London Code of Conduct

For principals and broking firms in the wholesale markets

Bank of England July 1995

Appendix 2

I INTRODUCTION

II GENERAL STANDARDS

III CONTROLS

IV DEALING PRINCIPLES AND PROCEDURES: A STATEMENT OF BEST PRACTICE

This edition of the Code supersedes that issued in May 1992.

Market notice 23 May 1997
Market notice 22 December 1997

Appendix 2

I INTRODUCTION

Aims

1 The London financial markets have a long-established reputation for their high degree of professionalism and the maintenance of the highest standards of business conduct. All those operating in these markets share a common interest in their health and in maintaining the established exacting standards.

2 The Code is applicable to most wholesale market dealings which are not regulated by the rules of a recognized investment exchange. These typically form part of 'treasury' operations and are undertaken in large amounts. A full list of the products covered and the appropriate size criteria are shown in the box opposite.

3 The Bank of England (the Bank) wishes to sustain the efficient functioning of the London wholesale markets in which these products are traded and to avoid over-burdonsome regulation; and believes that this Code is consistent with these objectives.

4 The Code has been developed in close consultation with market practitioners and will continue to be kept under regular review. A fuller description of the Bank's regulatory arrangements covering the wholesale markets, of which this Code is an integral part, is set out in the 'Grey Paper' (The regulation of the wholesale markets in sterling, foreign exchange and bullion) available from the Wholesale Markets Supervision Division of the Bank of England.

5 The Code sets out the general standards and controls which the management and individuals at broking firms (including electronic broking firms) and **'core principals'** (banks, building societies plus financial institutions authorized under the Financial Services Act 1986) should adopt when transacting business in the relevant financial products. Furthermore, the Chartered Institute of Public Finance and Accountancy and the Association of Corporate Treasurers commend the Code to their members, which also deal as principal in these markets, as best practice, to which they, too, should adhere.

Distribution

6 It is the responsibility of broking firms/core principals to seek to establish whether their UK based clients/counterparties have a copy of the Code. If they do not, they should send them one or advise them to contact the Bank direct. Where relevant, local authorities plus other institutions and companies in the UK are encouraged to adopt a similar approach.

7 The Bank will seek to make as many as possible **overseas based** firms aware that their wholesale market deals in the London market are undertaken in accordance with the London Code. If broking firms or core principals receive any questions from

overseas based firms about their wholesale market deals they should, where appropriate, make them aware of the Code's existence; and that copies can be obtained from the Bank. Non-core principals are encouraged to adopt a similar approach.

Compliance and complaints

8 **Compliance with the Code is necessary to ensure that the highest standards of integrity and fair dealing continue to be observed throughout these markets.** Breaches by those institutions which they supervise will be viewed most seriously by the Bank and by the Building Societies Commission; any such breaches may be reflected in their assessment of the fitness and propriety of these institutions. In addition, the Securities and Investments Board and the UK Self-Regulating Organisations expect those core principals which they supervise to abide by the Code when dealing in the wholesale markets.

9 If any principal (core or non-core) or broking firm believes that an institution supervised by the Bank has breached either the letter or the spirit of the Code in respect of any wholesale market transaction in which it is involved, it is encouraged – whether or not it is itself supervised by the Bank – to seek to settle this matter amicably with the other party. If this is not possible, the institution which is subject to the complaint should make the complainant aware that it can bring the matter to the attention of the Head of Wholesale Markets Supervision Division of the Bank of England. All such complaints will be investigated by the Bank. As a general rule the Bank will seek evidence from all parties named in the complaint and will wish to discuss this in detail with management of the institution subject to the complaint.

10 Where a breach of the Code by a bank or other firm listed by the Bank under Section 43 of the Financial Services Act (FSA) – a 'listed institution' – is established, and depending on how serious it is, the Bank may publicly reprimand individuals and/or the firms involved. It may also restrict a listed institution's activities or, if the breach is sufficiently serious to cast doubt on the competence of the firm or on its integrity, suspend or remove the offending firm from the list. The Bank will seek to promulgate its decisions as widely as it considers appropriate; in so doing the Bank will wish to consider the possible implications of making its findings known to others.

11 Since the compensation fund arrangements established under the FSA do not apply to any exempt business undertaken by listed institutions, if any breaches of the Code are found to have occurred, the offending institution will be expected to consider making appropriate redress to any damaged party or parties, bearing in mind any legal implications of so doing.

Appendix 2

Arbitration

12 In order to help resolve differences the Bank is willing, if asked, to arbitrate in disputes between firms it supervises. These arrangements are set out in more detail in paragraph 120.

PRODUCTS COVERED BY THE BANK'S WHOLESALE MARKETS ARRANGEMENTS

A: Cash Market Products

1 Sterling wholesale deposits.

2 Foreign currency wholesale deposits.

3 Gold and silver bullion wholesale deposits.

4 Spot and forward foreign exchange.

5 Spot and forward gold and silver bullion.

B: Instruments which are defined as investments in the Financial Services Act but which are outside the scope of the Investment Services Directive:

6 Over the counter (OTC) options (including warrants) or futures contracts on gold or silver.

C: Instruments which are defined as investments in the Financial Services Act and are within the scope of the Investment Services Directive:

7 Certificates of deposit (CDs), or other debt instruments, issued by institutions authorised under the Banking Act 1987, European authorised institutions, and by UK building societies, with an original maturity of not more than 5 years. (This class of instrument is included in the Financial Services Act under the generic term 'debenture').

8 Bank Bills (or bankers' acceptances)*

9 Other debentures with an original maturity of not more than 1 year (including non-London CDs and commercial paper).

10 Medium-term notes issued under the Banking Act 1987 (Exempt Transactions) (Amendment) Regulations.

11 UK local authority debt (bills, bonds, loan stock or other instruments) with an original maturity of not more than 5 years.

12 Other public sector debt with an original maturity of not more than 1 year (eg Treasury bills but **not** gilt-edged securities).

13 Any certificate (or other instrument) representing the securities covered in items 7 – 12; or rights to and interests in, these instruments.

14 OTC options (including warrants) or futures contracts on any currency (including sterling); interest rate; or items 7 – 13 above.

15 Interest rate and currency swaps, regardless of their original maturity; forward rate agreements, or any other 'contracts for differences' involving arrangements to profit (or avoid loss) by references to movements in the value of any of the instruments in 7 – 13 above; or the value of any currency; or in the interest on loans in any currency.

16 Sale and repurchase agreements ('repros'), sale and buybacks and stock borrowing and lending involving debentures, loan stock or other debt instruments, including gilts, of whatever original maturity where the repurchase of repayment will take place within twelve months.

Note 1 Instruments subject to the rules of a recognized investment exchange are **not** covered.

Note 2 Instruments denominated in foreign currencies, as well as in sterling **are** covered.

Note 3 Transaction by listed institutions may come within the Bank's supervisory framework even if one of the other parties to the transaction is operating abroad.

Note 4 The regulation of deposit-taking under the Banking Act 1987 is not affected in any way.

Note 5 The Government made clear in January 1988 that ordinary forward foreign exchange (and bullion) transactions fall outside the Financial Services Act; these nevertheless fall within the scope of the Bank's arrangements.

Note 6 Wholesale transactions between core principals in items 1 and 8 are not usually less than £100,000. For items 2 and 4, the usual minimum is £500,000 (or currency equivalent). For bullion (items 3 and 5), the relevant amounts are 2,000 ounces for gold and 50,000 ounces for silver.

Note 7 For items 7, 9 – 13, and 16, the minimum size of wholesale transactions is £100,000 (or the equivalent in foreign currency). For swaps, options, futures, forward rate agreements (FRAs) and other 'contracts for differences' (items 6, 14 and 15) the minimum underlying value is £500,000 (or the equivalent in foreign currency).

---

* With effect from 1 January 1996, following amendment to the Financial Services Act.

II GENERAL STANDARDS

Core principals and broking firms – and their employees – should at all times abide by the spirit as well as the letter of the Code when undertaking, arranging or advising on transactions in the wholesale markets.

Managers of core principals and broking firms must ensure that the obligations imposed on them and their staff by the general law are observed. Management and staff should also be mindful of any relevant rules and codes of practice of other regulatory bodies.

Responsibilities

- **Of the principal/broker**

13 All firms (core principals and brokers) should ensure that they and, to the best of their ability, all other parties act in a manner consistent with the Code so as to maintain the highest reputation for the wholesale markets in London.

14 Core principals which conduct non-investment business (see the box on page 3) with private individuals should have internal procedures which set out whether these individuals will be treated as retail customers or as wholesale market participants under the arrangements set out in this Code. The procedures set out in Part IV of this Code may not be relevant, directly, to such business.

15 It is essential that all relevant staff are made familiar with the Code and conduct themselves at all times in a thoroughly professional manner. In particular they must conduct transactions in a way that is consistent with the procedures set out in Part IV of this Code.

16 All firms will be held responsible for the actions of their staff. They must:

- ensure that any individual who commits the firm to a transaction has the necessary authority to do so.
- ensure that employees are adequately trained in the practices of the markets in which they deal/broke; and are aware of their own, and their firm's, responsibilities. Inexperienced dealers should not rely on a broker, for instance, to fill gaps in their training or experience; to do so is clearly **not** the broker's responsibility.
- ensure staff are made aware of and comply with any other relevant guidance that may from time to time be issued by the Bank.
- ensure that employees comply with any other regulatory requirements that may be applicable or relevant to a firm's activities in the wholesale markets.

17 When establishing a relationship with a **new** counterparty or client, firms must take steps to make them aware of the precise nature of firms' liability for business to

be conducted, including any limitations on that liability and the capacity in which they act. **In particular, broking firms should explain to a new client the limited role of brokers (see paragraphs 29 and 30 below).**

18 All firms should identify any potential or actual **conflicts of interest** that might arise when undertaking wholesale market transactions and take measures either to eliminate these conflicts or control them such as to ensure the fair treatment of counterparties.

19 All firms should **know their counterparty**. For principals this is essential where the nature of the business undertaken requires the assessment of creditworthiness. Before dealing with another principal for the first time in any product covered by this Code, core principals should ensure that appropriate steps (see Part III of this Code) are taken.

20 As part of the 'know your counterparty' process firms must take all necessary steps to prevent their transactions in the wholesale markets being used to facilitate **money laundering**. To this end firms should be familiar with the Guidance Notes published in 1995[1]. These make clear the very limited responsibilities name passing brokers have in this area; in particular banks (and others that use brokers) should **not** seek to rely on brokers to undertake anything other than identity and location checks on their behalf.

21 As a general rule core principals will assume that their counterparties have the capability to make independent decisions and to act accordingly; it is for each counterparty to decide if it needs to seek independent advice. If a non-core principal wishes to retain a core principal as its financial adviser it is strongly encouraged to do so in writing, setting forth the exact nature and extend of the reliance it will place upon the core principal. All principals should accept responsibility for entering into wholesale market transactions and any subsequent losses they might incur. They should assess for themselves the merits and risks of dealing in these markets. Non-core principals must recognize that it is possible for core principals to take proprietary positions which might be similar or opposite to their own.

22 It is good practice for **principals**, subject to their own legal advice, to alert counterparties to any legal or tax uncertainties which they know are relevant to a proposed relationship or transaction, in order that the counterparty may seek its own advice if it so wishes.

23 Management of **broking** firms should advise their employers of the need to ensure that their behaviour could not **at any time** be construed as having misled counterparties about the limited role of brokers (see paragraphs 29 and 30 below); failure to be vigilant in this area will adversely affect the reputation of the broking firm itself.

---

1 Available from the British Bankers' Association, 10 Lombard Street, London EC3V 9EL

- **Of the employee**

24 When entering into or arranging individual deals, dealers and brokers must ensure that at all times great care is taken not to misrepresent in any way the nature of any transaction. Dealers and brokers must ensure that:

- the identity of the firm for which they are acting and its role is clear to their counterparties/clinets to avoid any risk of confusion. This is particularly important, for instance, where an individual dealer acts for more than one company, or in more than one capacity. If so, he must make absolutely clear, at the outset of any deal, on behalf of which company or in which capacity he is acting.
- it is clearly understood in which products they are proposing to deal.
- any claims or acknowledgements about, or relevant to, a particular transaction being considered should, as far as the individual dealer or broker is aware, be fair and not misleading.
- facts believed to be material to completing a specific transaction are disclosed before the deal is done, except where such disclosure would reveal confidential information about the activities of another firm. Unless specifically asked for more information, or clarification, a dealer at a core principal will assume his counterparty has all the necessary information for this decision making process when entering into a wholesale market transaction.

25 When a deal is being arranged through a broker, the broker should act in a way which does not unfairly favour one client, amongst those involved, over another, irrespective of what brokerage arrangements exist between them and the broking firm.

Clarity of role

- **Role of principals**

26 The role of firms acting as principal is to deal for their own account. **All principals have the responsibility for assessing the creditworthiness of their counterparties or potential counterparties whether dealing direct or through a broking firm. It is for each principal to decide whether or not to seek independent professional advice to assist in this process.**

27 **It is also for the principal to decide what credence, if any, is given to any information or comment provided by a broker to a dealer. Where such information or comment might be interpreted as being relevant to a particular counterparty or potential counterparty, this does not alter the fact that the responsibility for assessing the creditworthiness of a counterparty, whether or not it is supervised, rests with the principal alone.**

28 Some firms may act as agent for connected or other companies as well as, or instead of, dealing for their own account. If so, such agents should:

- always make absolutely clear to all concerned the capacity in which they are acting (eg if they also act as principal or broker).
- declare at an early stage of negotiations the party for whom they are acting. It may be considered desirable to set out this relationship formally in writing for future reference.
- ensure that **all** confirmations make clear when a deal is done on an agency basis.
- when acting as agent for an unregulated principal, make clear at an early stage this qualification to potential counterparties; and include this on confirmations.

- **Role of brokers**

29 Typically the role of the specialist wholesale market broking firms in London supervised as such by the Bank is to act as **arrangers** of deals[1]. They:

- bring together counterparties on mutually acceptable terms and pass names to facilitate the conclusion of a transaction.
- receive payment for this service in the form of brokerage (except where a prior explicit agreement between the management of all parties to a deal provides otherwise).
- are **not** permitted, even fleetingly, to act as principal in a deal (even on a 'matched principal' basis), or to act in any discretionary fund management capacity[2].

30 It is accepted that, in providing the service specified in the previous paragraph, individual brokers may be called upon to give advice or express opinions, usually in response to requests from individual dealers. While brokers should be mindful of the need not to reveal confidential information about the market activities of individual clients, there is no restriction on brokers passing, or commenting, on general information which is in the public domain. Equally, there is no responsibility upon a broker to volunteer general information of this type. Where information is sought or volunteered individual brokers should exercise particular care. For instance, brokers

1 There are two exceptions to this rule. The first covers the specialist inter-dealer brokers, involved primarily in US Treasury bills, notes and bonds, which act as matched principals. The other exception is when name-passing broking firms are investing their own money; in such transactions, brokers must make clear to the relevant counterparties that they are acting as principal.

2 The relationship between an institution offering a discretionary or advisory management service and its clients in any of the financial products described in the box on page 223 falls outside the scope of this Code and, if it constitutes investment business within the terms of the Financial Services Act 1986, should be conducted in accordance with the requirements of the relevant Self-Regulating Organization.

do not have sufficient information to be qualified to advise principals on the creditworthiness of specific counterparties and to do so is not their role.

III CONTROLS

It is essential that Management have in place, and review regularly, appropriate control procedures which their dealing and other relevant staff must follow.

Know your counterparty

It is necessary for a variety of reasons, including firms' own risk control and the need to meet their legal obligations (e.g. on money laundering) for firms to undertake basic 'know their counterparty' checks before dealing in any products covered by this Code. Before agreeing to establish a dealing relationship in any of these wholesale market products, core principals should be mindful of any reputational risks which might arise as a result, and whether these risks might be greater when undertaking such transactions with non-core principals. In the absence of firm evidence to the contrary, non-core principals should be regarded as end-users (i.e. 'customers') of the wholesale markets.

31 In order to minimize the risks which they face it is desirable for core principals to have in place a clearly articulated approval process for their dealers and salespersons to follow before dealing for the first time in any wholesale market product with counterparties. This process, which should be appropriately monitored by management, should apply both when granting an initial dealing line for a product, and subsequently if changing or extending it to other wholesale products. Such a process might include the following considerations, which will need to be tailored to the type of transaction being considered:

- **With all counterparties**
  - What information is available to the core principal on the legal capacity of the counterparty to undertake such transactions? Is this information sufficient to make an informed decision on the legal risks it might face if it undertakes such business with the counterparty?
- **With customers**
  - Who initiated the request for the product relationship? Might this decision have been influenced by any product **advice** given by the core principal?
  - If advice is given was this subject to a written agreement between the parties; if not, should it be? Are both parties clear what reliance the customer is placing upon that advice?
  - What, if any, are the legal responsibilities the core principal might owe to the customer to whom advice is given in subsequently undertaking transactions in

that product? For instance, management might ask itself if it is being asked to advise on the customer's whole portfolio – which might put it in a different legal position than if it were advising on only part of the portfolio.

- Are there potential conflicts between the firm's interests and those of the potential customer? If there are how should they be managed; and does the customer need to be alerted?
- Have appropriate legal agreements between the core principal and the customer been enacted? Do they make clear the respective responsibilities of both parties for any losses? Do they make clear which party is responsible for decisions to close-out trades undertaken?

32 **Procedures should be in place to ensure that the information available to banks and other core principals,** upon which they will base their judgement on whether or not to open/extend a dealing relationship with a particular customer, **is carefully assessed on a broad product by product basis.**

33 Once a customer dealing relationship has been established in one, or more, wholesale market product(s) it is **strongly recommended that management at both parties periodically review it,** against the above criteria. It is also in their own interest for core principals to review periodically the totality of their business relationship with each customer against the same criteria.

- **Additional arrangements for small investors**

The Bank believes that it is in the interest of banks and other listed institutions for management to consider most carefully whether to grant or extend dealing facilities in OTC wholesale market products to 'small investors' (i.e. individuals or small business investors as defined under SFA rules).

34 The expectation at the time the FSA was introduced was that individuals (or other small investors) would not normally be dealing in the wholesale OTC markets, which are primarily for core principals and other professionals such as large corporates, that regularly use the markets and which should have professionally trained staff able to undertake such transactions on their behalf.

35 It is more likely, therefore, that small investors will ask for **advice** on the particular product being considered (for instance in terms of its risk profile, how this might differ from exchange traded instruments with which they might be more familiar, or how to value its worth over time, etc). It is the Bank's view (shared by the SIB) that where this is so they should **not** automatically be granted a new or extended dealing line for this product. If the product being considered is a derivative and/or leveraged, the Bank believes that it is in the interest of banks and other listed institutions to have in place a written agreement, which makes clear which products are concerned and the extent to which any reliance can be placed by the small investor on the advice given.

36 Where an FSA exempt product is involved (items 6–16 in the box on page 223) small investors should also be advised that by seeking to conduct such business with a s43 listed institution they would not have the protection of the FSA. The provisions set out in paragraph 21 above would apply.

37 The Bank believes it prudent for core principals to maintain, as accurately as they can, records of conversations – both internal or with the investor – material to their relationship. Where these are in written form, records must be kept in line with statutory requirements. Where tapes are the only record of specific transactions, management should consider very carefully whether some or all of these should be retained for a similar length of time to written records.

Dealing mandates

38 There has been growing interest in the use of dealing mandates as a means of clarifying the extent of a relationship between core principals and their customers, and their respective responsibilities. That in turn could help reduce the scope for errors. In the Bank's view it is appropriate for core principals to consider the merits of establishing dealing mandates to govern their relationship with non-core principals, but it is unlikely that mandates would be necessary between core principals. When deciding whether to initiate a mandate it is important that proper consideration is given by both parties to the manner in which the mandate is to be structured and subsequently administered.

39 It is good practice for both parties to agree what the mandate should and should not cover. To aid this process associations like the ACT and BBA may be able to guide their members on common practice. Where a mandate has been initiated, both parties should review it periodically; as a general rule, the onus is on the counterparty to notify the core principal promptly of any change necessary to an existing mandate.

40 While they can have a useful role in improving internal controls dealing mandates should **not** be used as a vehicle to pass all responsibility to another counterparty. They should not, therefore, weaken the standard set out in paragraph 16 – that all firms will be held responsible for the actions of their staff. Firms must, in particular, ensure that any individual who commits the firm to a transaction has the necessary authority to do so, and is aware of the terms of any mandate that has been agreed.

Confidentiality

41 Confidentiality is essential for the preservation of a reputable and efficient market place. Principals and brokers share equal responsibility for maintaining confidentiality. Principals or brokers should not, without explicit permission, disclose or discuss, or apply pressure on others to disclose or discuss, any

information relating to specific deals which have been transacted, or are in the process of being arranged, except to or with the parties directly involved (and, if necessary, their advisers) or where this is required by law or to comply with the requirements of a supervisory body.

42 Where confidential or market sensitive information is routinely shared by a London based firm with other branches/subsidiaries within its group it is for management to review periodically if this is appropriate. Where it is, the Bank believes that London management should be responsible and accountable for how such information is subsequently controlled – in particular they should make clear that such information should **at all times** continue to be treated as being subject to the confidentiality provisions of the Code. It is a responsibility of management to ensure that all relevant personnel are aware of, and observe, this fundamental principle.

43 Care should be taken over the use of open loudspeakers in both brokers' offices and principals' dealing rooms to ensure that they do not lead to breaches of confidentiality.

44 Situations arise where sales/marketing staff from core principals visit the offices of their customers; during such visits the customer may wish to arrange a transaction via the sales/marketing representative. Subject to proper controls this is perfectly acceptable. However, individual dealers or brokers should **not** visit each others' dealing rooms except with the express permission of the management of both parties. In particular a principal's dealer should **not** deal from within the offices of a broker or another principal. Brokers should never conduct business from outside their own offices. The only exception to these general rules might be when it is necessary for two unconnected institutions to share the same facilities as part of their agreed contingency arrangements. In such circumstances management should ensure appropriate arrangements are in place to protect counterparty confidentiality.

45 A principal should not place an order with a broker with the intention of ascertaining the name of a counterparty in order to make direct contact to conclude the deal; neither should direct contact be made to increase the amount of a completed trade arranged through a broker.

Location of back office functions

46 There is a growing trend towards locating front and back office functions in physically separate locations; indeed a number of the branches of international banks in London have relocated and consolidated their back office functions in their home country. Others have back offices outside London. The Bank's view is that there should be no objection to banks consolidating back-offices in a single location, even if that were overseas – provided that there are individuals in London with whom any deal or settlement queries can be resolved quickly.

47 At the same time the banking supervisors have reviewed whether it is still necessary in all cases, on control grounds, to maintain a physical segregation of back and front office staff within banks. They have concluded that whilst in most cases physical segregation is preferable, a lack of such segregation may be acceptable provided that it can be demonstrated that appropriate management controls are in place. For instance lack of segregation may be acceptable where computer logical access controls are in place. **Even so, it is essential that a strict segregation of duties between staff in the front and back office is maintained,** and especially that confirmations are sent direct to back office staff (see also paragraph 98 below).

Taping

48 Experience has shown that recourse to tapes proves invaluable to the speedy resolution of differences and disputes. The use of recording equipment in the offices of voice brokers and principals has become common; other means for monitoring 'conversations' are embodied within electronic broking systems now used in the markets. **The Bank strongly recommends taping by principals and brokers of all conversations by dealers and brokers** together with back-office telephone lines used by those responsible for confirming deals or passing payment and other instructions. The Bank expects firms which it supervises to use tapes. Any which do not tape all their front plus relevant back office conversations should review this management policy periodically and be prepared to persuade the Bank that there are particular reasons for them to continue with such an approach. This review should be repeated annually. Failure to tape will normally count against a firm if it seeks to use the arbitration process described in paragraph 120 to settle a difference, or is the subject of a complaint.

49 When initially installing tape equipment, or taking on new clients or counterparties, firms should take the necessary steps to inform them that conversations will be recorded. **Tapes should be kept for at least two months, and preferable longer.** Experience suggests that, with the growing involvement of the private banking divisions within core principals in selling wholesale products to small investors, taping of all conversations by salesmen/account officers in these areas is in the interests of core principals. The longer tapes are retained the greater the chances are that any subsequent disputes over transactions or where advice has been given, can be resolved satisfactorily. **Tapes which cover any transaction about which there is a dispute should be retained until the problem has been resolved.** Management should ensure that access to taping equipment and tapes, whether in use or in store, is strictly controlled so that they cannot be tampered with.

Deals at non-current rates

There is now widespread recognition that, as a general rule, deals at non-market rates should not be undertaken.

50 Banks and other listed firms are strongly discouraged from undertaking deals involving rolling-over an existing contract at the original rate. These should only be undertaken, if at all, on rare occasions and then after most careful consideration by both parties and approval, on a deal by deal basis, by their senior management. Senior management must ensure that proper procedures are in place to identify and bring to their attention all such deals **when they are proposed** so that they can be made fully aware of the details before reaching a decision on whether a particular trade should go ahead on this basis. Before reaching such a decision, senior management should seek written confirmation from the counterparty, also at senior management level, of the reasons for the transaction. This is essential not only because of the potential credit risk implications of rolling-over deals at original rates but also because failure to use current rates could result in the principal unknowingly participating in the concealment of a profit or loss, or in perpetration of a fraud. In order to provide a clear audit trail, there should be an immediate exchange of letters between the senior managements of both parties to any such deals to demonstrate that the above procedures have been followed.

51 However, if management accept that the application of non-market rates can be necessary to create deal structures which satisfy the legitimate requirements of counterparties, they should ensure proper controls are in place to prevent such arrangements from concealing fraud, creating unacceptable conflicts of interest, or involving other illegal activity. It is particularly important to ensure that there is no ambiguity in such transactions over the amounts which each counterparty is to pay and receive. It should, for instance, be possible to demonstrate from the documentation available to both parties that the combination of cashflows, coupons, and foreign exchange rates etc, used in such transactions produces a result that is consistent with the current market price for a straightforward transaction of similar maturity. **It is therefore essential that appropriate documentation is in place before any such deals are undertaken and that this is reviewed, by senior management, regularly so that they can satisfy themselves whether it remains appropriate to undertake further transactions on this basis.**

52 A specific area where there is sometimes pressure to conduct deals at non-current rates is in the foreign exchange market. In particular pressure can be placed on dealers undertaking a foreign exchange swap to avoid the immediate fixing of the spot price underlying the trade. **This practice is judged by practitioners in the London market to be unethical and is not appropriate practice for UK based institutions. Spot rates should be determined immediately after completion of the foreign exchange swap transaction.**

Dealing with unidentified principals

53 There has been a growing trend towards discretionary management companies dealing in wholesale market products on behalf of their clients. For its own

commercial reasons a fund manager may not wish to divulge the name of its client(s) when concluding such deals. Since this practice raises important considerations, particularly in terms of banks' ability to assess their credit risk to particular counterparties and to meet supervisory requirements on large exposures, the Bank is in discussions with the relevant market associations about it; and may in due course seek views from other supervisors in Basle on this practice. In the interim, before any institution transacts business on this basis its senior management should decide, as a matter of policy, whether they judge it appropriate to do so. In doing so, they should consider all the risks involved. They should fully document the decision which they reach.

After-hours dealing

54 Extended trading after normal local hours has become accepted in some markets, most notably foreign exchange. Dealing after-hours into other centres forms an integral part of the operations of many firms both in London and elsewhere. Such dealing can involve additional hazards – whether undertaken direct or via a broker. For example, when dealing continues during the evening from premises other than the principals' dealing rooms, one of the principals involved might subsequently forget, or deny, having done a deal. Management should therefore issue clear guidelines to their staff, both on the kinds of deal which may be undertaken in those circumstances and on the permitted limits of any such dealing. All deals should be confirmed promptly – preferably by telex or similar electronic message direct to the counterparty's offices – and carefully controlled when arranged off-premises. Management should consider installing answerphone facilities in the dealing area which dealers should use to record full details of all off-premises trades. These should be processed promptly on the next working day.

Stop-loss orders

54 Principals may receive requests from branches, customers and correspondents to execute transactions – for instance to buy or sell a currency – if prices or rates should reach a specified level. These orders, which include stop-loss and limit orders from counterparties desiring around-the-clock protection for their own positions, may be intended for execution during the day, overnight, or until executed or cancelled. Management should ensure that the terms of such orders are explicitly identified and agreed, and that there is a clear understanding with the counterparty about the obligation it has assumed in accepting such orders. Moreover, management needs to establish clear policies and procedures for its traders who accept and execute stop-loss and limit orders. Management should also ensure that any dealer handling such an instruction has adequate lines of communication with the counterparty so that the dealer can reach authorized personnel in case of an unusual situation or extreme price/rate movement.

Conflicts of interest

- **Dealing for personal account**

56 Management should consider carefully whether their employees should be allowed to deal at all for own account in any of the products covered by this Code. Where allowed by management, it is their responsibility to ensure that adequate safeguards are established to prevent abuse. These safeguards should reflect the need to maintain confidentiality with respect to non-public price-sensitive information and to ensure that no action is taken by employees which might adversely affect the interests of the firm's clients or counterparties.

- **Deals using a connected broker**

57 Brokers have a legal obligation to disclose the nature and extent of any material conflict between their own interests and their responsibilities to clients. To safeguard the independence of brokers they should give all their clients formal written notification of any principal(s) where a material connection exists (unless a client explicitly waives its rights to this information in writing); and notify any subsequent changes to this list of principals as they occur. For the purposes of this Code, a material connection would include situations where the relationship between the parties could have a bearing on the transaction or its terms, as a result for example of common management responsibilities or material shareholding links, whether direct or indirect. The Bank regards a shareholding of 10% or more in a broker as material; but, depending on the circumstances, a smaller holding may also represent a material connection.

58 Any deals arranged by a broker involving a connected principal must be at arm's length (i.e. at mutually agreed rates which are the same as those prevailing for transactions between unconnected counterparties).

Marketing and incentives

59 When listed institutions are operating within the boundaries of the Section 43 arrangements, they will not be subject to advertising or cold-calling rules since these would be inappropriate in such professional markets. Nevertheless listed institutions should take care to ensure that any advertisements for their services within the exempt area are directed so far as possible towards professionals.

60 In recent years a number of foreign exchange electronic broking services have begun operating in London. Understandably such firms have considered a range of marketing arrangements, in the form of incentives, to generate liquidity in their systems. After consultation through the Joint Standing Committee it was concluded that the principle that brokers should not make payments to banks for using their services should be strictly maintained. As with conventional voice brokers, the provision of discount arrangements is a legitimate marketing technique, even if these involve cross-product subsidization between different parts of the same group.

Entertainment, gifts and gambling

61 Management or employees must neither offer inducements to conduct business, nor solicit them from the personnel of other institutions. However it is recognized that entertainment and gifts are offered in the normal course of business and do not necessarily constitute inducements. Nevertheless, this is an area where the Bank receives a surprisingly high number of complaints about the potentially excessive nature of entertainment being offered. In response the Bank consulted practitioners during 1994 on how best to help facilitate a consistent approach across the London market. This reconfirmed that management should have a clearly articulated policy towards the giving/receipt of entertainment (and gifts), and ensure it is properly observed. It should include procedures for dealing with gifts judged to be excessive but which cannot be declined without causing offence. The policy should be reviewed periodically. In developing and implementing its policy, management should have regard to the potential adverse impact on the reputation of the firm, and the London market generally, of any adverse comment/publicity generated by any entertainment (or gifts) given or received.

62 The following general pointers have been identified which management ought to consider including as part of their policy:

- **Firms should have in place arrangements to monitor the type, frequency and cost of entertainment and gifts. Periodic control reports should be made available to management.**
- **Authorization and control procedures should be clear and unambiguous in order to ensure proper accountability.**
- **Policies should contain specific reference to the appropriate treatment for gifts (given and received). This policy should specifically preclude the giving (or receiving) of cash or cash convertible gifts.**
- **In determining whether the offer of a particular gift or form of entertainment might be construed as excessive, management should bear in mind whether it could be regarded as an improper inducement, either by the employer of the recipient or the supervisory authorities. Any grey areas should be cleared in advance with management at the recipient firm(s).**
- **Firms should not normally offer entertainment if a representative of the host company will not be present at the event.**

63 These procedures should be drawn up bearing in mind that the activities of dealers of some of the principals active in the markets may be governed by statute. For instance, offering hospitality or gifts to officers and members of local authorities and other public bodies is subject to the provisions of legislation that carries sanctions under criminal law. One of the most onerous requirements of this legislation is that any offer or receipt of hospitality is, prima facie, deemed to be a criminal offence, unless the contrary is proved.

64 Similar guidelines should also be established on gambling with other market participants. **All these activities carry obvious dangers and, where allowed at all, it is strongly recommended that they are tightly restricted.**

Abused substances (including drugs and alcohol)

65 Management should take all reasonable steps to educate themselves and their staff about possible signs and effects of the use of drugs and other abused substances. The judgement of any member of staff using such substances is likely to be impaired; dependence upon drugs etc makes them more likely to be vulnerable to outside inducement to conduct business not necessarily in the best interests of the firm or the market generally and could seriously diminish their ability to function satisfactorily.

IV DEALING PRINCIPLES AND PROCEDURES: A STATEMENT OF BEST PRACTICE

Scope

Deals in the London wholesale markets (defined by the products covered in the box on page 223) should be conducted on the basis of this Code of Conduct.

66 Whilst this Code is designed for the London markets, its provisions may extend beyond UK shores, for example where a listed UK broker arranges a deal involving an overseas counterparty. Where deals involving overseas counterparties are to be made on a different basis in any respect, for example because of distinct local rules or requirements, this should be clearly identified at the outset to avoid any possible confusion.

Overseas market conventions

The trading of currency assets in London should follow recognized trading conventions that have been established internationally or in specific overseas markets, provided they do not conflict with the principles of this Code.

67 Where foreign currency-denominated short-term securities issued overseas are traded in London, there may be important differences in dealing practice compared with the trading of London instruments, partly reflecting the way the instruments are traded in their domestic markets. The London Code is intended to be complementary to any generally accepted local standards and practices for such instruments traded in London. The Bank would expect firms trading these instruments in London to abide by any such local conventions.

Procedures

- **Preliminary negotiation of terms**

Firms should clearly state at the outset, prior to a transaction being executed, any qualifying conditions to which it will be subject.

68 Typical examples of qualifications include where a price is quoted subject to the necessary credit approval; finding a counterparty for matching deals; or the ability to execute an associated transaction. For instance principals may quote a rate which is ‘firm subject to the execution of a hedge transaction’. For good order’s sake it is important that firms complete deals as quickly as possible; the onus is on both sides to keep each other informed of progress or possible delays. If a principal’s ability to conclude a transaction is constrained by other factors, for example opening hours in other centres, this should be made known to brokers and potential counterparties at an early stage and before names are exchanged.

69 In the Euronote and commercial paper markets, principals should notify investors, at the time of sale, of their willingness or otherwise to repurchase paper. Investors should also be notified, before the sale, of any significant variation from the standard terms or conditions of an issue.

- **Undertaking derivative transactions with end-users (i.e. 'customers' of the market)**

It is important before derivative transactions are undertaken with a customer, that dealers are satisfied that appropriate 'know your counterparty' procedures (see section III above) have been implemented for the product under consideration.

70 When a core principal is dealing with any customer of the market in leveraged or derivative products it is good practice for its dealers to assist their opposite number by using clear concise terminology. It is however the responsibility of each party involved to seek clarification, before concluding a deal, on any points about which they are not clear. Each party should also consider whether it would be helpful for the core principal to send by electronic means (telex or fax) a pre-deal message setting out the terms upon which the deal will be priced and agreed by both parties. While this may not be judged appropriate for some customers (e.g. an experienced large corporate), **it is likely to be helpful to send pre-deal messages to small investors (as defined earlier).** Such a message may also be particularly useful, for instance, where the product involved is relatively new to the customer; or where the individual dealer acting on behalf of the customer is not the regular contact point for undertaking such trades with that customer. The sending or receipt of such a message is not a substitute for the confirmation procedures described below.

71 The existence, or not, of such a message should not however be taken as undermining in any way the principle that each party must accept responsibility for entering into such trades and any losses that they might incur as a result of doing so. There are, of course, circumstances in which this principle might be brought into question; for instance if the dealer at the core principal had deliberately misled the customer by knowingly providing false and/or inaccurate information at the time the deal was being negotiated. It is therefore very important that great care is taken not to mislead or misinform.

72 To help minimize the scope for error and misunderstanding the Bank strongly recommends that management require their dealers to use standard pre-deal check lists of the key terms that they need to agree when entering into leveraged and/or derivative transactions.

- **Firmness of quotation**

All firms, whether acting as principal, agent or broker, have a duty to make absolutely clear whether the prices they are quoting are firm or merely indicative. Prices quoted by brokers should be taken to be firm in marketable amounts unless otherwise qualified.

73 A principal quoting a firm price (or rate) either through a broker or directly to a potential counterparty is committed to deal at that price (or rate) in a marketable

amount provided the counterparty name is acceptable. In order to minimize the scope for confusion where there is no clear market convention, dealers quoting a firm price (rate) should indicate the length of time for which their quote is firm.

74 It is generally accepted that when dealing in fast moving markets (like spot forex or currency options) a principal has to assume that a price given to a broker is good only for a short length of time – typically a matter of seconds. However, this practice would be open to misunderstandings about how quickly a price is deemed to lapse if it were adopted when dealing in generally less hectic markets, for example the forward foreign exchange or deposit markets, or when market conditions are relatively quiet. Since dealers have prime responsibility for prices put to a broker, the onus in such circumstances is on dealers to satisfy themselves that their prices have been taken off, unless a time limit is placed by the principal on its interest at the outset (e.g. 'firm for one minute only'). Otherwise, the principal should feel bound to deal with an acceptable name at the quoted rate in a marketable amount.

75 For their part brokers should make every effort to assist dealers by checking from time to time with them whether their interest at particular prices (rates) is still current. They should also do so when a specific name and amount have been quoted.

76 What constitutes a marketable amount varies from market to market but will generally be familiar to practitioners. A broker, if quoting on the basis of small amounts or particular names, should qualify the quotation accordingly. Where principals are proposing to deal in unfamiliar markets through a broker, it is recommended that they first ask brokers what amounts are sufficient to validate normal market quotations. If their interest is in a smaller amount, this should be specified by the principal when initially requesting a price from or offering a price to the broker.

77 In the swap market, considerable use is made of 'indicative interest' quotations. When arranging a swap an unconditional firm rate will only be given where a principal deals directly with a client, or when such a principal has received the name of a client from a broker. A principal who quotes a rate or spread as 'firm subject to credit' is bound to deal at the quoted rate or spread if the name is consistent with a category of counterparty previously identified for this purpose (see also paragraph 82 below). The only exception is where the particular name cannot be accepted, for example if the principal has reached its credit limit for that name, in which case the principal will correctly reject the transaction. It is not an acceptable practice for a principal to revise a rate which was 'firm subject to credit' once the name of the counterparty has been disclosed. Brokers and principals should work together to establish a range of institutions for whom the principal's rate is firm subject to credit.

- **Concluding a deal**

Principals should regard themselves as bound to a deal once the price and any other key commercial terms have been agreed. Oral agreements are considered binding. However,

holding brokers unreasonably to a price is viewed as unprofessional and should be discouraged by management.

78 Where quoted prices are qualified as being indicative or subject to negotiation of commercial terms, principals should normally treat themselves as bound to a deal at the point where the terms have been agreed without qualification. Oral agreements are considered binding; the subsequent confirmation is evidence of the deal but should not override terms agreed orally. The practice of making a transaction subject to documentation is **not** good practice (see also paragraphs 107 – 109). In order to minimize the likelihood of disputes arising once documentation is prepared, firms should make every effort to agree all material points quickly during the oral negotiation of terms, and should include these on the confirmation. Any remaining details should be agreed as soon as possible thereafter.

79 Where brokers are involved, it is their responsibility to ensure that the principal providing the price (rate) is made aware immediately it has been dealt upon. As a general rule a deal should only be regarded as having been 'done' where the broker's contact is positively acknowledged by the dealer. A broker should never assume that a deal is done without some form of oral acknowledgment from the dealer. Where a broker puts a specific proposition to a dealer for a price (e.g. specifying an amount and a name for which a quote is required), the dealer can reasonably expect to be told almost immediately by the broker whether the price has been hit or not.

- **Passing of names by brokers**

Brokers should not divulge the names of principals prematurely, and certainly not until satisfied that both sides display a serious intention to transact. Principals and brokers should at all times treat the details of transactions as absolutely confidential to the parties involved (see paragraph 41 above).

80 To save time and minimize frustration, principals should wherever practicable give brokers prior indication of counterparties with whom, for whatever reason, they would be unwilling to do business (referring as necessary to particular markets or instruments). At the same time brokers should take full account of the best interests and any precise instructions of the client.

81 To save subsequent awkwardness, principals (including agents) have a particular obligation to give guidance to brokers on any particular features (maturities etc) or types of counterparty (such as non-financial institutions) which might cause difficulties. In some instruments, principals may also wish to give brokers guidance on the extent of their price differentiation across broad categories of counterparties. Where a broker is acting for an unlisted (or unsupervised) name he should disclose this fact as soon as possible; the degree of disclosure required in such a case will usually be greater. For instance, credit considerations may require that such names be disclosed to a listed principal first (as in the swap market), in order that the listed principal may quote a rate at which it is committed to deal. Equally, disclosure of difficult names may be necessary since this may influence the documentation.

82 In all their wholesale market business, brokers should aim to achieve a mutual and immediate exchange of names. However this will not always be possible. There will be times when one principal's name proves unacceptable to another and the broker will quite properly decline to divulge by whom it was refused. This may sometimes result in the principal whose name has been rejected feeling that the broker may in fact have quoted a price (rate) which it could not in fact substantiate. In such cases, the Bank will be prepared to establish with the reluctant principal that it did have business to do at the quoted price and the reasons why the name was turned down, so that the aggrieved party can be assured the original quote was valid without, of course, revealing the reluctant party's name.

83 In the sterling and currency deposit markets, it is accepted that principals dealing through a broker have the right to turn down a name wishing to take deposits; this could therefore require predisclosure of the name before closing the deal. Once a lender has asked the key question 'who pays', it is considered committed to do business at the price quoted with that name, or an alternative acceptable name if offered immediately. The name of a lender shall be disclosed only after the borrower's name has been accepted by the lender. Conversely, where a borrower is taking secured money there may be occasions when it will wish to decline to take funds, through a broker, when the lender's name is passed.

84 In the case of instruments like CDs, where the seller may not be the same entity as the issuer, the broker shall first disclose the issuer's name to the potential buyer. Once a buyer has asked 'whose paper is it', the buyer is considered committed to deal at the price quoted. Once the buyer asks 'who sells it' it is considered committed to deal with the particular seller in question (or an alternative acceptable name, so long as this name is immediately shown to the buyer by the broker). The name of the buyer shall be disclosed only after the seller's name has been accepted by the buyer. The seller has the right to refuse the particular buyer, so long as it is prepared at that time to sell the same amount at the same price to an alternative acceptable name immediately shown to it by the broker.

85 In the CD markets a price quoted is generally accepted as good for any name 'on the run'.

- **Use of intermediaries**

Brokers must not interpose an intermediary in any deal which could take place without its introduction.

86 An intermediary should only be introduced by a broker where it is strictly necessary for the completion of a deal, most obviously where a name switch is required because one counterparty is full of another's name but is prepared to deal with a third party. Any fees involved in transactions involving intermediaries must be explicitly identified by the broker and shown on the relevant confirmation(s).

87 Where a broker needs to switch a name this should be undertaken as promptly as possible, bearing in mind that this may take longer at certain times of the day; or if

the name is a particularly difficult one; or if the deal is larger than normal. In no circumstances should a deal be left overnight without acceptable names having been passed.

- **Confirmation procedures**

Prompt passing, recording and careful checking of confirmations is vital to minimize the possibility of errors and misunderstanding whether dealing direct or through brokers. Details should be passed as soon as practicable after deals have been done and checked upon receipt. The passing of details in batches is not ***recommended. For markets where standard terms are applicable e.g. under standard documentation, it is recommended that confirmations conform to the formats specified for the market or instrument concerned.***

(a) Oral deal checks

An increasing number of practitioners find it helpful to undertake oral deal checks at least once a day, especially when using a broker.

88 Particularly when dealing in faster moving markets like foreign exchange, but also when dealing in other instruments which have very short settlement periods, many principals now request regular oral deal checks – whether dealing through brokers or direct – prior to the exchange and checking of a written or electronically dispatched confirmation. Their use can be an important means of helping to reduce the number and size of differences particularly when dealing through brokers or for deals involving non-London counterparties. It is for each firm to agree with its broker(s) whether or not it wishes to be provided with this service; and, if so, how many such checks a day it requires. When arbitrating in disputes, the Bank will take into account the extent to which principals have sought to safeguard their interests by undertaking oral checks.

89 If a single check is thought to be sufficient, the Bank sees merit in this being undertaken towards the end of the trading day as a useful complement, particularly where late deals are concerned, to the process of sending out and checking confirmations.

90 As a matter of common sense, the broker should always obtain acknowledgement from a dealer on completion of the check that all the deals have been agreed or, if not, that any identified discrepancies are resolved as a matter of urgency. Lack of response should not be construed as acknowledgment.

(b) Written/electronic confirmations

In all markets, the confirmation provides a necessary final safeguard against dealing errors. Confirmations should be dispatched and checked carefully and promptly, even when oral deal checks have been undertaken. The issue and checking of confirmation is a back-office responsibility which should be carried out independently from those who initiate deals.

91 A confirmation of each deal must be sent out without delay. This is particularly essential if dealing for same day settlement. As a general rule the Bank believes all participants in the wholesale markets should have, or be aiming to have, in place the capability to dispatch confirmations so that they are received and can be checked within a few hours of when the deal was struck. Where the products involved are more complex, and so require more details to be included on the confirmation, this may not be possible; nevertheless it is in the interest of all concerned that such deals are confirmed as quickly as is practicable. The Bank recommends that principals should enquire about any confirmations which have not been received within the expected timescale.

92 It is not uncommon in the derivatives markets, and perfectly acceptable if the two principals involved agree, for only **one** party (rather than both) to the deal to send out a confirmation. But where this is so, it is imperative not only that the recipient checks it promptly, but that it also in good time responds to the issuer of the confirmation agreeing/querying the terms. For good order's sake it would also be imperative that the issuer of the confirmation has in place procedures for chasing a response if one is not forthcoming within a few hours of the confirmation being sent.

93 All confirmations should include the trade data, the name of the other counterparty and all other details of the deal, including where appropriate the commission charged by the broker. Some principals include their own terms and conditions of trading on their written confirmations. To avoid misunderstandings, any subsequent changes should be brought specifically to the attention of their counterparties.

94 In many markets, it is accepted practice for principals to confirm directly all the details of transactions arranged through a broker; the broker should nevertheless also send a confirmation to each counterparty.

95 All principals are reminded that the prompt sending and checking of confirmations is also regarded as best practice in deals not arranged through a broker, including those with corporates and other customers.

96 Wherever practicable the Bank wishes to discourage the practice in some markets of sending two confirmations (e.g. an initial one by telex, fax or other acceptable electronic means) followed by a written confirmation, which if posted could easily not arrive until after the settlement date and could cause confusion and uncertainty. For this reason, the Bank believes that wherever practicable a single confirmation should be sent promptly by each party, if possible by one of the generally accepted electronic means now available (notably the ACS system, SWIFT, fax or telex). Where this is not practicable, for instance in more complex derivative transactions, firms should indicate (e.g. on the preliminary confirmation) that a more detailed written version is to follow. The Bank does not believe that it is good practice to rely solely on an oral check.

97 It is valid that principals check confirmations carefully and immediately upon

receipt so that discrepancies can be quickly revealed and corrected. Firms that check within a few hours of receipt would be complying with best practice.

98 As a general rule, confirmations should not be issued by or sent to and checked by dealers. This is a back-office function. Where dealers do get involved in these procedures they should be closely controlled. The most common instance where it may sometimes be thought helpful to mark a copy of the confirmation for the attention of the person who has arranged the deal, in addition to the back office, is in markets requiring detailed negotiation of terms (notably those involving contracts for differences). Certain automated dealing systems produce confirmations automatically; provided these are received in the back office no additional confirmation need be sent.

99 Particular attention needs to be paid by all parties when confirming deals in which at least one of the counterparties is based outside London, and to any consequential differences in confirmation procedure.

- **Payment/settlement instructions**

Instructions should be passed as quickly as possible to facilitate prompt settlement. The Bank strongly recommends the use of standard settlement instructions; their use can make a significant contribution to reducing both the incidence and size of differences arising from the mistaken settlement of funds.

100 The use of standard settlement instructions (SSIs) continues to increase in London. International acceptance of the benefits of many SSIs is an important next step. In order to facilitate still greater usage of SSIs the BBA now maintains a directory of London based institutions that use them. The Bank wishes to encourage firms that it supervises, that do not already do so, to draw up plans to move towards using SSIs as soon as possible. A major advantage of using SSIs is that they remove the need to confirm payment details by phone.

101 The guidelines set out in Schedule 2, which have been drawn up in consultation with practitioners, set out a framework which it is hoped principals will aim to adopt when using SSIs for wholesale market transactions. The guidance notes emphasize that SSIs should only be established via confirmed letter or authenticated SWIFT message, and **not** by SWIFT broadcast. While many firms comply with this guidance, difficulties have been encountered where some insist on using SWIFT broadcasts. Having raised the matter with SWIFT it is clear that broadcast messages remain unsuitable for the purpose of changing SSIs and are non-binding on recipients. SWIFT is currently looking at developing a new message for this purpose. In the interim, however, the majority view is that banks which receive notice from a counterparty of the amendment of an SSI by a SWIFT broadcast should be free to act upon such notice if they so wish. They should seek authentication of the message by way of sending confirmation of the arrangement, making clear when and for what deals the new instructions will be implemented. Until that process is complete the original instructions will be deemed still to be operative.

102 It has been the practice in the domestic sterling market that brokers pass payment instructions. In view of the increasing use of SSIs, the domestic sterling market should be moving away from requiring this service from brokers. Brokers should therefore only be expected to pass payment instructions in very unusual circumstances or in certain deposit markets where the counterparty is a non-core principal (such as a local authority).

103 Similarly brokers do not pass payment instructions in the foreign exchange and currency deposits market where the counterparties are both in the UK. It is for banks to agree with brokers the basis on which they will be able to pass such instruction for deals using a non-UK counterparty; all such instructions should be passed with minimum delay. It is intended that, with the hoped for increasing use of SSIs internationally, brokers will cease providing payment instructions involving overseas counterparties in due course.

104 Where SSIs are not being used, principals should ensure that any alteration to original payment instructions, including the paying agent where this has been specifically requested, should be immediately notified direct to the counterparty. This notification should be supported by written, telex, or similar confirmation of the new instructions.

105 While it is important that payment instructions are passed quickly, it is equally important that principals have in place appropriate procedures for controlling the timing of their instructions to correspondent banks to release funds when settling wholesale market transactions. A recent survey by G-10 central banks suggested that there is a wide gap between the best and worst controls practised in the markets; failure to maintain effective controls over payment flows can significantly increase the risks that institutions face when dealing in the OTC wholesale markets.

- **Fraud**

106 There is a need for great vigilance by all staff against attempted fraud. This is particularly so where calls are received on an ordinary telephone line (usually in principal to principal transactions). As a precautionary measure, it is strongly recommended that the details of all telephone deals which do not include pre-agreed settlement instructions should be confirmed by telex or similar means without delay by the recipient, seeking an answer-back to ensure the deal is genuine.

- **Terms and documentation**

It is now common for wholesale market deals to be subject to some form of legal documentation binding the two parties to certain standard conditions and undertakings. The Bank endorses the use, wherever possible, of such documentation (which typically will take the form either of signed Master Agreements exchanged between the two parties or can take the form of standard Terms). Core principals should have procedures in place to enable documentation to be completed and exchanged as soon as possible.

107 It is in the interest of all principals to make every effort to progress the finalization of documentation as quickly as possible. In some markets, such as repo, or in other circumstances such as those described in paragraphs 31 and 51, documentation should be in place before any deals are undertaken. More generally, however, the Bank believes the aim should be for documentation to be in place within three months of the first deal being struck. Failure to agree documentation within this timescale should cause management to review the additional risks that this might imply for any future deals with the counterparty concerned. Factors which may influence managements' views include whether they can take comfort on their legal position from the mutual confirmation of terms with a particular counterparty; or where the delay is in putting in place multiple master agreements for products that are, in the interim, subject to previously agreed documentation.

108 Some documentation in common usage provides for various options and/or modifications to be agreed by mutual consent. These must be clearly stated before dealing. Firms should make clear at an early stage, when trading any of the above mentioned products, if they are not intending to use standard terms documentation. Where changes are proposed these should also be made clear. For other wholesale instruments, where standard terms do not yet exist (e.g. barrier options), particular care and attention should be paid to the negotiation of terms and documentation.

109 Some outstanding transactions might still be subject to old documentation (e.g. the 1987 ISDA) that results in one-way payment provisions. The use of such provisions is **not** recommended. Banking supervisors worldwide have indicated that such transactions will not be eligible for netting for capital adequacy purposes and the Bank supports moves to amend such clauses where they are still in existence. Non-core principals are encouraged to co-operate with core principals in this objective.

- **Stock lending and repos**

Where sale and repurchase (or stock borrowing and lending) transactions are entered into, proper documentation and prior agreement of key terms and conditions are essential.

110 The Bank expects core principals to abide by the relevant codes drawn up by market practitioners. When undertaking stock lending transactions the Stock Borrowing and Lending Committee Code of Guidance should apply. With the advent of a gilt repo market the Gilt Repo Code of Best Practice should be adhered to.

111 The Gilt Repo Code will apply not only to gilt repo, but also to other transactions involving gilts which have similar effect and intent, including secured lending (of money and gilts) e.g. under the gilt-edged stock lending agreement; lending of gilts against collateral; and buy/sellbacks (whether or not under a Master Agreement). The Bank also believes that the general standards set down in the Gilt Repo Code will be relevant when undertaking other, non-gilt, repo activity covered by the London Code.

- **Assignments of transfers**

Assignments should not generally be undertaken without the consent of the parties concerned.

112 Assignments have become increasingly common in the derivatives market. Principals who enter into any wholesale market transaction with the intention of shortly afterwards assigning or transferring the deal to a third party should make clear their intention to do so when initially negotiating the deal. It is recommended that the confirmation sent by the principal should specify any intent to assign and give details of the procedure that will be used. The subsequent documentation should also make provision for assignment.

113 When a principal is intending to execute such a transfer it must obtain the consent of the transferee before releasing its name. If the principal proposes to use a broker to arrange the transfer, consent from the transferee for this to happen must also be obtained. The transferee has an obligation to give the principal intending to transfer sufficient information to enable the transaction to be conducted in accordance with the principles of best practice set out elsewhere in the Code. Where the transaction is conducted through a broker, this information should likewise be made available to him. In particular, the information from the transferee should include details of the type of credit the transferee is prepared to accept, and whether he is seeking any sort of reimbursement for the administrative costs that might be incurred. Principals and brokers arranging a transfer or assignment should also agree the basis of pricing the transfer at an early stage of the negotiations. When arranging assignments, it is important for participants to observe the general principle set out elsewhere in the Code that there should be mutual disclosure of names. Finally it should be noted that proper, clear documentation is as important for transfers as for the origination of deals.

Settlement of differences

If all the procedures outlined above are adhered to, the incidence and size of differences should be reduced; and those mistakes which do occur should be identified and corrected promptly. Failure to observe these principles could leave those responsible bearing the cost, without limit on size or duration, of any differences which arise. Except in the foreign exchange market, all differences must be settled in cash.

114 In all the wholesale markets (including foreign exchange) if a broker misses a price he is required by the Bank to offer to close the deal at the next best price if held to the deal. The broker must then settle the difference arising by cheque (or, if both sides agree, points if it is a foreign exchange transaction); **principals should always be prepared to accept this cash settlement since to do otherwise would put the broker in breach of the Code. It is unprofessional for a dealer to refuse to accept a difference cheque and insist the deal is honoured;** individual brokers facing this situation should

advise their senior management who, if necessary, should raise the matter with management of the client. The Bank is keen to be advised of any persistent offenders.

115 Where brokers are used to arrange derivative products like barrier options, they should not be held liable for disputes between principals that arise where there is a disagreement over whether a certain spot level has or has not been reached in sufficient quantity to trigger the option. Nor should brokers be cited as independent referees in such transactions unless they have explicitly agreed to do so before the deal is struck.

116 As noted above, the prompt despatch and checking of confirmations is of paramount importance. Non-standard settlement instructions should be particularly carefully checked, and any discrepancies identified promptly upon receipt, and notified direct to the counterparty, or to the broker (in circumstances described earlier).

117 Where difference payments arise because of errors in the payment of funds, principals are reminded that it is the view of the Bank and the Joint Standing Committees that they should not benefit from undue enrichment by retaining the funds. Technological developments have resulted in faster and more efficient mechanisms for the delivery and checking of confirmations. This means that when brokers pass payment instructions that cannot be cross-checked against direct confirmation details, their liability in the event of an error should be limited to 24 hours from when the deal was struck. This limit on the broker's liability is not intended to absolve brokers of responsibility for their own errors; rather it recognizes that once payments do go astray the broker is limited in what action it can directly take to rectify the situation.

118 In the foreign exchange and currency deposit markets arrangements have been drawn up to facilitate the payment of differences via the Secretary of the Foreign Exchange Joint Standing Committee[1]. In the foreign exchange market only, and only with the explicit consent of principals, brokers may make use of 'points' to settle differences. Even then their use will only be permitted if arrangements for management control, recording and reporting of points consistent with the requirements laid down by the Bank (see Annex 1) have been established.

119 Listed broking firms must agree their own procedures with the Wholesale Markets Supervision Division of the Bank before using 'points'. The informal use of 'points' between individual dealers and brokers is not acceptable. Using 'points' in lieu of cash to settle differences is not permitted in any market other than foreign exchange. As a matter of prudent housekeeping, all differences should normally be settled within 30 days from the date the original deal was undertaken.

---

1 All requests for settlement via these arrangements should be marked for the attention of The Secretary, Foreign Exchange Joint Standing Committee, Bank of England Dealing Room (HO-G), Bank of England, Threadneedle Street, London EC2R 8AH. They should be accompanied by a written report of the circumstances resulting in the difference.

Arbitration procedure

120 The Bank is prepared to arbitrate in disputes between firms it supervises about the application of the Code, or current market practice, to specific transactions in wholesale market products. As a condition for doing so the Bank will expect the parties to have exhausted their own efforts to resolve the matter directly. All parties must then first agree to the Bank taking such a role and to accept its decision in full and final settlement of the dispute. In doing so, the Bank may draw on the advice and expertise of members of the Joint Standing Committees or other market practitioners as it feels appropriate. Requests for arbitration should be addressed to the Bank's Wholesale Markets Supervision Division. The Bank will not normally arbitrate in any dispute which is subject to, or is likely to be subject to, legal proceedings. Paragraphs 48 and 49 of the Code, on taping, and paragraphs 88–90, on oral deal checks, are especially relevant to firms considering recourse to these arrangements.

Commission/brokerage

Brokers' charges are freely negotiable. Principals should pay brokerage bills promptly.

121 Where the services of a broker are used it is traditional practice for an appropriate brokerage package to be agreed by the directors or senior management on each side. Any variation on a particular transaction from those previously agreed brokerage arrangements should be expressly approved by both parties and clearly recorded on the subsequent documentation; this should be the exception rather than the rule. Under no circumstances should a broker pay cash to a principal as an incentive to use its service (see also early section on Marketing).

122 Although brokers normally quote dealing prices excluding commission/brokerage charges, it is perfectly acceptable, and not uncommon, in some derivative markets for the parties to agree that the broker quotes rates gross of commission and separately identifies the brokerage charge. Equally there may be circumstances when the broker (or principal) and client may agree on an acceptable net rate; if so it is important that the broker (or principal) subsequently informs the client how that rate is divided between payments to counterparties and upfront commission. In such cases it is essential that all parties are quite clear that this division will be determined no later than the time at which the deal is struck; and that a record is kept.

123 The Bank is aware that some principals fail to pay due brokerage bills promptly. **This is not good practice** and can significantly disadvantage brokers since overdue payments are treated by the Bank, for regulatory purposes, as a deduction from their capital base.

Appendix 2

Market conventions

Management should ensure that individual brokers and dealers are aware of their responsibility to act professionally at all times and, as part of this, to use clear, unambiguous terminology. This is even more important when dealing with non-core principals, whose staff may be less experienced in dealing in these markets.

124 The use of clear language is in the interests of all concerned. Management should establish internal procedures (including retraining if necessary) to alert individual dealers and brokers who act in different markets (or move from one market to another) both to any differences in terminology between markets and to the possibility that any particular term could be misinterpreted. The use of generally accepted concise terminology is undoubtedly helpful. In those markets where standard terms and conditions have been published individual dealers and brokers should familiarise themselves with the definitions they contain.

125 Standard conventions for calculating the interest and proceeds on certain sterling and currency instruments, together with market conventions regarding brokerage, are set out in Schedule 1.

Market disruption/bank holidays

126 There have been instances of general disruption to the wholesale markets which have, in turn, resulted in interruptions to the sterling settlement systems and consequent delays in sterling payments. It has been agreed by the Joint Standing Committees that in such unexpected circumstances the Bank should determine and publish the interest rate(s) which parties to deals affected by such interruptions should use to calculate the appropriate interest adjustment (unless all the parties to the deal agree instead on some other arrangement – such as to continue to apply the existing rate of interest on the original transaction or as provided for in the relevant documentation). The Bank shall have absolute discretion in its determination of any interest rate(s), and shall not be required to explain its method of determining the same and shall not be liable to any person in respect of such determination.

127 Occasionally unforeseen events mean that market participants will have entered into contracts for a particular maturity date only to find, subsequently, that that day is declared a public holiday. It is normal market practice in London to extend contracts maturing on a non-business day to the next working day. But to minimize possible disputes market participants may need to agree settlement arrangements for such deals with their counterparties in advance.

MARKET CONVENTIONS

1 Calculation of interest and brokerage in the sterling deposit market

- **Interest**

On CDs and deposits or loans this is calculated on a daily basis on a 365-day year. Interest on a deposit or loan is paid at maturity, or annually and at maturity, unless special arrangements are made at the time the deal is concluded.

On secured loans the discount houses and Stock Exchange money brokers do not pay interest at intervals of less than 28 days. The current general practice is to calculate at the close of business on the penultimate working day interest outstanding on secured loans to the last working day of each calendar month and to pay the interest thereon on the last working day of the month.

- **Brokerage**

All brokerage is calculated on a daily basis on a 365-day year and brokerage statements are submitted monthly.

2 Calculation of interest in a leap year

The calculation of interest in a leap year depends upon whether interest falls to be calculated on a daily basis or an annual basis. The position may differ as between temporary and longer-term loans.

- **Temporary loans**

Because temporary loans may be repaid in less than one year (but may, of course, be continued for more than a year) interest on temporary money is almost invariably calculated on a daily basis. Thus any period which includes 29 February automatically incorporates that day in the calculation; in calculating the appropriate amount of interest, the number of days in the period since the last payment of interest is expressed as a fraction of a normal 365-day year, not the 366 days of a leap year, which ensures that full value for the 'extra' day.

Examples:

Assume last previous interest payment 1 February (up to and including 31 January) and date of repayment 1 April (in a leap year). Duration of loan for final interest calculation = 29 days (February) + 31 days (March) = 60 days.

Calculation of interest would be

$$P \times \frac{r}{100} \times \frac{60}{365} =$$

Assume no intermediate interest payments. Loan placed 1 March and called for repayment 1 March the following year (leap year). Total period up to and including 29 February = 366 days. Calculation of interest would be

$$P \times \frac{r}{100} \times \frac{366}{365} =$$

This is in line with banking practice regarding interest on deposits which is calculated on a 'daily' basis and no conflict therefore arises.

- **Longer-term loans**

The following procedure for the calculation of interest on loans which cannot be repaid in less than one year (except under a TSB or building society stress clause) was agreed between the BBA and the Chartered Institute of Public Finance and Accountancy on 12 December 1978.

(a) Fixed interest

The total amount of interest to be paid on a longer-term loan at fixed interest should be calculated on the basis of the number of complete calendar years running from the first day of the loan, with each day of any remaining period bearing interest as for 1/365 of a year.

Normal practice for the calculation of interest in leap years is to disregard 29 February if it falls within one of the complete calendar years. Only when it falls within the remaining period is it counted as an additional day with the divisor remaining at 365.

Example: 3½ year loan, maturing on 30 June of a leap year.

First 3 years' interest: $P \times \frac{r}{100} \times 3 =$

Final 6 months' interest: $P \times \frac{r}{100} \times \frac{182}{365} =$

Certain banks, however, require additional payment of interest for 29 February in all cases, and it was therefore agreed that:

both the original offer or bid, and the agent's confirmation, must state specifically if such payment is to be made; and

the documentation must incorporate the appropriate phraseology.

Interest on longer term loans should be paid half-yearly, on the half-yearly anniversary of the loan or on other prescribed dates and at maturity. **To calculate half yearly interest payments** the accepted market formula is:

$$P \times \frac{r}{100} \times \frac{d}{365} =$$

Where d = actual number of days

Although, with the agreement of both parties, the following is sometimes used:

$$P \times \frac{r}{100} \times \frac{1}{2} =$$

(b) Floating rate

Interest on variable rate loans, or roll-overs, which are taken for a fixed number of years with the rate of interest adjusted on specific dates, should be calculated in the same manner as for temporary loans.

3 Brokerage and other market conventions in the foreign exchange and currency deposit markets

- **Brokerage**

(a) General (foreign exchange and currency deposits)

Brokerage arrangements are freely negotiable.

These arrangements should be agreed by directors and senior management in advance of any particular transaction.

(b) Currency deposits

Calculation of brokerage on all currency deposits should be worked out on a 360-day year.

Brokers' confirmations and statements relating to currency deposits should express brokerage in the currency of the deal.

In a simultaneous forward-forward deposit (for example one month against six months), the brokerage to be charged shall be on the actual intervening period (in the above example, five months).

- **Other market conventions**

Currency deposits

Length of the year

For the purpose of calculating interest, one year is in general deemed to comprise 360 days; but practice is not uniform in all currencies or centres.

Spreads and quotations

Quotations will normally be made in fractions, except in short-dated foreign exchange dealings, where decimals are normally used.

Call and notice money

For US dollars (and sterling), notice in respect of call money must be given before noon in London. For other currencies, it should be given before such time as may be necessary to conform with local clearing practice in the country of the currency dealt in.

4 Calculations in the foreign currency asset markets

- **Euro-commercial paper (and other such instruments)**

The net proceeds of short-term interest-bearing and discount Euro-commercial paper, on which interest is determined on a 360-day basis, are calculated in the same manner as those for short-term, interest-bearing and discount CDs.

Formula for non-interest bearing Euronotes quoted on a 'discount to yield' basis:

$$\frac{N}{1 + \left(\frac{Y}{100} \times \frac{M}{360}\right)} = \text{Purchase consideration}$$

where

N = Nominal amount or face value
Y = Yield
M = Number of days to maturity

Example:

A Euronote with a face value of US \$5 million and with 90 days to run is sold to yield 7.23% per annum.

$$\frac{5{,}000{,}000}{1 + \frac{(7.23 \times 90)}{(36{,}000)}} = \$4{,}911{,}229.53$$

- **US Treasury bills (and other US discount securities such as bankers' acceptances and commercial paper)**

The quoted trading rates for such assets are discount rates. The price of the asset is calculated on the basis of a 360-day year.

The market price (Pm) on a redemption value of \$100 can be calculated as follows:

$$Pm = 100 - \frac{(M \times D)}{(\ 360\ )}$$

where

M = days to maturity or days held
D = discount basis (per cent).

GUIDELINES FOR EXCHANGING STANDARD SETTLEMENT INSTRUCTIONS (SSIs)

These guidelines have been drawn up by the Bank of England in consultation with practitioners. While the parties to SSIs are free to agree changes to the detail on a bilateral basis, it is hoped that this framework will be useful and as such followed as closely as possible.

When **establishing** SSIs with a counterparty for the first time these should be appropriately authorized internally before being issued. It is desirable that SSIs be established by post (and issued in duplicate, typically under two authorized signatories). However authenticated SWIFT message can also be used if necessary.

Cancellation or amendment of a standard instruction should ideally be undertaken by authenticated SWIFT; tested telex is also an unacceptable means when cancelling or making amendments. SWIFT broadcast is **not** an acceptable means for establishing, cancelling or amending SSIs.

A mutually agreed **period of notice** for changing SSIs should be given; typically this will be between 10 working days and one month. Some parties may also wish to provide for changes to be made at shorter notice in certain circumstances.

Recipients have a responsibility to acknowledge acceptance (or otherwise) of the proposed/amended SSI within the timescale agreed (see above). Failure to do so could result in a liability to compensate for any losses which result. In the case of written notification this should be undertaken by the recipient signing and returning the duplicate letter.

Recipients should also confirm the precise date on which SSIs will be activated (via SWIFT or tested telex).

Instructions should be issued for each currency and wholesale market product. Each party will typically nominate only one correspondent per currency for foreign exchange deals and one per currency for other wholesale market deals. The same correspondent may be used for foreign exchange and other wholesale market deals.

As a general rule, all outstanding deals, including maturing forwards, should be settled in accordance with the SSI in force at their value date (unless otherwise and explicitly agreed by the parties at the time at which any change to an existing SSI is agreed).

The SSI agreement for each business category should contain the following:

- the nature of the deals covered (for example whether they include same day settlement or only spot/forward forex deals).
- confirmation that a single SSI will apply for all such deals with the counterparty.
- the effective date.

- confirmation that it will remain in force 'until advised'.
- recognition that no additional telephone confirmation of settlement details will be required.
- recognition that any deviation from the SSI will be subject to an agreed period of notice.

When operating SSIs on this basis, the general obligations on both parties are to ensure that:

- they apply the SSI which is current on the settlement date for relevant transactions.
- confirmations are issued in accordance with the London Code of Conduct; the aim should be to send them out on the day a deal is struck.
- confirmations are checked promptly upon receipt in accordance with the London Code. Any discrepancies should be advised by no later than 3.00 pm on the business day following trade date, if not sooner.

Annex 1

OPERATING A DUAL BROKING SYSTEM IN THE LONDON FOREIGN EXCHANGE MARKET

Notice issued by the Bank of England, 24 October 1989*

1 The Bank's enquiries of foreign exchange market participants in March 1989 established that opinion was divided on use of the 'points' system in London**. The Bank has considered with the FECDBA and the Joint Standing Committee the kind of steps necessary to allow those institutions wishing to retain the use of points to do so, whilst ensuring that points are not used in deals with banks which reject this system. It has been agreed that the following general arrangements will be established.

2 Management in all banks (and other active market participants) will be expected to have internal rules for their dealers to minimize the scope for differences and to discourage dealers from acting unprofessionally, for example by 'stuffing' brokers.

Participating banks

3 Each broking firm will approach all their clients (based in the UK or overseas) at the appropriate management level to establish whether, in order to be provided as far as possible by the broker with the current firm price service, they are prepared to sign a client letter accepting the broker's involvement in points arrangements. Those banks which do agree client letters are referred to here as 'participating banks'.

4 Banks which explicitly accept the use of points in this way will be assumed to have given their informal consent to the practice. The arrangements described here are deemed satisfactory in the foreign exchange market because it is a professional market in which best execution is not normally expected. Obviously in abnormal circumstances, where a broker agrees to provide best execution to a client or the client is not a market professional or the broker performs an advisory or discretionary function*** to a client, there must be full disclosure to the client of the broker's interest and explicit informed prior consent.

5 Signing such a client letter will **not** of itself commit any bank to **lending** points to brokers or to the use of positive points in lieu of cash payment for any differences. Any such decision should be taken quite separately by management and would require appropriate record keeping and reporting arrangements to be established.

---

* The Bank introduced a complementary Notice (February 1994) to all banks and brokers setting out the detailed requirements for brokers operating a 'points' broking system in London; copies are available from the Wholesale Markets Supervision Division at the Bank of England. Note: this Notice may be amended from time to time.

** Examples of typical situations generating 'negative' and 'positive' points are set out in the Appendix.

*** See paragraphs 29 and 30 of the July 1995 Code regarding the Role of Bankers.

Non-participating banks

6 For 'non-participating banks' which decline to provide a client letter, a broking firm will need to consider on a case-by-case basis whether it is prepared to continue to provide a broking service, and if so on what terms. Where a service continues to be provided, the broking firm will be required to take the following steps to ensure that these banks are not unwittingly involved in deals where there is an undisclosed benefit to the broker:

(i) The broker will advise the management of these non-participating banks that it may no longer provide as firm a price service; banks will be expected to take steps to inform their dealers that the broker cannot be held to a price. Any attempts to 'stuff' a broker should in the first instance be brought to the attention of management in the broking firm; they in turn should raise it at the appropriate level with the bank(s) concerned. Any bank dealers attempting to pressurize a broker should be subject to internal disciplinary procedures. Furthermore, if necessary, brokers will have recourse to the Bank of England to complain.

(ii) Each broking firm will establish to the Bank of England's satisfaction appropriate arrangements to enable it to distinguish non-participating from participating banks. The precise means by which this distinction is achieved are likely to vary between broking firms depending, inter alia, on the number of non-participating clients each broker has; the manner in which they receive a service (whether over an open voice box system or over an ordinary telephone line); and the number and volume of deals involved.

(iii) Any differences payable by the broker resulting from mistakes will normally be settled by cheque; where London banks are concerned, it is recommended that cheques be paid through the established FECDBA mechanism*. As a matter of equity, banks should also accept that any differences resulting from mistakes on the part of their dealers should be payable to the broker through the same procedures.

(iv) An up-to-date list of names distinguishing participating from non-participating banks will be maintained by the broker, with copies provided to all appropriate members of staff. The Bank of England will also be provided with a copy of the current list.

(v) Any 'cross-overs' involving a non-participating bank will, subject to acceptability of names, be completed either at a mutually acceptable middle rate or by the introduction of an intermediary bank; if an intermediary is introduced, none of the benefit to it from such a deal will accrue to the broker.

* See paragraph 119 of the July 1995 Code for details of the arrangements which superseded the FECDBA mechanism.

(vi) In the event of a 'name switch' becoming necessary involving one or more non-participating banks, the broker will reserve the right to adjust the brokerage charges to compensate. Any such adjustment should be arranged between management in both the broking firm and the bank(s) concerned.

7 Management in broking firms active in forex have indicated to the Bank that this framework forms an acceptable basis for accommodating banks' differing requirements for broking services. Its operation will be kept under close review by the Bank and by the Joint Standing Committee, and the first six months of operation will be regarded as experimental.

8 The Bank will require brokers to maintain records of deals involving points, including any such deals arranged involving correspondent brokers. These must ensure that accurate and verifiable points' tallies are kept on a deal by deal basis, and must be backed by rigorous management systems and controls. These requirements have been discussed with the broking firms concerned and are set out in a separate paper which has been provided to all listed brokers for implementation to the Bank's satisfaction.

9 The Bank accepts that on rare occasions individuals will inevitably make mistakes, when (positive) points may wrongly be taken by a broker from a deal involving a non-participating bank. Systems will therefore need to be in place in each broking firm to identify any such errors promptly and to ensure that full rectification takes place immediately so that no positive points accrue to the benefit of the broker. Any such adjustment will leave the original deal undisturbed. The Bank will monitor closely the frequency of any such errors in each firm; if they reveal an inability to distinguish participating from non-participating banks, the Bank may require a broking firm to give up the use of points altogether.

Arrangements for monitoring participating banks

10 In parallel to these arrangements for brokers, the Banking Supervision Division of the Bank will wish to be notified by those UK authorized banks which decide that they must be prepared to accept positive points to settle differences arising with broking firms. They will wish to discuss with these banks from time to time how these arrangements will work, including importantly the record keeping arrangements in place to enable individual transactions involving points (both negative and positive) to be identified.

Appendix 2

EXAMPLES OF SITUATIONS GIVING RISE TO POINTS IN FOREIGN EXCHANGE DEALING

'Negative points'

1 Suppose a broker quotes sterling at $1.8030/1.8035. Bank A hits the $1.8030 bid for 5 mn. However, before the broker could let Bank A know, this price had been withdrawn by the market maker who had originally indicated to the broker a willingness to deal at the rate. The market for sterling has moved to $1.8025/1.8030.

2 When told that the bid price of $1.8030 was no longer available, the trader at Bank A insists on selling 5 mn at the original price.

3 Suppose the broker accepts responsibility for not withdrawing the price quickly enough, or values highly his relationship with Bank A, and therefore agrees to be held to the price. He searches the market and finds Bank B (a participating bank) who is willing to help the broker by agreeing to buy from Bank A at $1.8030 (and hopefully sell to the current bidder in the market at $1.8025); the broker is committed to make good the $2 500 loss which results from Bank B doing the two trades. This dealer has lent the broker 25 'points' (i.e. 5 'points' per 1 mn in a 5 mn deal).

'Positive points'

4 The $2 500 (25 'points') obligation of the broker in the above example to Bank B could obviously be settled in cash if Bank B so wished. Or Bank B may be prepared to see it reduced by the broker's ability to put to Bank B other transactions that produce a profit to Bank B's dealing position of at least $2,500. This might be achieved in various ways, one of which is as follows.

5 Suppose at some later time the market for sterling stands at $1.8070/75. This might reflect prices put into the broker as follows: Bank A bidding at 1.8070; Bank C is offering at 1.8075. Suppose two unrelated Banks, X and Y, simultaneously have a respective need to sell/buy 5 mn. Bank X hits the 1.8070 bid; Bank Y the 1.8075 offer. The broker now has these latter two banks committed to deal in opposite directions at overlapping rates (in this example equal to the market spread). The broker may, at its discretion, offer both these deals to Bank B.

6 The consequences of this would be:

(i) Bank X has sold sterling at the (market) rate desired;

(ii) Bank Y has bought sterling at the (market) rate desired;

(iii) by being given both deals Bank B earns a profit of $2 500 equal to the spread; it may, or may not, decide to reward the broker for this 'service' in the form of offsetting these 'positive points' against the 25 negative points the broker owes.

Annex 2

LONDON INSTRUMENTS

The London Code of Conduct defines best market practice for secondary transactions. The act of issuing debentures (including CDs, commercial paper and medium-term notes) is not an investment activity under the Financial Services Act 1986, but such primary issues are expected to comply with the Bank's market guidelines. The Bank believes that as great a degree of homogeneity as possible at the primary issuing stage in the short-term paper markets assists good order in those markets. It reduces the scope for investor confusion about the nature of the instrument being traded and thereby facilitates market trading.

Such homogeneity is achieved in the CD market by the Bank's guidelines on Certificates of Deposit in London, together with a booklet issued by the British Bankers' Association setting out in detail the requirements covering the issuance of CDs. These identify the standard terms and conditions under which London CDs are issued. A similar degree of homogeneity is also achieved in the sterling Commercial Paper and Medium Term Note markets through both the Bank's Market Notice incorporating guidelines on this subject and the underlying statutory instrument which provides exemptions from the deposit-taking prohibition in the Banking Act and therefore permits regular issuance by non-deposit-taking entities.

Copies of the Bank's current notices on CDs, and Commercial Paper and Medium-Term Notes, may be obtained from the Bank's Gilt-Edged and Money Markets Division (telephone 0171-601 3100); any questions on either of these subjects may also be directed to the Bank on the same number.

The Bank is willing to co-operate with market participants in any of the other wholesale markets where similar standards and homogeneity would be desirable.

Appendix 2

BANK OF ENGLAND
LONDON EC2R 8AH

Clive Briault
Head of Division
Capital and Wholesale Markets
Supervision & Surveillance
Tel 0171-601 4019
Fax 0171-601 5827

23 May 1997

To all listed institutions

Dear Sir/Madam

For the Attention of the Compliance Officer

MARKET NOTICE: GREY PAPER AND LONDON CODE

This market notice offers guidance on a number of issues that relate to the Grey Paper and London Code of Conduct: the treatment of private individuals as wholesale counterparties; the authorisation of custody activities; changes to the corporate debt regime introduced by the Banking Act (Exempt Transactions) Regulations 1997; and the settlement of differences.

(1) The Treatment of Private Individuals as Wholesale Counterparties

The Bank has dealt with a small – but increasing – number of cases where listed principals have not treated individuals dealing in large-size transactions which fall within the Grey Paper regime in accordance with the standards expected of them under the Grey Paper and the London Code of Conduct. In particular, the Bank has investigated a number of complaints from private individuals who have been sold a derivative and/or leverage product where the individual customer has not fully understood the risks inherent in the product. In these cases the appropriate 'know your counterparty' checks were not followed by listed firms to the standards expected under the Code. Furthermore, in some cases, listed firms have not appreciated that where they undertake a transaction of sufficient size in a relevant Financial Services Act Schedule 5 product, the customer becomes a wholesale counterparty under the Grey Paper regime.

As a consequence, listed firms are reminded:

- of the 'know your counterparty' requirements of the London Code (page 6). The Grey Paper regime is intended for bona fide wholesale market professionals dealing in the relevant set of products;
- that where individuals are involved as counterparties, listed firms must:
  - consider most carefully whether to deal with such 'small investors' in OTC wholesale market products. It is the Bank's view that such an extension should

by no means be automatic. Listed firms should, for example, be in no doubt that the individual understands fully the risks inherent in the product concerned;

- ensure that customer dealing relationships are appropriately and periodically reviewed;
- have a clearly articulated approval process for dealers and salespersons to follow (Code para 31).

- that the Grey Paper and Code requirements on record-keeping and taping apply to private clients as well as to other counterparties (note Code paras 37, 48–49; Grey Paper paras 60–65);
- of the importance of having in place two-way written agreements where derivative or leveraged products are involved, irrespective of whether advice is being offered (Code para 35);
- of the legal and Grey Paper requirements regarding the identification of wholesale counterparties and the issue of an appropriate warning and subsequent reminders (Grey Paper paras 16, 70–74 and Annex; Code para 36).

In any future cases where the Bank discovers that a listed firm's treatment of inexpert private individuals – or other inexpert counterparties – has fallen below the standards expected of them under the Code, the Bank will view such failures most seriously. Listed firms are therefore reminded of the range of sanctions at the Bank's disposal (as set out in paragraph 10 of the London Code).

(2) Custody Authorisation

With effect from 1 June 1997, the custody of investments will become an authorisable activity regulated by the SFA or IMRO. These new custody provisions will apply where the custodian both safeguards and administers the assets (or makes arrangements for this).

As indicated in the SIB's consultative paper (no 107, March 1997), custody of investments will not generally fall within the exemption under Section 43 of the FS Act. Ordinary portfolio custody services will therefore not have the benefit of the Section 43 exemption. Where exempt transactions such as repo are undertaken as an ancillary service by a custodian, the arranging of the transaction would fall to the Bank for regulation, but the custody element will require authorization. The custody element of hold-in-custody repo will also require authorization.

(3) Exempt Transactions: Issue of Debt Securities of One Year or Over

On 18 March, the Bank issued an explanatory memorandum on the effect of certain changes to the corporate debt regime introduced by the Banking Act 1987 (Exempt Transactions) Regulations 1997, which took effect on 3 April 1997. With regard to secondary market transactions conducted under Schedule 5 of the Financial Services Act, these changes have the following implications for product coverage:

- All transactions in issues of unlisted debt with an original maturity of not more than five years will now be subject to the Bank's Section 43 arrangements. Previously only those unlisted debt instruments with a maturity of one year or less, medium-term notes with a maturity of one to five years, and debentures with a maturity of not more than five years issued by institutions authorized under the Banking Act 1987, building societies and certain European institutions, fell under Section 43.
- As a consequence, the product coverage table (page 2 of the Grey Paper, page 3 of the Code) is revised as follows:
  - (i) Item 7 now refers to: all CDs with an original maturity of not more than five years which are issued by institutions authorized under the Banking Act 1987, European authorized institutions and by UK building societies;
  - (ii) item 9 becomes 'Commercial paper';
  - (iii) delete old item 10 which refers to medium term notes;
  - (iv) new item 10 to read 'Other debentures with an original maturity of not more than five years'. Under the next Exempt Transactions Regulations, unlisted debt securities will no longer be subject to a maximum maturity of five years, but only those with an original maturity of no more than five years will fall under the Grey Paper. Trading in such securities falls under Section 43 for regulation irrespective of their currency denomination.

These changes are included in the revised product table (attached).

(4) Settlement of Differences

The Bank has become aware of an increasing number of cases where principals are unwilling to accept cheques from brokers in settlement of differences arising in a range of Schedule 5 transactions. In a number of instances it appears that principals have insisted that the broker finds them a name at the quoted price even though this automatically puts the broker in breach of the Code, since they are not allowed to take positions. If held to the deal, brokers are required by the Bank to offer to close the deal at the next best price. Treasury managers are therefore asked to remind their dealers of their responsibilities under the Code, and especially of paragraphs 114 and 118. Principals should always be prepared to accept cash settlement, except in the foreign exchange market where subject to mutual agreement the use of 'points' may apply.

Market participants should also be aware that brokers have to report all large differences to the Bank. In view of the recent reports concerning market practice, principals and brokers are advised that the Bank may itself choose to investigate the reasons why a large difference has arisen and that the Bank will need to be satisfied that the Code has not been breached.

Yours faithfully

Clive Briault

Products covered by the Bank's wholesale markets arrangements

A: Cash market products:

1 Sterling wholesale deposits.

2 Foreign currency wholesale deposits.

3 Gold and silver bullion wholesale deposits.

4 Spot and forward foreign exchange.

5 Spot and forward gold and silver bullion.

B: Instruments which are defined as investments in the Financial Services Act but which are outside the scope of the Investment Services Directive:

6 Over the counter (OTC) options (including warrants) or futures contracts on gold or silver.

C: Instruments which are defined as investments in the Financial Services Act and are within the scope of the Investment Services Directive:

7 All certificates of deposit (CDs) issued by institutions authorized under the Banking Act 1987, European authorized institutions and by UK building societies, with an original maturity of not more than 5 years.

8 Bank bills (or bankers' acceptances).

9 Commercial paper.

10 Other debentures with an original maturity of not more than five years.

11 UK local authority debt (bills, bonds, loan stock or other instruments) with an original maturity of not more than 5 years.

12 Other public sector debt with an original maturity of not more than 1 year (e.g. Treasury bills, but not gilt-edged securities).

13 Any certificate (or other instrument) representing the securities covered in items 7 – 12; or rights to, and interests in, these instruments.

14 OTC options (including warrants) or futures contracts on any currency (including sterling); on interest rates; or on the instruments listed in items 7 – 13 above.

15 Interest rate and currency swaps, regardless of their original maturity; forward rate agreements, or any other 'contracts for differences' involving arrangements to profit (or avoid loss) by reference to movements in the value of any of the instruments in items 7 – 13 above; or the value of any currency; or in the interest on loans in any currency.

16 Sale and repurchase agreements ('repos'), sale and buybacks and stock borrowing and lending involving debentures, loan stock or other debt

instruments, including gilts, of whatever original maturity where the repurchase or repayment will take place within twelve months.

Note 1 Instruments subject to the rules of a recognized investment exchange are not covered.

Note 2 Instruments denominated in foreign currencies, as well as sterling, are covered.

Note 3 Transactions by listed institutions may come within the Bank's supervisory framework even if one of the other parties to the transaction is operating abroad.

Note 4 The regulation of deposit-taking under the Banking Act 1987 is not affected by these arrangements in any way.

Note 5 The Government made clear in January 1988 that ordinary forward foreign exchange (and bullion) transactions fall outside the Financial Services Act; these nevertheless fall within the scope of the Bank's arrangements. However, as explained by the Securities and Investments Board in consultation document 89 issued in August 1995, certain margined products in foreign exchange and bullion do constitute investment business within the meaning of the FSA.

Note 6 Wholesale transactions between core principals in item 1 are not usually less than £100 000. For items 2 and 4 the usual minimum is £500 000 (or currency equivalent). For bullion (items 3 and 5) the relevant amounts are 2000 ounces for gold and 50 000 ounces for silver.

Note 7 For items 7–13 and 16, the minimum size of wholesale transactions is £100 000 (or the equivalent in foreign currency). For swaps, options, futures and forward rate agreements (FRAs), or other 'contracts for differences' (items 6, 14 and 15), the minimum underlying value is £500 000 (or the equivalent in foreign currency).

Note 8 Items 7–10 fall within the Financial Services Act under the generic term 'debenture', irrespective of their currency denomination.

BANK OF ENGLAND
LONDON EC2R 8AH

Clive Briault
Head of Division
Capital and Wholesale Markets
Supervision & Surveillance
Tel 0171-601 4019
Fax 0171-601 5827

22 December 1997

To all listed institutions

Dear Sir/Madam,

For the Attention of the Compliance Officer

MARKET NOTICE: GREY PAPER AND LONDON CODE

This market notice offers guidance on a number of issues relating to the Grey Paper and London Code: wholesale counterparty arrangements; using independent sources for marking-to-market; taping; electronic confirmations; and the use of SSIs. I would be grateful if you would ensure that this Notice is promulgated as appropriate within your organization.

(1) Wholesale counterparty arrangements

In the last Market Notice (23 May 1997) the Bank reminded firms of the Grey Paper's requirements for the treatment of private individuals who become wholesale counterparties. We have since discovered some failures to comply with the Bank's requirements among institutions dealing with more professional counterparties.

A particular area of concern is where dual regulated firms fail to maintain systems to distinguish transactions that fall within the scope of the Bank's arrangements (set out on page 3 of the Code) from those subject to the requirements of another UK regulator. This can lead to a failure to warn wholesale counterparties of their status under the Financial Services Act and to notify them that certain transactions will be governed by the London Code. This constitutes a serious breach of the Grey Paper and a failure to monitor regulatory boundaries appropriately. One firm has been privately reprimanded for failing to identify its wholesale counterparties for some years.

Listed firms are required to maintain adequate systems and controls to ensure that the requirements in the Grey Paper can be met at all times. You should ensure that all relevant business areas within your firm are fully aware of the scope of the Bank's arrangements for wholesale counterparties.

(2) Good practices in obtaining data for mark to market purposes

A note is attached which provides some guidance on obtaining external data for the purposes of marking to market OTC transactions and for brokers who may be supplying some of this data. A number of market participants have asked for clarification of where responsibilities lie, and of what the Bank sees as good practices, in the acquisition and supply of such data.

(3) Taping

The European Council and European Parliament have reached agreement on the Directive concerning the processing of personal data and the protection of privacy in the telecommunications sector (formerly known as the 'ISDN Directive'). This seeks to protect individuals from having their communications interfered with (including through listening, tapping or other surveillance) without their consent, except where this is legally authorized. Member States have until 24 October 2000 to bring this part of the Directive into force. The Directive may have implications for the London Code's stance on taping, which we are considering, but for the time being the current requirements in the London Code remain unchanged. The Code already includes a reference (paragraph 49) to firms taking the necessary steps to inform new clients or counterparties that conversations will be recorded.

(4) Electronic confirmations

Paragraph 96 of the Code recommends that a confirmation should be sent promptly using, if possible, one of the generally accepted electronic means now available (e.g. ACS system, S.W.I.F.T., fax or telex). Following discussion with practitioners, we can clarify that the use of an electronic trade matching system, such as TRAX, is also suitable for this purpose.

(5) Standard Settlement Instructions

The Code strongly recommends that principals use standard settlement instructions for wholesale market transactions, which should be established by confirmed letter or authenticated S.W.I.F.T. message. When using S.W.I.F.T. to amend or cancel SSIs it is recommended that authenticated messages are used; broadcast messages are not considered suitable for this purpose. As indicated in the Code (para 101), S.W.I.F.T. has been seeking to develop their service in this area and they have recently launched the SSI/FX Directory Service which covers foreign exchange, money market and derivative SSIs. The service allows authenticated exchange of SSIs as recommended in Schedule 2 of the Code. It also makes it unnecessary for subscribers to send acknowledgement to each other, since subscribers must act upon messages received and make necessary changes to their internal records, provided a sufficient notice period is given (in line with Schedule 2). Non-subscribers, however, should continue to send acknowledgement of any changes in SSIs. More generally, firms should continue to follow the recommended procedures in the Code whenever notification of an amendment to an SSI is received by S.W.I.F.T. broadcast.

(6) Information available on the Bank's web-site

Details of the Bank's regulatory arrangements are now available on the Bank's web site at http://www.bankofengland.co.uk/wmsd.htm. You may wish to access this facility and to advise your wholesale counterparties of its existence.

Yours faithfully

Clive Briault

Appendix 2

GOOD PRACTICES IN OBTAINING DATA FOR MARK TO MARKET PURPOSES

This note is intended to provide guidance for principals when obtaining external data for the purposes of marking to market OTC transactions and for those brokers who may be supplying these data. A number of market participants have asked for clarification of where responsibilities lie, and of what the Bank sees as good, or sound, practices in the acquisition and supply of such data. It is clear that there is a wide range of practices among participants; this guidance is intended to outline the main principles which participants should consider, rather than to be overly prescriptive as regards methods.

The general principles

- Principals who engage in trading should undertake regular prudent and consistent valuation of their mark-to-market trading positions. For many such positions, quoted prices will be the best guide to a fair valuation.
- Principals need to have in place appropriate procedures for the independent checking of mark-to-market trading positions by the middle and/or back office.
- Brokers can play a useful role in the market as one of the sources of external data for valuation purposes. Where they do so, this service should be governed by the same considerations as apply to other relations between brokers and principals, where the London Code states 'it is ... for the principal to decide what credence, if any, is given to any information ... provided by a broker to a dealer'. Firms may enter into specific bilateral agreements about the reliance to be placed on any service supplied but, absent these, all principals are responsible for their own actions.

Acquisition of data

Where principals are seeking to acquire external data for valuation purposes, they should also consider the following:

- Where possible, the Bank would expect the prices (and volatilities) used in mark-to-market calculations to be checked by an area of the principal which is independent of the front office.
- Screen services, brokers and other third party providers can all be useful sources of data. In some areas such as where markets are particularly thin or illiquid, principals may consider exchanging historical data with other principals.
- Where independent prices are not available, a series of checks should be put in place to ensure that all prices are measured on a prudent basis.
- Screen prices showing the bid-offer spread are widely available for many products. Where available, these will often be the most appropriate source,

though principals should also consider how these data have been constructed and what they represent. Are they, for example, last actual trade and if so how long ago did it occur? From which market were they obtained and at what time? If the prices are not actual trades on what basis were they calculated (e.g. interpolation)? What size was the trade representative of? Is this price based on a liquid market?

- Where principals seek external data for specific transactions/instruments, they should specify in appropriate detail what data they require. Principals should state the appropriate characteristics on which they want the estimate to be based e.g. mid-market, indicative or firm prices, close out prices, the size of deal for which the price is generally good, at the money prices etc.

Supply of data by brokers

In supply data, brokers should consider:

- Whether appropriate back office controls are in place to ensure the data are appropriately calculated and recorded. The procedures for supplying data should be fully documented.
- Stating the precise conditions under which the estimates were constructed (mid-market, at the money, last trade, size etc.) They should also ensure that they provide data to principals on a consistent basis.
- Indicating an appropriate disclaimer of liability where appropriate, in addition to the general presumption of the Code outlined above.
- Where possible, data should be provided by the broker's back office function independent of the brokers.
- Where data are provided by fax (or fax equivalent), particular care is taken to ensure that the appropriate procedures are followed.
- Where markets are particularly illiquid, whether the broker can give any guidance on, say the number of principals trading the product to which the price refers.
- Subjecting the supply of data procedures to periodic compliance and internal and external audit review.

Bank of England

December 1997

Glossary

Algorithm: A set of rules that specify a method of carrying out a task, e.g. an encryption algorithm states the rules to be followed to produce the encrypted message.

ANSI (American National Standards Institute): ANSI is the principal standards making body in the US.

APACS (The Association for Payment Clearing Services): APACS is the organization which is responsible in the UK for matters relating to money transmission and payment clearing activities generally. There are 23 members of APACS and three autonomous clearing companies operating under the umbrella of APACS – BACS Limited, CHAPS Clearing Company Limited, and Cheque and Credit Clearing Company Limited. (See Chapter 2.)

Asymmetrical: Irregularity between the opposing sides of an object, on either sides of a line. If you take a square and draw a line across it from half way down one side, to half way down either of the adjacent sides, the two sections created will not be identical but together form the whole.

Asymmetrical encryption: A process which permits the key used for encryption to be different from the key used for decryption. Both keys are intrinsically linked.

Authentication: Authentication ensures the integrity of the data by preventing it from being tampered with or changed without the recipient becoming aware of it and acts as a check on the identity of the sender of the information. 'End to end' authentication verifies that the transaction created at the user's office contains exactly the same information when it arrives at the receiving bank. (See also MAC.)

BACS (Bankers' Automated Clearing System): BACS provides an electronic batch processing clearing service within the UK. (See Chapters 2 and 4.)

Banking system: This term may be used in two different contexts. In a global context, 'banking system' refers to the infrastructure of banks within a country and how they deal with clearing each other's cheques and other payment instructions. Alternatively, a 'banking system' may refer to a system provided by a bank which provides cash management services for corporate clients, reporting transactions over their accounts and portfolios throughout the day. It enables payments to be initiated and it reports information in the most appropriate format to enable companies to manage their various accounts and portfolios in the most effective manner. Banks sometimes also describe their banking systems as 'treasury systems'. (See also Treasury system.)

Certificate: A commonly used method for the control of encryption keys, i.e. 'key management'. A key certificate contains information that uniquely identifies the authorized key and its user. The key certificate is in encrypted electronic form and is typically contained within one of the operating security devices.

CCITT (Consultative Committee International for Telegraphy and Telephony): The CCITT is the international body which sets standards for telecommunications. The X-series standards, e.g. X.25, X.400, etc, are the standards produced by the CCITT for digital communications systems.

CHAPS (Clearing House Automated Payment System): CHAPS provides a same-day guaranteed sterling electronic credit transfer service within the UK. (See Chapter 2.)

Clearing House: This description dates back to the time when all the banks which were members of the Bankers' Clearing House – the 'clearing banks' – met every day to exchange or clear all cheques drawn on each other. The Town Clearing, which was a low volume same-day value paper clearing operating within a limited area in the City of London, ceased operation in February 1995.

Cryptography: The art of writing in cypher or code.

Digital signature: The result of encrypting a hash total to protect a message from denial of origination by the sender, usually involving asymmetric encryption to produce the signature.

EDI (Electronic Data Interchange): EDI describes a technique which enables the computer-to-computer transfer of structured information, usually between companies which are trading partners. Typically this may be the ordering of materials, invoicing and settlement. (See Chapter 10.)

EDIFACT: See UN/EDIFACT.

EFT (Electronic Funds Transfer): EFT is a method of transferring funds from one bank account to another (whether in the same bank or not), with the instructions being transmitted to the bank using a dedicated electronic system. The term can cover a wide range of systems, including CHAPS, BACS, SWIFT and systems specific to banks, such as NatWest MTS.

Encryption: The process of encryption converts the texts and the numbers in a message into a code which is unintelligible to human beings without a decryption key and a conversion table. In the US the standard encryption algorithm is DES (the Data Encryption Standard), although some banks use their own proprietary algorithms. Encryption of data can either be carried out using a physical device or using integrated software. On receipt of messages at the receiving bank, they are decrypted by the bank prior to processing. A popular analogy is an English to German dictionary: if trying to interpret a German word, the English to German dictionary would be almost, useless because all the references are alphabetical in English. The book is available to the public but the German word could probably only be found with considerable luck.

Hash: An arithmetic calculation at the end of a string of data, which represents the entire contents of that string.

Key: When used in the context of encryption, a series of numbers which are used by an encryption algorithm to transform plaintext data into encrypted (cyphertext) data and visa versa are known as the keys.

Logical security: The techniques that can be applied to maintain the security of a system, other than those that are physical or organizational, e.g. cryptography.

Lockbox: A PO box address to which debtors can post cheque remittances. Advice of receipt and local cheque clearance are key features.

MAC (Message Authentication Code): A 'message authentication code' is a unique value generated by using an algorithm. It is generated through a complex mathematical computation, using each character in a message such as a payment instruction (be it a number, a letter or a punctuation mark). The purpose of a MAC is to ensure that a message has been received from a specific sender and that it has not been altered or tampered with after it has been approved by the originator. Any change in the content of the message whatsoever will also change the MAC. The MAC calculated by the sender is transmitted with the instruction and, on receipt, the receiving bank's system automatically recalculates the MAC for the message using a cryptographic key known only to the sender and receiver so that any amendment is immediately obvious. (See also Authentication.)

Organizational security: Different activities undertaken at various levels within an organization, e.g. checking the procedures undertaken by different parties.

Physical security: Safeguards that are physical, e.g. padlocks and lockable safes.

Private key: A cryptographic key which can be used for decryption as well as encryption. It is unique to the user and is not available to others. It is the opposite of a public key – see below.

Public key: A cryptographic key which is used for data encryption, and which cannot be used for decryption. The contents can be freely published.

RTGS: Real Time Gross Settlement. (See Chapter 2.)

SMART card: A SMART card is a plastic card containing a microchip which contains a personal identification number (PIN) or some other code unique to the holder. These cards can be used either as access control devices to funds transfer systems or as an authorizing key. Often the code contained on the microchip will be used in calculating the MAC on a funds transfer message.

SWIFT (Society for Worldwide Interbank Funds Transfer): This is an international system owned and used by international banks to advise each other of payments to be made and accounts to be debited and credited.

TAN: Transaction Authenticating Number.

TARGET: Trans European Automated Real Time Gross Settlement Express Transfer. (See Chapter 2.)

Treasury system: A treasury system can be defined as a database of treasury transactions with facilities for recording information about those transactions and additional facilities for analyzing and reporting the transactions. Different systems concentrate on different aspects of treasury transactions. Systems supplied by banks are likely to interface closely with EFT and banking systems. (See Chapters 9 and 10.)

UCC4A (Uniform Commercial Code 4A (US)): This is a comprehensive US law relating to wholesale funds transfers. (See Chapter 6.)

UNCITRAL (The United Nations Commission on International Trade Law): See Chapter 6.

UN/EDIFACT (United Nations/EDI for Administration Commerce and Transport): UN/EDIFACT is the international standard which specifies the requirements for EDI messages. The Security Joint Working Group has proposed three segments for inclusion in EDIFACT syntax. These are the SEC (security), CER (certificate) and RES (result) segments. The SEC segment specifies the type of security to be applied to a message in which it is included. The CER segment (for use with the SEC segment) contains details of a digital signature scheme to be applied to the message and the certified public key to be used to verify the signature. The RES segment (for use with the SEC segment) contains any security result, such as digital signature, which is to be applied to the message. (See Chapter 10.)

X-series standards: These standards (e.g. X.25, X.400, etc) are produced by the CCITT to cover digital communication systems. (See also CCITT.)

Index

Index

Index